THE COST OF BEING
UNDOCUMENTED

ONE WOMAN'S

RECKONING

WITH AMERICA'S

INHUMANE

MATH

ALIX DICK & ANTERO GARCIA

BEACON PRESS, BOSTON

BEACON PRESS
Boston, Massachusetts
www.beacon.org

Beacon Press books
are published under the auspices of
the Unitarian Universalist Association of Congregations.

28 27 26 25   8 7 6 5 4 3 2 1

This book is printed on acid-free paper that meets the uncoated paper
ANSI/NISO specifications for permanence as revised in 1992.

Text design and composition by Kim Arney

*Library of Congress Cataloguing-in-Publication
Data is available for this title.*
Hardcover ISBN: 978-0-8070-1494-3
E-book ISBN: 978-0-8070-1495-0
Audiobook: 978-0-8070-2082-1

The authorized representative in the EU for product safety and compliance
is Easy Access System Europe 16879218, Mustamäe tee 50,
10621 Tallinn, Estonia: http://beacon.org/eu-contact

For AC—Alix

For Stella & Joey—Antero

And to our fathers

CONTENTS

A Note on Our Research Process vii

INTRODUCTION The Balance 1

CHAPTER 1 The Cost of Time 9

CHAPTER 2 The Cost of Being Mexicana 23

CHAPTER 3 The Cost of Living in a Cartel War 35

CHAPTER 4 The Cost of Border Crossing 55

CHAPTER 5 The Cost of Employment. 73

CHAPTER 6 The Cost of Love 91

CHAPTER 7 The Cost of Faith 113

CHAPTER 8 The Cost of Mental Health 129

CHAPTER 9 The Cost of Healthcare 145

CHAPTER 10 The Cost of Dreaming 150

CONCLUSION Reckoning with Inhumane Math 169

Acknowledgments 181
Notes 185
References .197
Index 213

A NOTE ON OUR
RESEARCH PROCESS

This book is written from Alix's first-person point of view, giving voice to her lived experience as an undocumented immigrant. However, there is a "we"—Alix and Antero—that went into researching and writing it. We want to tell you how our unique research partnership came about, and how the costs described in this book brought us together.

In 2019, Antero hired Alix as a nanny to help care for his newborn twin daughters. This working relationship plays out in the background of parts of this book. We weathered the pandemic together, and two years in, we recognized our shared interests in centering the voices typically pushed to the margins of society.

In his work as an educational researcher at Stanford University, Antero regularly centers the expertise of youth, who are otherwise sidelined in the very research that dictates their educational futures.[1] And, as you'll see in the chapters that follow, Alix has spent much of her life working on issues like immigrant rights and the needs of people experiencing homelessness. We are both committed to storytelling and scholarship as tools for social justice. And we were both interested in exploring how individuals labeled "undocumented" were confronting the everyday challenges of life during and beyond the pandemic. We discussed historical and sociological research approaches to exploring this topic. Building from this, we embarked on an awkward experiment: for the first year that we conducted research for this project, Alix still worked for Antero's family. This led to a sometimes uncomfortable power dynamic that we discussed openly and acknowledge here.

Research authorities advise against the kind of power imbalances at the forefront of this research relationship. However, the systems that dictate such concerns typically reduce people like Alix to research subjects, while granting people like Antero the authority to conduct research *on* other people. We rejected these predetermined roles. Ours was a relationship built from a relentless pursuit of justice and birthed from a shared investment in the care of two growing toddlers. When Antero's twins turned three and started attending a local preschool, our research partnership continued without the added layer of caregiving.[2]

PLÁTICAS AND THE "MIRROR METHOD"

Many popular social science books rely on the tools of economics and quantitative data. Such books draw on large-scale surveys, randomized control trials, census data, and economic reports to offer incisive looks into social inequality, racism, sexism, and poverty. We build on these bodies of work throughout this book while also deviating from their methodological approaches. We used a set of research tools less familiar to most readers, first and foremost the Chicana feminist tradition of *pláticas*, or talks. *Plática*[3] dates back to scholarship from the 1970s and '80s and centers the "everyday"[4] expertise of individuals who may not hold traditionally recognized scholarly credentials. It recognizes their embodied and lived experiences. As Cindy O. Fierros and Dolores Delgado Bernal write, a Chicana feminist lens is not solely about an analytic approach; rather, it embodies "who we are and requires us to grapple with our activist-scholar role, embrace alternative ways of knowing, and confront those aspects of ourselves that render us the colonized or the perpetrator."[5] This tradition centers people who would usually be considered research subjects as co-constructors of knowledge, leaning into "relations of reciprocity and vulnerability and researcher reflexivity."[6]

During our weekly pláticas, we sat, *platicando* (talking) about our lived experiences, the histories we draw from, and the ways social science data shaped our understanding of it all. Some scholars might refer to these as, in methodological parlance, semi-structured interviews, but

that assumes that one of us was the interviewer and the other the inter-
viewee—a premise that we reject.

As we sketched out the initial outline for this book, we reached out to
friend and fellow researcher Leigh Patel. She noted that this kind of work
reflects the regular forms of knowledge production that the academy
often overlooks: "That is what happens in communal living—knowledge
is always made collectively. . . . the biggest thing that qualitative research
has going for it is the fact that it's relational."[7]

For this book, we pushed this method one step further, collaboratively constructing our pláticas as spaces for what Alix calls our "mirror
method." We did not just co-construct knowledge. We codesigned the
study that is this book to emphasize how readers might come to learn
about the experiences of being undocumented. This was an experiential
process that shaped our pathways for collecting archival data, interviewing individuals, and writing the book.

Our work was and continues to be *relational*. One of our primary
methods is dialogic: we talked, we listened, we reflected out loud with
one another.[8] The raw data for large portions of how we worked on
this book do not look particularly fancy. They look like the two of us
engaged in lengthy, sometimes heated, conversations.

Cultural anthropology and ethnographic approaches privilege the
lone scholar venturing into the exotic wilds of a given research site for
prolonged periods—out and away. We chose instead to go *in* and *toward*.
During our pláticas, we focused on finding a vocabulary for the embodied and embedded memories that are otherwise ineffable. Alix might
not be able to put to words how her "brown body knows"—referencing
the qualitative scholarship of Cindy Cruz—but this process allowed her
to uncloak the tacit knowledge of labor abuse, domestic violence, and
workplace sexual harassment she carries with her.[9] Our ideological and
theological differences, too, shaped our conversations. For example, Antero's agnostic worldview contrasted regularly with Alix's faith-based un-
derstandings of purpose and God. We had prolonged conversations about
terms that are fundamental in this book: feminism, Christianity, activism.
We sometimes disagreed about the varied suffixes to describe Latino/a/

ex/e individuals. These conversations were not about hashing out who was right or who might convince whom but about getting to a shared understanding of the purposes and truths that underlie individuals and society.[10] This was, for us, the hard work of qualitative research: bringing our full and vulnerable selves to understand the truths around us.

DATA, ANALYSIS, AND WRITING

There is an expansive and somewhat lucrative market for qualitative software tools that help researchers organize, sort, and code their qualitative data. Contrary to what might be assumed, qualitative data such as interviews, transcribed pláticas, and written observations can, like numerical data, be coded thematically to illuminate patterns and triangulate insights. Digital products purport to speed up and support researchers in this process. However, for the most part, they are not particularly useful and contrary to the aims of this book. Digital coding software often takes researchers away from the human perceived experiences and from ourselves as interpreters of life around us. It also often reinforces the dispassionate dispositions we are expected to maintain in research environments.

One of our early conversations led to Alix reflecting on the ways her undocumented status is "convenient" for the US economy. The opening paragraphs of the introduction that follows this section are an edited version of that musing. This framework of costs and their benefits became a kind of coding structure for the data we collected. As we organized themes of varied costs, we knew not all of them would fit into a single book.

Methodologically, we tried to account for our full selves without quantification and without purely putting personal pain on voyeuristic display.[11] To get to Alix's narrative as the central driver for this book, we engaged in discursive analysis of the transcriptions of our pláticas and of various other texts such as written reflections, legal documents, and photographs. We analyzed activist social networks and online spaces to help us understand undocumented policies and immigrant rights movements. We interviewed scholarly experts, family members, friends, pastors, doctors, landlords, and health insurance agents.

Member checking is an important component of ethnographic research. Traditionally, a researcher might take their work back to the site where they conducted their research and ask participants if the findings they developed accurately depict their experiences. This is how researchers "check" if their findings match the views and beliefs of their participants. We didn't member check most of Alix's narrative because this work is closer to traditions of autoethnography, memoir, and decolonial research practices.[12] We did, however, revisit the family members and friends who played central roles in Alix's narrative. More importantly, we frame the chapters in which they appear as an accounting of Alix's life with the recognition that there are parallel pathways in the lives of others. We also knew that this book would not cover the entirety of some mythological universal undocumented experience. Instead, large portions of some chapters, like "The Cost of Love" and "The Cost of Mental Health," deviate from generalizable experiences. Applying our mirror method meant seeing one person's vulnerable self and knowing that her experiences of harm and loss might reflect emotions present in all of us.

Substantial academic research has been written through conducting research *on* vulnerable communities generally, and *on* undocumented youth and families in particular. While this work generates important insights into the precarious experiences of these communities, it is often conducted in ways that "other" and extract their life. Our methods took these concerns to heart and additionally looked at existing methodological writing about research *with* immigrant and undocumented individuals and families.[13] We shifted to this personal approach because Western academic research has a pernicious legacy of harming individuals and communities, from the racist medical scholarship of the Tuskegee Institute to the legacy of the HeLa cells that were cultivated without the consent of Henrietta Lacks to social science practices like the Stanford Prison Experiment and Stanford's ongoing heraldry of eugenics.[14]

Researchers have an overt responsibility to conduct our research morally and ethically. Institutional review boards (IRBs) are a central means of protecting research participants, researchers, and, of course, the universities that house them. They are the first step in any research study that Antero undertakes, and the research for this book was no exception.

Except that our IRB protocol was rejected.

In a note sent back to Antero, the Stanford IRB stated:

> This protocol is being returned to you because, based on the information provided in this application, the IRB has determined that this project does not meet the definition of "research" as defined in 45 CFR 46, which requires the results to contribute to generalizable knowledge. In the future, if you decided to increase the sample size of your study, please contact us as your project may require IRB review.

We don't dispute the fact that this research revolves around one individual, and Stanford's response is in line with how social science research is framed. However, we are seeking to transgress this particular border. Across the hundreds of pages of reflection that led to this book, we deliberately avoided generalizing from Alix's experiences. If we truly want to understand the costs of immigration policy in the United States, this book presupposes that generalizability is a hurdle—a border—to overcome. Readers must recognize the individual voices, perspectives, and contributions of Alix, her family members, and the countless other individuals that are otherwise lumped into grotesque, blanket characterizations that misrepresent their actual strengths and desires. Ultimately, the IRB determination allowed us to continue our research. Because it was not defined as "research" in the eyes of Antero's employer, we were at liberty to continue collaborating together as a non-generalizable activity.

ON WRITING

Given the sensitive nature of this work, Antero initially proposed writing up our research using the same anonymizing steps that are expected in approved IRB protocols. He proposed that we would publish our findings as an anonymous case study of an undocumented perspective during and beyond the pandemic. We would give Alix a pseudonym and mask many of her personal details. This is the familiar pathway for qualitative research publication. It is the assumption of how you do ethical research *on* vulnerable communities. Alix, however, had other plans.

Alix felt that it was imperative for her identity to be maintained, as a form of advocacy and also so that she could be properly credited for the self-expression and reflection she had given to the research. Recognizing the extractive nature of research, we discussed how the formally trained researcher often benefits from systems of subject anonymity. As Leigh Patel said in a conversation, these scholarly systems "come from these settler colonial ideas that one can *own* knowledge." Anonymized subjects allow researchers to claim ownership over findings that are often developed on the backs of individuals who do not have postgraduate university degrees.

There were many fits and starts before we found the "right" voice for this book. We ultimately realized that the best approach would be to write in the first person, the "I" always representing Alix,[15] with the actual writing done collaboratively. Every interview mentioned in this book was conducted together. We wrote and reviewed each sentence as a team. We compiled many of the accounts of Alix's life from our plática transcripts, from written material passed back and forth in email and on Google Docs, and through lengthy voice memos.

Once a rough draft was in place, we edited it together both in real time and asynchronously. Alix would identify words that sounded out of place, while Antero would find narrative gaps. Together, we coalesced around the same sentiment that had carried us through our pláticas.

The production of this work didn't require complicated tools. It did require trust, a willingness for tears to be shed as a part of our collective research process, and moving the language toward a simpler vernacular of shared understanding. We agreed that *stories* were how we would portray Alix's immigration experience. Leigh Patel encouraged us to lean into narrative and storytelling as our mode of communication: "Narratives ignite our imagination. I imagine that's part of why you want to write the book in a way that actually reflects and honors your relationship over the years, and maybe really hit that this is research, this is knowledge." This is why, in our first chapter, we ask a question that centers Alix and her "I:" "Why am *I* here?"

Of the many borders we've encountered throughout this book, the border between academic writing and public access has been a surmountable one. In 2022, as we were in the middle of writing this book, we decided to launch *La Cuenta*, an online publication that invites other writers and storytellers to join us in our accounting for undocumented life. Each week, we curate voices from a growing community of undocumented creators. While this book is a cumulative accounting of the costs of living in this country for one individual labeled undocumented, *La Cuenta* brings together short snippets of the lives of others.

If writing is a human act of reciprocity, as described by Robin Kimmerer in *Braiding Sweetgrass*,[16] how might our writing create closeness with an unseen reader, with an uncertain tomorrow? Can we build emotional fortitude with an unknown? Can our words and images and banter build the nest that might incubate a better tomorrow *now*? And can we do this together, collectively? Ultimately, our research approach for this book—and *La Cuenta*—has been one that calls for broader and more inclusive methods. With important exceptions, the majority of scholarship that impacts the well-being of minoritized communities is written by folks outside of those groups. They are speaking *for* others, rather than *with* or *as* them. Qualitative research, despite its name, often belies a lack of caring about the quality of the relationships at the center of this work. Our research partnership was born out of an unexpected, shared interest in each other's well-being and how the pandemic opened pathways for understanding and learning alongside each other.[17] It shouldn't take global catastrophe for research to center care.

THE BALANCE

If you ask me what it's like to move through life as an undocumented person in the United States, I'll tell you it is an exhausting mental game. You have to trick yourself into believing you're going to be okay. Otherwise, how could you even step outside? Legal surveillance is everywhere, and police checkpoints are frequent in Southern California, where I live. Contrary to how you're portrayed in news and media coverage, it's not like you can keep your existence a secret. The IRS, the DMV, the police, they all know you exist. There are records that you surrender to the whims of the government—like proof of address and documentation of your identity—in order to do the simple tasks of living, such as getting a driver's license or receiving your pay.[1] Those records then ensnare you. You are, conspicuously, *documented* in your process of living "illegally" in this country. The US government is aware that you are working because, although you lack a Social Security number, you are assigned a personal identification number that you use to pay taxes each year. They know how to find you because of your proof of address. If they have a reason to come get you, they will. The smallest traffic infraction or an altercation at a grocery store could be enough to incite your deportation. But if they don't have a reason, they're going to take advantage of you instead. Even though we work, we are denied the basic forms of help that most Americans can depend upon; no access to consistent healthcare in most parts of the country and no 401(k) or other retirement benefits are just two examples. Because—and this is the crux of how my physical, emotional, and spiritual well-being have been taken away from me—the presence of undocumented immigrants is convenient for the United States. Your time, your labor, your ingenuity: this country extracts these from you cheaply, with no safety net proffered in return.

The scars of the past hardships that brought me to this country intermingle with my fear of Border Patrol—a fear that is triggered by even the most banal of activities. From showing my driver's license at a bar to getting on the freeway to go to work, each public act feels like stepping on thin ice.

In 2011, I fled my home country, Mexico, and landed in the United States in a daze of loss, clutching the hand of my little brother, AC. We were seeking refuge from a war—a war of drug cartels—that the US refuses to acknowledge, meaning the government will not allow us to claim refugee status. I do everything in my control to live in accordance with the legal system in this country. Despite the label I've been assigned, there isn't anything "illegal" about me.

ON "THE COST"

In 2010, Harvard economist Raj Chetty and his research team suggested that a high-quality kindergarten teacher is worth $320,000 per year, based on the wage earnings and life outcomes of their students.[2] This, of course, is far more than actual teacher salaries, which averaged $61,000 that year.[3] There is a yawning gap between the value that these teachers produce and the salary our society is willing to pay. In this spirit, I work throughout this book to illuminate the actual value of the services the US has extracted from me while also denying me the rights of citizens.

Although I express this value as a sum, in truth, it exceeds mere dollar amounts; it's too overwhelming to fully comprehend. The tally also includes intangibles: Rocío Rosales, an associate professor at UC Irvine who has spent years studying the lives of *fruteros* (fruit vendors) in Los Angeles,[4] has identified losses such as the "cost of memory." "What does it mean to miss years of your parents' lives, to miss a funeral, to miss the act of mourning with your family? . . . There are all these young men and women who are living in Los Angeles and across the US, who are missing out on creating memories with their families in Mexico. In terms of the price that undocumented immigrants pay, that's one of the heaviest: that when you are in the US, you might never see your family again."

Rosales's reflection gets to the historical and structural factors that push people to migrate to the US in the first place. American culture often frames a person's choice to migrate as driven solely by their individual concerns. Jonathan Rosa, a linguistic anthropologist at Stanford, notes in an interview with me, that "the prevailing, dominant narrative around immigration and around everyday life in the United States, is just kind of focused on individual-level choices that are imagined as only coming from a single person, an individual person, and only impacting that person."

Rosa goes on, "There is actually a long history of US wealth being built through extraction from the very places that then prompt people to migrate to the United States. And then our entire economy is built on the labor of people who are held in a perpetual stasis as portable and vulnerable."

Becoming undocumented is something that the United States did to me. But that's not who I am. The "cost" in the title of this book is one that was imposed upon me, dehumanizing me and treating me as little more than labor. I am seen as a statistic, not as an individual with dreams and desires. Unseen in the eyes of this country are the ways I spend my time making films, creating stories, and collaborating on social justice movements. I've always been driven by words and by helping the world around me. When I was younger, I assumed that the only way I could help people and transform unjust systems was by becoming a lawyer. I never thought I would be someone in the kinds of dire need that I detail in this book. After years of pursuing the prerequisites to a law degree, accumulating debt in the process, I realized that access to higher education is closed off to me in the United States. Forced to drop out of college, I shifted my efforts. Today I produce films, collaborate on research, and write stories as my primary means of bettering this world.

And so, despite the heavy costs of life in immigration limbo, I've still been able to thrive and transform my community. The growth of the US is in*debt*ed to the individual suffering in marginalized communities, as well as to our bright moments of success. The researcher Leigh Patel writes: "Although rarely acknowledged, the nation owes a great debt to the many cultures it has exploited for the purposes of accumulating property as whiteness. . . . The nation owes debts not only to those who have suffered under its project of settler colonialism, but also to those populations who have manifested, under challenging obstacles, success and stability."[5]

One of the hardest aspects of trying to offer a summary of the costs of undocumented American life is the fact that these costs overlap and compound.[6] The cost of being an undocumented immigrant overlaps with the cost of existing as a racialized multilingual Mexican woman in a white supremacist culture. My limited access to medical care is compounded by my inflexible work schedule and a lack of paid time off. When you are undocumented, finding a job you "want" isn't an option, and flexible schedules or paid time off are not up for negotiation. The stress of navigating these difficulties intertwines with my mental health. And so on.

ORGANIZING AND RESEARCHING THE COSTS

Each of this book's ten chapters accounts for one specific cost of my life as an undocumented American. This accounting is grounded in the overarching narrative of my arrival in the US and my struggle to build a life here. These chapters share the broad strokes of a younger me thriving on one side of a border before global forces and local dangers forced me to merely survive on the other side. The first three chapters detail a childhood and young adulthood spent in Mexico. Readers might wonder what these chapters have to do with the cost of being undocumented in the US. The answer is that global markets, Western cultural attitudes, and a never-ending drug trade created pivotal and precarious moments in my life long before I arrived here, ultimately making my experiences in the US even harder.

It took all of my strength and emotional energy to share these stories with you, and know that I—and any individual labeled undocumented— could fill this book ten times over with additional costs. As I unwrap the private parts of my life for you, it might surprise you to know that I am a deeply private person. Many of the stories I share in this book are new even to most of my friends and family. Excavating them has been an incredibly difficult process. To protect the people I have been close to, and to avoid retaliation from people who wish me harm, many of the names, locations, and corroborating details have been changed. I am sharing these stories because this country spends too much time *talking about* and not nearly enough time *listening to* people like me. With the exception of a few nuanced, singular memoirs, there aren't many places where you'll find our voices.[7] Specifically, Jose Antonio Vargas's *Dear America*, Karla Cornejo Villavicencio's *The Undocumented Americans*, and Julissa Arce's *My (Underground) American Dream* have been important touchstones for this book. This book adds to those voices, but also goes a step further by situating my personal experiences within the larger context of scholarship on immigration policy, immigration history, and ethnographic research. Together, these research approaches explore the limits of empathy and redefine how readers can support and understand individuals like me.[8]

I am also sharing this book with you because I want to convey a complicated feeling that many other undocumented immigrants can relate to. I hold a deep love for the United States, even as I am often furious with its treatment of me. I am grateful for how this country has protected me from the violence that would have killed me in Mexico, even if, lately, the inaccessibility of healthcare here has nearly taken me out. Yet I've been able to access an abundance of beautiful opportunities in this country. Opportunities to create films, to lead organizations that better the lives of people in my city, to write this book. Putting these feelings side by side, it may seem like I am in a codependent relationship. And so, as I will write bitterly in the pages to come, remember that I carry a deep love for this country, and I hurt when this country hurts.

Lastly, I write this book to speak to and alongside my immigrant community. For every family that has ever been separated by borders and immigration policies, I write this for you. For us. I wish that my suffering was not relatable and that this was not a book that needed to be written. And so, I write, hoping if I illuminate my truth, it might help many of us, collectively.

A WARNING

In many ways, my story may not be what you expect. I didn't cross the border with a coyote—I flew in on a tourist's visa. I wasn't brought here as a child, innocent of my undocumented status—I made the decision to take these risks as an adult. I am not one of the famous Dreamers; I do not qualify for Deferred Action for Childhood Arrivals (DACA).[9] My story is my own, and, like the stories of all human beings, it is filled with contradictions. I am a dutiful and pious daughter in one paragraph and a confidant to the children of one of Mexico's most prominent drug cartels in another. I am an activist organizing a large-scale humanitarian campaign for the unhoused only to find myself rattled and broken by insecurity and developing English proficiency.

We don't talk about people being "documented." It's a label that exists largely only for those that lack it. Labeling people as *un*docu-mented—something Americans do to roughly 11 million people in their country—defines us as incomplete, not of equal value, not fully existing. While the media has painted broad pictures of us as a monolithic entity, the full spectrum of who we are, the dreams we harbor, and the desires we suppress are not fully shown. In this way, my story is a singular ac-counting of the mounting costs of my lived experiences.

The costs of my survival in this country include multiple descriptions of (my own and others') physical and mental abuse, work exploitation, drug use, and attempted suicide. These were not easy memories to excavate, and they will not be easy to read. I want you to take care of yourself and consider if my costs might be too much for you as a reader at any given time. The stories will be waiting when you're ready to pick this book up again.

PROPINA

These stories are an accounting, but they are also my gift to you. A *pequeño regalo* (small gift).[10] Since 2022, I have been coediting *La Cuenta*, an online publication that centers the voices of undocumented storytell-ers. At the end of each weekly story, our contributors offer a *propina*—an action item, an offering for the reader to take away with them. When *La*

Cuenta publishes a story about undocumented motherhood or higher education or the perils of E-Verify, for example, it is followed with links to resources or poems or other ways to stay engaged. In the same spirit, I want readers to consider each chapter of this book as a set of narratives to guide dialogue and spur action. If my research and experiences connect with you, I hope you'll share them with your friends and colleagues, and I hope you'll reevaluate the narratives of immigration and "legality" that litter the news today.

We are not that different, you and I. I want you to work alongside me in building a different, more compassionate world, where our similarities drive toward a balanced-out accounting of everyday life. In the words of activist Lilla Watson, "If you have come here to help me, you are wasting your time, but if you have come because your liberation is bound up with mine, then let us work together." The first step toward our collaboration is understanding. Take out your ledger book and tally with me as we begin our accounting of the cost of being undocumented.

CHAPTER 1

THE COST OF TIME

A healthy life should have a past that can be cherished, a present that offers challenges and joys, and a future to look forward to. However, because of my circumstances, my past has nothing for me. It is just a house that used to be my family's, ransacked of my childhood belongings, sitting in a now unfamiliar city. My present is filled with mounting costs, all to live in a country that does not always tolerate me. And my future is a series of bleak prospects and dead ends.

People very rarely ask why I am living in the United States in the first place. It frustrates me that the circumstances that bring the undocumented community to this country are overlooked or depicted as problematic stereotypes. It is convenient to not have to know me and my truth. It's easier to keep me in an exploited position that way. The United States profits from not acknowledging why I am here. But as I share in this chapter the costs of my past, my present, and my uncertain future, I will begin with the painful story that brought me from there to here, from then to now.

THE PAST

I grew up in a very wealthy family in the Mexican state of Sinaloa during the 1990s and 2000s. If you were walking the streets of my hometowns of Culiacán and Navolato during those years, you might have heard delivery trucks playing the jingle for my family's chain of *tortillerías*: "Tortilla's Alix!" The chain was named after me, and the tortillerías were a cornerstone of my family's wealth. My sister and I grew up working in several of the nearby shops. Before becoming entrepreneurs, my father practiced business law and my mother was a private school director and teacher. By the time I was a young child, they had both left those careers to focus on building their grocery empire.

My family had multiple houses and a collection of cars. I grew up among nannies and housekeepers. We were raised with conservative, Apostolic/Pentecostal Christian values. My parents instilled in me and my two siblings, alongside lessons of humility and respect for everyone, the fact that money was an illusion that could disappear. This is why my parents felt it was so important for my sister and me to work in our family's business from an early age. Sinaloa had long been a center of drug cartels. The escalating violence in my city and the threats of extortion directed at our family's businesses meant that we never took our comfort for granted.

These lessons were shared quietly and deliberately. My dad was a natural introvert, though also an energetic and exuberant person. He would speak only when he had something important to say. He talked and moved slowly. He was a calming, steady presence for me, an angel. He had so much peace in his heart that it overflowed into the corners of our home. My childhood is soundtracked by my dad playing hymns on our family's piano. He loved me and my siblings more than anything.

In 2008, when I was in college, my dad started to invest in projects that involved collaborating with people beyond his established network. A family friend introduced him to someone interested in partnering to expand our chain of stores across Mexico, perhaps even internationally. My dad took on a substantial loan from this investor. The opportunity, however, came at an unfortunate time. The global economy took a turn for the worse, and our lives started to go downhill. Sales went down as people in the city were forced to make do with less money, buying fewer extra groceries or tortillas. My dad began working endless hours, as longtime employees had to be let go.

It seemed like everybody in my country was losing money. Businesses were shutting down. Many people around us were losing their houses and cars. The particularities of life in Sinaloa made this situation even more adverse. At the time, 90 percent of the cocaine in the US was being smuggled in from Mexico, much of which was controlled by cartels in Sinaloa. Escalating feuds between cartels and with the Mexican and US governments made life in Sinaloa all the more dangerous. Gunfire in the streets, robberies in broad daylight, and kidnappings were daily occurrences. Families that had the means fled the area. My family, too, had plans to move and open shops in Cabo. We also knew that our family's debt would follow us to another state. We delayed our departure, hoping to first make a substantial dent in the money we owed. And yet, despite his efforts, my dad found himself unable to make payments to his new business partner.[1]

One of my parents' biggest fears was that my sister, my brother, or I would get caught up in the life of the cartels. Because of those fears, they perhaps protected us too much. We weren't allowed, for example, to listen to the popular *narcocorridos* that glorified the gruesome cartel crimes on the streets of Culiacán.

Corridos are a genre of narrative ballads in Mexico, and narcocorridos focus that form on cartel violence. Cati de los Ríos, an associate professor at UC Berkeley, explained to me over a Zoom call, "Narcocorridos were blowing up in the late '90s and 2000s. Around 2010, the [Mexican] government started banning them, prohibiting them on the radio. Kids were basically not allowed to listen to them. And that's also kind of why, a lot of *corridistas* in Mexico would come to Los Angeles and find refuge with certain record labels because they felt like, 'Okay, we're less likely to be sued for defamation or killed on this side if we sign with [record labels in the US].'"

Explaining her years-long work listening to, interviewing, and observing Mexican youth writing and listening to corridos within California, de los Ríos is careful to make clear that the violent narcocorridos were only a portion of the corridos that circulate more widely: "A lot of the kids, yes, would listen to narcocorridos. But it would also not necessarily be a blueprint for how to live life. It was, for them, a kind of reading and learning about the horrors of capitalism and the drug war."[2]

This glorified drug war was front and center for my family. The stress of the new financial reality brought on by that war, in addition to the global downturn, weighed heavily on my father. The house grew quieter as he retreated into himself, trying to find a way to dig us out of mounting debt. Within months, his hair went gray, and his once lithe figure became alarmingly thin. By 2009, an old man had replaced the person I'd known as my dad.

This was when he started selling our cars, our businesses, and our houses. Things started getting tense at home, but I was too young to understand that my dad was in a living nightmare.

Two years later, in late 2010, when I was nineteen years old, my father gathered us for a very hard conversation. It was the five of us: my dad, my mom, my older sister, Cindy, my eight-year-old brother, AC, and me. At the table where we'd shared Christmas dinners and laughed as a family, my father slouched in a seat diagonal from me, not at his customary position at the head. He breathed out slowly, controlling his voice. He told us that he'd found out that his new business partner had been laundering money for one of the major drug cartels in Sinaloa. This meant that the business partner was an incredibly dangerous man. Fuzzy details of our lives became clearer to me; the new bodyguards my father had suddenly hired as security for our house now made sense. My family had hired bodyguards before, when I was younger and cartel-related violence had gotten especially bad, but the appearance of this additional security had been a surprise. At the time, we didn't know that the debt we owed would become the breaking point for us as a family. That we would be broken apart.

As my father spoke, it became clear that the heaviness he was carrying was killing him. We kept our emotions in check for one another, no one wanting to cry, as we listened to my exhausted father. I broke down silently, wiping away my tears so that my dad would see me as strong. I stood and paced anxiously in the dining room, too agitated to stay seated, as my dad said, "You know what? We're going to have to sell the other houses. We're going to keep this house because *this* is our home. We're going to sell all the cars. At the end of the day, I don't care if we lose material things. I'm just really scared that our lives might be in danger."

The danger turned out to be greater than my siblings and I could have known at the time. My parents were hiding from us the fact that cartel members had been in regular contact with my dad, and that he had sold some of our cars and our houses to keep them away from us. While Cindy, AC, and I could see our wealth draining, we couldn't see how desperately my dad surrendered our belongings in an attempt to protect us.

At the end of the conversation, my dad said something that has stayed in my heart: "We're losing everything. But look, it's the five of us. We're not going to focus on what we don't have anymore, which is money. *We're going to focus on what we have left: the five of us.*"

He said that two more times. *We're going to focus on what we have left: the five of us. We're going to focus on what we have left: the five of us.*

I think of that sentence every single day of my life.

When I heard that, I realized that we were probably going to end up homeless. But hearing my dad say "the five of us" gave me comfort. I was reminded that hardships happen in life. We might lose all the luxuries of wealth, but that was okay. We would still have each other. That night I slept, knowing I had my family.

THE DAY I LOST IT ALL

I am eighteen months younger than my sister, but we were both always treated like "older sisters." If you are an older sister in Mexico, you are like a mom. We pretty much had to raise our little brother as a team, because that was the cultural expectation. As a result, I developed a lot of the skills I rely on today. My parents might have worked hard, but so did we.

One of my tasks at home was cooking. I loved cooking because my dad appreciated it so much. He was always so grateful when I cooked a special dish just for him. One afternoon in December 2010, I decided to make him *camarones en crema* while he was at work. He loved seafood.

I had done a really nice job preparing that dish and was excited for him to come home.

But he never came home to eat that meal. Just before six o'clock, one of his employees began shouting outside for my sister: "Cindy! Cindy! Cindy!"

Cindy and I went to the window. The employee told us our dad was going to the hospital in an ambulance. He had fainted.

My sister and I grabbed our keys, went to the hospital, and waited for hours to see him, as my mom stayed by his bedside. Finally, she came out and told us something I didn't fully understand: "Your dad fainted, and he woke up without his memory." I had just seen my dad that morning. How could he have no memory?

For three days, the doctors tried to figure out what was wrong. On the third day, a doctor told us that my dad had five cancerous tumors in his brain. They were the reason he didn't remember anything.

The doctor then added that the effects of the tumors on his brain and his perception were why the doctors had been forced to tie my dad to the bed. My mom had been hiding that information from us. She had been protecting us from the reality that my dad had been trying to escape the hospital, screaming that he had to go home.

My dad stayed in that bed for thirty-two days. On January 2, 2011, he regained his memory for three minutes. He told us, "I'm going to go with God very soon." He was crying. And he said that things might not get easier right now, but that we had to trust God that at some point things would get better. He told Cindy and me, "All the time, I have been telling you girls how to be strong, wise, and brave. The most important thing that you need to do is to protect your brother and to protect each other. Your lives are in danger, so you have to be careful with every single move that you make. You have to stay safe."

That night, I slept on the cold hospital floor next to his bed. Even though it was uncomfortable, I was so grateful to lie next to my dad one last time. When I heard his breathing go ragged at six in the morning, I stood up. He was struggling to breathe. I held his hand because I thought he might be having a bad dream.

What happened next was one of the biggest blessings in my life. I saw my dad pass away. I saw how he took his last breath. Even though it was a nightmare to go through, it was an honor to witness.

There was no use trying to collect myself. I walked into the hallway and everybody was there: my grandparents, my mom, my sister, and the doctor. As soon as they saw my face, they knew he was gone.

I followed them back into his room. I now wish I hadn't done that, because I regret seeing what I saw. The doctors tried to revive him by putting all these things on his chest, but nothing helped. I knew nothing was going to bring him back.

I was the person who had to tell the rest of our family and friends that my dad was dead. And then came the moment my dad had prepared me for: telling my brother. When I hugged him and told him the news, he was destroyed completely. So was I. He told me, "Hey, we're going to be okay. We are going to be just fine." He grabbed my face with unfamiliar confidence. I think his firm grip was God reminding us that, like my dad had said, things might be bad, but we would be okay. At that time, my sister and I were in college. Now we would not be able to finish. We still owed lots of money and our lives were in danger. My father's death did not wipe away our balance and we had no more money to pay for security or bribes. An unspoken law of Sinaloa is that if you cannot pay cartels back with money, you will eventually pay with your life.

Seeking help from friends or family in other Mexican cities would be putting them at risk. Because we had no money or resources to hide in any other states, we had to leave the country.

Outsiders don't understand that in Mexican states like Sinaloa, if somebody wants to kill you, they can hire an assassin for $100 and that person will kill you. Finding a hit man is as easy as going on Amazon and getting a package delivered. I love Mexico with all my heart, but I cannot deny how easy it is to commit crimes there. The US, on the other hand, runs background checks on Mexicans wishing to enter the country, making it impractical for those with a criminal record to cross the border. The surveillance that I went through in order to get a tourist visa to the US meant that violent criminals would not follow my family here.

I had a life in Mexico. I had friends, family, school, and a church. I had a favorite restaurant. I had a spot at the beach where the sun kissed my nose all year long. All that was taken away from me because I needed to stay alive. If I had stayed in Mexico, I can assure you that I would be dead.

We had a family friend in Georgia who offered to hide us from the people who wanted to kill us. AC and I would go to live with them. At the time, I was twenty and he was nine. My mom and sister were going to stay in Mexico to try to pay our debts by selling what remained of our houses, cars, and belongings. They would move from city to city as they did this, never staying in one place for long.

Years have passed, each one bringing new surprises. My mom is still trying to process our collective losses. As for me, I never got the chance to grieve my dad. I was in the United States trying to make a living and learning how to be a mom for my little brother.

THE EXORBITANT COSTS
OF "COLORED PEOPLE'S TIME"

My past holds nothing for me, but it is also something that I can never escape. This is true for so many of the undocumented individuals in this country. Our past takes its daily toll on us. The present offers us no peace either. Our current moment is one of anticipating things going badly, as they have too often gone. In this way the present is a temporal period that is also taxed. Literally.

Although undocumented people don't have Social Security numbers, most tax forms have a place to enter an Individual Taxpayer Identification Number (ITIN) instead. This is utilized by tax-paying undocumented individuals like me. Every year, undocumented workers pay more than $11 billion in taxes. Estimates are that 75 percent of us pay taxes each year. A decade and a half ago, a report from the Congressional Budget Office suggested that the two decades of tax revenue considered in the report did not "exceed the cost of the services [immigrants] used."[3] It was a purely financial conjecture, as such findings do not speak to the cultural and social benefits we ineffably bring to this nation of immigrants. More recent research emphasizes that most immigrants have a "net present value" of zero dollars, meaning that we essentially pay for ourselves over time, not actually burdening the US social system.[4]

I pay these taxes willingly and try not to think too hard about where my money goes. It's an odd feeling to do things right in a place that does not welcome you. US citizens, once they are of eligible age, receive Social Security and Medicare. If they are low-income, they may receive Medicaid at any age. I hand over income but do not receive the same benefits as my neighbors. This makes it impossible for me to imagine a future in which I can be healthy and secure.

Anthropologists—who are predominantly white—have lately been coming to a new understanding of non-Western conceptions of time. The foundations of our conceptualization of time as linear derive from thirteenth-century European Christianity, which viewed time as "a segment of eternity" and considered time to be godly in its manifestation. Previous, non-Christian civilizations, however, conceptualized time as cyclical. Anthropologist Carol Greenhouse in her study on the politics of time, *A Moment's Notice*, shows what time means within different societies, depending on how people choose to use the moments of their day. Her case studies—which range from legal histories of time in the US to the links between land and temporality in China—suggest that our conception of time can evolve. Our workday routines, our time commuting and existing in particular places, our perceptions of adolescence and growth—all of these are elastic, though I continue to feel the aching pull of the past when I remember my father and his words.

History would suggest that when one established perception of time butts against another, remarkable (and often violent) changes occur. In her analysis of the downfall of the Aztec Empire, for example, Greenhouse suggests that Emperor Moctezuma's interpretation of the arrival of conquistador Hernán Cortés as the return of the deity Quetzalcóatl stemmed from him misreading the cyclical Aztec calendar. The perceptions of time and its function as a harbinger of prophecy led to the Spanish conquest of South America. The costs of time have brought down entire civilizations in our past, as they may very well do again in the future. As Ursula Le Guin writes, "Any human power can be resisted and changed by human beings."[5] If society's perceptions of time are fueled by imagination, storytelling, and confronting new possibilities, a speculative imagination voiced by the marginalized must wind our clocks to a new kind of present.

This necessary work toward a new future, however, does not change the fact that the undocumented are currently forced to endure the painful costs of time in the present. One conception of modern time is a racist stereotype you might be familiar with: "colored people time" or other variations like "Black people time" or "Mexican time." This term carries the assumption that the named group of people inherently runs *late*. That they are less organized, respectful, hardworking, or capable. That they will roll into social gatherings hours later than expected. What's not acknowledged is how this term assumes that the "correct" perception of time is essentially "white" time.

Let us recognize that the cost of time in this country is extracted from the undocumented across several dimensions. First, racist policies steal our futures, making it impossible for us to benefit from the systems of social welfare that we pay into. Second, we are often separated from our past by borders that we cannot cross. This past is, instead, a debt we pay through grief. My constant fear of assassins is rooted in my past. Finally, racist *cultural* orientations of time—the capitalist workweek that pushes my life forward, and tropes like "colored people time"—assume an inferiority in how we live in the present.

STOLEN FUTURES

While ample research has been conducted on young undocumented immigrants and their educational and career opportunities in the US, there is scant information on the undocumented elderly.[6] This is despite the fact that this population is not only equal in size to the youth population of Dreamers often at the center of policy debates, it is expected to double in the next decade.

We are much more than the aches and pains that ail us. Yet the majority of data about the undocumented elderly focuses on health concerns. To be clear, health is indeed of central importance to this group.

This community is often denied consistent access to healthcare while simultaneously needing to work longer hours—often in physically demanding environments—in order to make ends meet. Nearly every aspect of undocumented life trickles into how the body is shaped, exhausted, and broken by these circumstances.

Aging therefore comes faster for this group. Treatable illnesses, work-related injuries, and dental complications transform into bigger, endemic issues. These all fall on the shoulders of a population that is less likely to have money for treatment, let alone retirement.

These are compounding problems: We contribute taxes in the present, funding public healthcare and retirement programs from which we cannot benefit. We then inevitably suffer treatable medical issues that worsen over time. And, because of legal restrictions to hiring us and providing us retirement plans, we're compelled to take jobs that do not allow us to amass the savings that would cushion us in times of medical emergency. Our future is typically a bleak one.

A policy brief released in 2019 by the Center for Social Innovation identified three familiar barriers impeding older undocumented adults' access to medical services.[7] The first barrier was language: if an individual could not speak English, they were not comfortable accessing services. The second was their fear that they would be asked questions about their immigration status; this fear of deportation remains a consistent deterrent, even in emergency situations. Finally, the costs of healthcare remain prohibitively high.

In the *New England Journal of Medicine*, Ricardo Nulia describes the revolving door of emergency care that offers undocumented immigrants a bare minimum level of care, just enough to survive from one day to the next. While federal law requires emergency departments to stabilize the symptoms of patients who come in for care, critically ill undocumented immigrants often cannot access long-term treatment or even hospice care that might make end-of-life pain more manageable. Those with terminal illnesses "are admitted from the emergency department with severe pain or organ failure, we stave off death well enough for them to be discharged, and very soon, they return . . . until the day they don't."[8] Morbidly, some of the community relief efforts for undocumented communities that sprang up during the COVID-19 pandemic included only financial support for funerals and repatriation—sending bodies *back* to a country they likely have not called home in decades. More than 40 percent of undocumented individuals in this country have been here for more than fifteen years, according to data from the Migration Policy Institute.[9]

I see these statistics and wonder where I will be when I am older. Bleak options await me in the future, while cartels haunt my past.

The limited research on the undocumented elderly fails to look at these individuals as anything more than laboring bodies or at their futures as anything more than illness. This is a self-fulfilling prophecy and a great loss for our society. We could learn so much from the undocumented elderly. In an alternative future, they could proffer knowledge, generosity, and insights that could fundamentally transform our society. A more empathetic beginning to this work requires seeing the undocumented elderly as more than future liabilities. They are family. They deserve rest, dignity, room to reflect and to contribute to society in ways that are not physically or spiritually backbreaking.

Recently, some psychologists have started to identify pre-traumatic stress disorder (pre-TSD) as a condition afflicting young people who fear the climate catastrophe to come. Likewise, a fear of imminent illness during the pandemic has also been linked to pre-TSD.[10]

Like post-traumatic stress disorder (PTSD), the symptoms of pre-traumatic stress are substantial: "The resulting symptoms (e.g., fear, anger, vulnerability, uncertainty, irritability, concentration difficulties, insomnia, appetite disturbances) are so intense as to negatively affect daily functioning," reports the American Psychological Association. While there is not yet consensus in the medical world about the symptoms of pre-TSD, the label offers recognition for understanding the lived costs of the undocumented perception of time: our anxiety about our future slowly eats away at our mental and physical well-being. Across multiple interviews and personal experiences, it is clear that this community does everything to persist in the present moment. Even as we are burdened by the traumas of the past, we receive nothing from our society with which we can build a future.

The costs of time consistently deny the full humanity of the undocumented. The corridos of the past wreak havoc and fear. The future imagines undocumented individuals as only bodies to deal with and dispose of. And the present is an expensive limbo of stereotyping, fear, and cut wages.

BEFORES AND AFTERS

Our lives are divided into a series of befores and afters—moments that irrevocably alter the terrain of where we'll go and who we'll become.

Before my father died. And after.

Before loss and drug cartels sent me across geographic borders and time zones. And after.

Before the US saw me as "illegal." And after.

There are also events that cleaved the world long before I was born. Before borders made people illicit. And after. This cleaved world may still unite at some future point, if borders are abolished.

As I unwillingly face the cost of the uncertain future I was handed, I think about the millions of other undocumented people in this country and wonder how they are dealing with this same anxiety. We collectively exhale a black cloud each day, trying to keep this stress inside of us. Lately, I've been wondering what the future looks like if I continue to stay in the United States. I don't know how much longer I can live like this.

Being in the United States is a battle with time. I left all of me in the past and had to rebuild myself through therapy, networking, and careful steps to avoid deportation. Regardless of how much I disagree with this country and how much it dehumanizes me, I retain love for the possibility of what America might become. Even though I don't feel safe, I know I'm alive because I came here. I am a resident who loves this country, yet I am only *harbored* here, not even tolerated by most people. I want this place to shelter me *safely*.

Recently, I was catching up with some of my LA friends on a Zoom call. Back when the pandemic started, they'd decided to rent a beach house so they could surf while isolating. They lived there for much of the worst of the pandemic, surfing every day.

Now they're all back at home. They have well-paying jobs, futures secure. So while we were on Zoom, they began talking about how perhaps, when they grow older and are ready to retire, they could buy a house together in Hawaii or at the beach here in California. Then they could "just be free." It was the kind of playful daydreaming backed with real financial and legal possibility. It certainly *could* be a reality someday if they wanted it to be. For them.

I love these friends. But they just have no idea what my life is like. Sure, they know I'm undocumented, but in our conversations, it's always clear that no one fully understands what that means for me. They always assume that it's a small legal loophole that will be easy to fix eventually. I don't think of myself as a jealous person, but the truth is, I am jealous—of my friends' ability to visualize themselves in the future.

It terrifies me that I'm not even able to dream of a future for myself when I'm older. It's one of the reasons I keep asking myself, "Is it even worth staying in the US?" But I do not have other safe options for living right now. I'm caught in the double bind of undocumented living: a perilous past is forcing me into an uncertain future. I don't know what the decades might throw at me. But I also don't know where I'll be a year from now, or in six months. The future is five minutes from now, and in that time, my world could suddenly collapse, again.

CHAPTER 2

THE COST OF
BEING MEXICANA

Growing up, I was always proud to be Mexicana.[1] It wasn't until I arrived in the US that the world told me that I shouldn't be. But being Mexicana is a gift. I love knowing that I belong to the land of dreamers, of hardworking and good-hearted people. And yet, being Mexicana also came with its own challenges.

Throughout my childhood, it was a tradition for one of my mom's sisters and her family to come visit us during the spring break or in the summertime. My family's house had a swimming pool, a luxury I look back on fondly. I love being in the water, and Sinaloa's temperate weather meant it was warm year-round.

I wasn't able to fully enjoy the pool the way my cousins did, though. They dressed in colorful bikinis, while I hid my swimsuit under a huge shirt and loose shorts. I knew that my body was not *good enough* for the rainbows of bikinis that everyone around me wore. I was twelve years old, and I knew—compared to everyone else in my family—I was too big, too curvy, and too brown.[2]

We usually spent the whole day in the pool, from eight in the morning until late into the evening, when a parent would finally pull us, shriveled and sated, out of the water and into bed. Our days were an endless loop of playing, laughing, and gorging on junk food.

That junk food, pillaged from my family's stores, was a key feature of those summer days. Each time we gathered, we splayed out a small monument of candy, chips, and other treats by the poolside for all of us to snack on. But one day during that summer, I turned down all of the Ruffles, Doritos, and Oreos. My family was weirded out—junk food had always been my thing, and everyone knew it.

Not eating wasn't the only reason I felt bad that day. I was also fatigued and had a headache. But I still spent the requisite amount of time dipping my body in the water, so as not to call attention to myself. I didn't want my aunt and cousins to know the real reason.

A few weeks earlier, my mom had started reading a book about a trendy new no-carb diet that it seemed everybody was on. She started following the diet and encouraged Cindy and me to do it with her. At first, I followed the diet when I was around my mom but secretly ate whatever I wanted at school. But after a few weeks, I couldn't take it anymore: the lack of energy, the constant headaches and nausea, and missing out on the junk food I loved. The short-lived diet was just one more reminder that my body wasn't good enough. The assault on self-worth starts far too young for a Mexicana, as it does for women all over the world.

When I was in fifth grade, I was running past one of the teachers, late to class for some reason, when he admonished me: "It's a good thing you're running because you are getting pretty fat." I remember another elementary teacher commenting with surprise, "You're actually pretty!" and then adding, "Just don't get fat."

This was the early 2000s, and diet culture was the only thing you saw on TV, in magazines, and in the movies. The beauty standards around me were impossible to achieve: impossibly thin yet also impossibly buxom, and of course, impossibly white. There was no one that looked like me in popular culture. Paris Hilton was the pinnacle of attractiveness. A tiny blond person: in Paris's catchphrase, "That's hot." By the time I was in middle school, it felt like eating disorders were the norm among the girls I knew. If you didn't have one, there was something wrong with you. So I had to try to be normal, right?

Instead, as a twelve-year-old girl, hungry for acceptance from my mother and for the carbs that I was expected not to consume when I was at home, I was overwhelmingly depressed. Every day, I had a headache and lived in the anxiety of my mom discovering I hadn't been following our diet. But, of course, as the weight melted away from my mother's and sister's arms and bellies, they saw that my body was doing the opposite.

I'm still scared of food. I instinctively flinch at the sight of heavy and greasy dishes. I still love the junk foods of my childhood, but I've been conditioned to not accept them when they're offered. I look at calories on the back of packages like they are my enemy. And I am not alone in this. Many of the women I know have similar phobias.

When I was a little girl, I was super slim. I could eat whatever I wanted, and God knows, I did! But when puberty hit in middle school, it came at me hard. I suddenly had what seemed like huge hips and a butt that nobody asked for. I hated it. It's what a naturally growing body does when it hits puberty. But that's not how my mom or her sisters saw it. To them, I was just *fat*.

My aunts made comments about my body every time I saw them. Instead of "Hello," the first thing they would say was *Te tienen en engorda* (They're fattening you up), like an animal to be cooked. Panic attacks preceded every family gathering.

Being a woman has always been suffused with these anxieties. Every single day a new fear is unlocked: a new part of your body turns out to be not the right size or shape or complexion. It feels like your genius and your creativity are deemed worthless. Your biggest task is to just *be* pretty for the world. I am grateful that I grew up with a father who enveloped me in love. My dad always made me feel like I was pretty. Like I was enough. But he was the exception. Growing up in the noise and pettiness of the world, with so many people telling you that you are not pretty enough or white enough or friendly enough ("You should smile more"), it is too easy to believe them. During that summer of baggy shirts and hunger cramps, I began to realize that to be Mexicana is to be in a constant battle against what aunts and mothers and the media—and your own mind—say about you.

I started to realize that the smaller I made myself, the more people approved of me. The quieter I was—the easier I was to be around—the better. I felt like I was born a square, but I had to mutilate my edges to become the circle that the world expected me to be.

BEING BROWN

For as long as I can remember, people constantly compared me to Cindy. While I had dark brown hair and light brown skin, Cindy was blond, light-skinned, and incredibly smart. Genes are funny that way. She didn't struggle with any of her classes and never had to spend much time doing homework. She took to dance naturally and planned to become a professional ballerina. She had the rhythm, she had the attitude. In contrast, I felt rhythmless in my growing limbs.

Cindy was never comfortable with the comparisons between us. She was always my protector and reassured me that in her eyes I was special, beautiful. And yet our differences were profound, and my family and teachers were not shy about pointing them out. My kindergarten teacher was the first in a long series of teachers to ask me why Cindy and I didn't look alike. "Do you have different parents?" she asked. No, I explained, our parents are the same. While my teacher questioned my genetics, my classmates told me—bluntly, as kids do—that Cindy was *so* pretty. And that I was *not so* pretty. In traditional Mexican culture, skin tone is a major component of evaluating a person's beauty. The same kindergarten teacher once told me, "If you didn't play so much in the sun, you wouldn't be so *prieta* [a pejorative word to describe dark brown skin]. You would be as light as your sister." Lighter skin, of course, reflects colonial, European heritage and dark skin implies more Indigenous roots. Colorism runs deep in our culture, even if we are starting to awaken to the cultural lies we've been told.[3]

My family started to make a painful running joke of our differences. Clearly, they said, it was impossible for me and Cindy to be blood sisters. I was obviously adopted. For a few years, I wondered if there was actually some truth behind the jokes. My mom's father had come to Mexico from Germany, marrying my Mexican grandmother. Most of the family members on my mom's side were light-skinned and blond. The jokes reinforced the idea that I didn't look German. They implied that, even in Mexico, I was not white enough.

Even though blond hair and light skin are rare in most parts of Mexico, it is still a part of the culture's aspirational beauty standards. That's still largely the case today. People associate lighter skin with higher status. Isabel Wilkerson's book *Caste: The Origins of Our Discontents* sheds light on how light skin and caste systems are found in systems of privilege across the world.[4]

My relationship with Cindy has been complicated from the earliest days of our childhood. She never held her light-skinned privilege over me. She tried to take care of me and protect me from the outside world, even though I never asked for it. She was sometimes overprotective of me, more like a parent than a sister. She acted as if she were responsible for everything that I did. It was suffocating. At the time, I found her constant presence and bossiness more annoying than endearing. Looking back, I can see how my sister's persistence in my life was due to her love for me. But I don't think she's ever realized how much her efforts sometimes made me feel judged by her. It would lead to a rupture in our relationship as adults. We are in a good place now, but it took years for us to repair it.

BEING GOOD

Since I knew I wasn't the pretty kid or the athletic kid or the good dancer kid or the smartest kid, I decided I would be the *easy* kid.

Cindy gave my parents a hard time. If my mom said, "You cannot have candy," Cindy would probe and question and rebut. She needed to know the rationale behind my mother's choice to deprive her of candy. My parents thought Cindy would grow up to become the world's best courtroom lawyer, and had we been able to stay in Mexico and finish college, I think this could have come true. However, some people criticized Cindy for being too outspoken, the same people who praised me for being quiet and for "knowing my place." I reasoned that if I was quiet and said yes to everything, I would be loved and admired.

I started doing a lot more for people, and I started to ask for less for myself. It got to the point where I preferred to live in discomfort than bother anyone around me. Looking back, I can see the hunger headaches by the pool as a culmination of those years of silent sacrifice. I became the kid that never talked back. I became the kid that never snuck out to parties. Good. Humble. A real team player. I wonder if that could have ever been enough for the world.

I silenced not just my desires but my basic needs. Asking my mom to make me breakfast in the morning, even just cereal, felt like a huge burden on her. Since she and my dad were either getting ready for work or out the door by the time I awoke, I saw my hunger as an imposition. Most of the time, as a result, I went to school hungry. There were real perks to being invisible and never asking for anything. My silence was treated as sweetness. My people-pleasing was seen as good-natured. The smaller I became, the better my life became for me. I would have shrunk myself out of existence if I could have.

When my brother was born, I was nine years old, and he gave me the perfect opportunity to cement my self-sacrificing persona. Acting as his primary caretaker alongside Cindy came naturally to me—I've always loved children and babies—but I took it to an extreme, because that was my role in the family.

In Mexican culture, there is this image of the sacrificial wife who stays dutifully with her husband her whole life. Even if he hits her, even if he comes home with a neck full of hickeys, this wife becomes a wonderful woman by persisting and fighting for her marriage. Long before marriage was even something I was considering in any relationship, I became fixated on embodying that perfect mixture of duty and loyalty and subservience. I learned to believe that this was not only the correct way but the only way to live. The more I gave of myself—to AC, to my family, to friends—the better a person I thought I was.

EXOTIC SURVIVAL

Throughout Mexico, especially in Sinaloa and Jalisco, the girlfriends and wives of narco bosses sport a look known as *buchona*, with light skin, large breasts, tiny stomachs, and big butts.[5] This has shaped conceptions of what beautiful Mexican women look like.[6] I had childhood friends who went in, as thirteen- and fourteen-year-olds, for multiple rounds of cosmetic surgery such as liposuction and butt and breast implants. This sculpted, fake look was a part of Mexican beauty culture that ultimately spilled across the border.

When Cindy and I moved to Atlanta as young women, I became exotically desirable. My thick accent, my fuller hips, and my shyness that was often read as demure or coy: all of this made me the invocation of the "hot" Latina archetype made famous by actresses that look like Sofía Vergara. I had been the object of some crushes back in Mexico, but nothing prepared me for the onslaught of unwanted male attention that I encountered in the US.

In Georgia, the first time I ventured to the mall with a friend, three different men tried to pick me up. I wasn't used to the boldness of young American dudes. I was going up the escalator when I heard a deep voice shout, "Hey, you dropped something!" Turning around, I saw a tall, blond young man. My English was bad, and I was scared that I had lost something or that this dude was going to hurt me. He smiled and shifted approaches: "You're really pretty—can I have your number?" I fell back on the go-to line that I had used in the past: "That's so sweet, but I have a boyfriend." My imaginary boyfriend got me out of most of these encounters, but he wasn't always enough. These kinds of pickups force women into tactical threat assessment, stressful interactions we experience throughout our lives. I've found that it's a cost that knows no borders.

"You have the most beautiful accent," said the man who kept returning to the section of the restaurant I was working in. "I love your accent," said the community college professor who was supposed to be helping me get my associate degree. "Your accent is so beautiful." "Where is your accent from?" "Your accent is so unique." "It's so attractive." "It's so sexy."

I learned to speak English by copying the phrases and pronunciations I heard in movies and TV shows. I didn't even know I had an accent until people pointed it out, as part of the "whole package" they saw in my exotic appeal: "I find how you speak so sexy." It was—and is—relentless.

And it wasn't just my voice. Men became infatuated with what I represented: a Mexican woman is supposed to be controlling but carefree, intense but loving, passionate but submissive, possessive but wholesome. Ready to cook dinner for her man and also throw hands if anyone ever threatened him. Men can't—and won't—see the real me, and that erasure is benign compared to the threats of violence that men can wield. I experience the danger that comes with being desired but not the privilege of being loved fully.

Surviving cartels in Mexico taught me early on that danger had a particular look: it was usually male. One of the habits I developed while growing up in Mexico—one that I had hoped to shed in the US—was the routine practice of trying to decide if a guy is "safe" or "a threat." Sadly, this skill has only been sharpened since coming here. The data on harassment is overwhelming: 81 percent of women have experienced sexual harassment, according to a 2018 report by the National Sexual Violence Resource Center.[7] The majority of women in the US have been catcalled. Sorry, let me clarify: the majority of women in the US have been catcalled *before they turned eighteen*, a statistic that includes 13 percent of girls younger than eleven.[8] From the man in a Chevrolet truck following me as a child in Sinaloa to the tech bros in the Bay Area, I've been catcalled in a variety of languages—"compliments" that add to the fear I've experienced as I've tried to make myself smaller in this country. I've learned that, if my guard is ever let down, even the seemingly nicest men in this country will not hesitate to devour me.

A GIRLHOOD ROBBED

For decades, Lilia Soto has researched the migration experiences of girls in transnational families. "It seemed to me that something had been done to them in terms of their girlhood in the process of migration," she told me on Zoom. Currently an associate professor in Chicana/o studies at UC Davis, she reflected, "I felt like it *robbed* them of something."

Soto's book, *Girlhood in the Borderlands: Mexican Teens Caught in the Crossroads of Migration*, is anchored in the interviews she conducted with young women who'd been separated from their fathers (though sometimes—when the world, its economy, and legalities permitted—later reunited). Work opportunities dictated these separations, with fathers typically migrating north alone for seasonal labor in the US. Soto herself grew up in a transnational family: she was born in California but spent much of her childhood in Mexico before her family reunited with her father back in California's Napa Valley. Reflecting on this childhood, Soto says, "There's an emotional and psychological trauma that I experienced growing up without my father; it's hard for me to imagine who would I have become if my father had been around."

As Soto rattled off internal question after internal question, my mind, too, spun out the possibilities of who I might have been if I had not been driven out of my home country by loss and necessity. Her questions conclude with two that are most salient to my Mexicana identity: "How would I have felt in terms of relationships with men, whether as companions or as friends? What would my life have been?"

Getting new, unwanted attention from men: these costs might not be unique to being undocumented. But what you have to understand is that, once we arrived in Atlanta, my entire life reduced to survival and adaptation. In the constant stress of looking over my shoulder and clearing a path for my brother, America took away my opportunity to enjoy my youth.

Nearly every cost that I tally in this book stems from being Mexicana. I've had to siphon off one dream at a time. Long before I was undocumented, I wanted to study law, earn academic degrees, and become an advocate for immigrant legal rights. In contrast with the stereotypes of immigrant youth, I am the first person in my family who *didn't* finish college.

I also hadn't realized that my aunts' voices had stowed away with me when I crossed into the US. Whenever I tiptoed into new relationships and opportunities here, the memory of their judging words overshadowed my confidence. I knew my body was both not good enough and a reason to be afraid. It was easier to execute things for other people's happiness than to advocate for myself. Each day, I further suppressed who I was—a process I'd been practicing for two decades.

Media depicts people in their twenties and thirties having the time of their lives and establishing professional roots that will grow into future successes. From *Gossip Girl* to *Sex and the City*, the American television shows that I watched in my fleeting spare time sent messages of what idealized life as a young woman looked like. I should have been having fun and dating and exploring the world. I should have gotten to ease into womanhood, to take the world in, one sip at a time. All that goes out the window as you start looking for places to sleep each night, when every extra penny goes to your brother's happiness. The US cost me the opportunity to discover who I was at the time I needed it most. As I write this now—*still* in debt and concerned about paying next month's rent—I know that life won't ever give me a second chance. I'm *making* this chance now, tallying these costs for you and for the world.

Colonizer mentality was very present when I was growing up. Whiteness was cleaner and purer: I internalized this as fact in Mexico and then came to see it manifested even more clearly in the US. Americans assume that my being Mexican means I am here to steal your job, not learn English, and live off the charity of this country. I encountered this every time I walked out into the world, sought out work, or opened my mouth and let my foreign tongue speak. And yet, I am still so proud of what Mexico represents and what it's taught me. Mexico is *why* I am now the loving and bold version of me that the world is getting to meet now. As I tally my Mexicana costs in the next few chapters, what becomes clear is that I wouldn't have survived these costs if I hadn't ultimately let my stronger self out.

ACCEPTING BEAUTY

I'm sitting at the beach in Half Moon Bay. The ocean always seems to find me at my most introspective. I'm telling my friend Sandra about feeling wrung out—a parched shell of myself. The waves roll in dutifully, obliging us in their own people-pleasing ways. I am so exhausted. I am an immeasurable distance away from a home that is no longer my home. I miss my dad. And I wish I hadn't bent my body into the duty of others for so long with nothing to show for it. I maintain an unending list of wounds and illnesses inside of me that I need to fix. Every day, the overbearing future gets closer to devouring me.

"I don't think you realize you are one of the bravest humans I've ever met."

Sandra's voice jolts me from my spiral of toxic thoughts. I hear her words, and they unlock me.

Sandra reminds me that I'm not trash because I made mistakes or because I let Mexico, and then the US, trample over me. She helps me see a different, truer version of myself: strong and beautiful and valued by so many good people in this world. "This is who *I* see," Sandra explains, and then I start to see her too. I am raising an incredible young man, and I am touching the lives of creative leaders around me, shaping the world through my actions and letting a little bit of my beauty shine through on my communities. I've never felt deserving of praise, and so it takes time for me to acclimate to Sandra's words. She reminds me that my heart is good. When I came to America, I was a kid raising another kid. My upbringing as a Mexican girl prepared me for this. I'd always imagined that American women were different. Perhaps more independent, with more agency and control over the gazes and thoughts and hands and power of men. I'd hoped that America would be a utopia where I could dress freely, take up space in a body I was able to accept. It's cost me my youth and my career, but I've realized that Mexicana is me. It is my greatest means of survival. It is how I preserve the greatest parts of who my father was, who my brother is becoming, and how I am shaping the world.

CHAPTER 3

THE COST OF LIVING
IN A CARTEL WAR

During the summers when I was growing up, my sister and I were tasked with opening one of the family supermarkets each morning. One day when I was fourteen, I was driving to the store at 5:30 a.m. I was sitting at a red light on the boulevard when I saw something strange: three heavy objects swaying from the pole of the traffic light.

They were bodies, still dripping blood—the remains of three people who had been executed and displayed on one of Culiacán's biggest streets. At that time of the morning, the hit men had likely just left.

Those three bodies haunt my dreams to this day. They are a reminder of the unnamed war that ultimately compelled me to come to the United States: The war that traumatized me long before I ever stepped foot here. The war that forced people in my hometown to witness over and over again dead bodies on display in different configurations. The war that normalized fear. To live in Sinaloa is to know that there may always be a body swaying on the next corner.

If you search for Sinaloa on Google, you'll see beautifully illustrated travel guides alongside reports of gruesome cartel violence. These dualities are embedded in the outside world's perceptions of Sinaloa, and they are also internalized in how I learned to move through my hometown, Culiacán, as a young woman. The verdant state of Sinaloa was ideal for growing opium in the first half of the twentieth century, and the drug trade circulated around the area as a result, eventually expanding into a variety of drugs. For decades, Sinaloa has been at the center of the ongoing fight to control the lucrative drug trade in and out of Mexico. Widespread corruption has greatly complicated this fight; sadly, the cartels exert control over aspects of the Mexican government as well. The US and the world at large have benefited economically from the Mexican government's complicity in cartel activity. Popular American television shows and films, like *Narcos* and *Sicario*, sensationalize the narco culture of wealth, excess, and violence—exactly what every Sinaloan has become desensitized to. Of course, an hour-long episode, a two-hour movie, or a season of TV can never approximate the dizzying contrasts of life in an active war zone, not recognized as such by its inhabitants or the world at large.

Sinaloa is more than a narrative backdrop. It was my home, and the lessons of violence and familial love that I learned there eventually became a training ground for my survival within the United States.

Growing up, I memorized the names and traits of the cartels just as you might keep track of sports teams from one season to the next. There was Cártel del Golfo and Cártel de Juárez. There was the Mafia Mexicana, Caballeros Templarios, and Cártel de los Arellano Félix. And there was Cártel de los Soles and Cártel del Milenio and La Familia Michoacana, La Nueva Familia Michoacana, and Los Metros. The city was filled with violent men, and as a teenage girl, I had to hone my acting and lying skills to fend off the ones who tried to pick me up. And I have lost more friends to drugs and murder than these pages could properly account for. Instead, let the words here act as a eulogy to the lives of my friends, my family, my kin who have been lost but not forgotten in the ongoing fight for control of Sinaloa and the global drug trade.

To tell you the history of my region of Mexico is to recite the folklore of the cartels. I know the names and lives of their leaders, just as an American schoolchild might memorize the biographies of the Founding Fathers. In Sinaloa, the names and legacies of narcos were woven into the landscape: that school and this church were developed by a narco benefactor, this shop and that street were sites of historic cartel bloodshed. We layered a social map of drugs and money on top of our commutes.

This history was required knowledge because it dictated who you dated, who you respected, who you paid, and how you responded when you walked down the street, followed by a man in a red Chevrolet truck.[1]

GROWING UP IN A CHANGING CITY

I spent my childhood living between the small town of Navolato and the city of Culiacán. In Navolato, the rustic setting felt like everyone in town knew each other and each other's business. Culiacán is one of the biggest cities in Sinaloa. Both places felt like home and our houses were close to the network of business my family owned in both locations. Spending my childhood living in both areas exposed me to poor farming communities that worked the land and the extremely wealthy families of Culiacán who sent privileged children to private schools. For my parents, it was important for their children to spend time in both settings and learn how to connect with people from all backgrounds. Navolato was known as the hometown of one of the world's most famous cartel leaders, Amado Carrillo Fuentes. He was born into a poor family on December 17, 1956, and worked his way up to become the head of El Cártel de Juárez. He was known as *El Señor de los Cielos* (Lord of the Skies) because he'd been one of the first narcos to effectively use airplanes to transport drugs from Colombia to Mexico.

Although Fuentes was a towering figure who shaped the modern drug trade, he led a relatively quiet life, particularly after the death of his collaborator, Pablo Escobar. Fuentes dreamed of an anonymous life. He, like many narcos who would follow, underwent several facial surgeries in an effort to become unrecognizable. However, during one of his surgeries, he died. Allegedly.[2] The idea of one of the world's most wanted criminals dying on an operating table, away from any witnesses, sounded like the kind of sleight of hand that Fuentes dreamed of. The surgeons who'd botched the procedure were buried in cement. According to the official history of my hometown, Fuentes's life ended in 1997. But his life and legacy as one of history's greatest criminals lived on.

I was just seven years old when Fuentes (and his surgeons) died. I'd heard the stories about him but didn't understand their implications.

Instead, I knew Amado Carrillo Fuentes as a man deeply respected throughout Sinaloa. He had invested money in our schools, churches, and hospitals. My neighbors spoke of him affectionately and reverently. He'd done more for the people of Sinaloa than the Mexican government ever would, most people agreed. Families wanted their kids to "make it" in the same way that Amado Carrillo Fuentes had, even if they didn't condone his crimes. He was, perhaps, our version of the American Dream. By investing in Sinaloa, Fuentes helped sell the appeal of narco culture.

Cartels were romanticized seemingly everywhere—except at my house. After Fuentes died, my parents predicted our area would soon become more dangerous. When Amado Carrillo Fuentes had been overseeing El Cártel de Juárez, there had been unspoken limits to the violence. Women and children had been protected, and Fuentes had kept the state of Sinaloa "safe." But his death ushered in a new era.

After Fuentes died, his brother Vicente took his place as the cartel's primary drug lord. But Vicente's position was precarious. Every other cartel smelled the weakness of change, wanted the valuable Sinaloa territory for themselves, and sought to claim Amado Carrillo Fuentes's throne. As cartels from other states started to seek dominance here, my little town, once a safe place, became one of Mexico's most dangerous cities.

The police never interfered in any of the violence I witnessed. Effectively, the police *are* the cartels. The few police officers who didn't want to participate in the drug trade were either paid off or killed. This corruption funneled into every profession. If you were a lawyer, a doctor, or a local business owner, the cartels generally dictated how you operated and for whom. They eventually came for my family's businesses.

When I was ten, the cartels started stealing kids. The news frequently showed stories of white vans abducting children in front of schools, selling their organs on the black market, and then leaving the bodies outside of the parents' houses. These were the years when my dad first hired bodyguards to surround the house. The cartels also purchased billboard ads and plastered them with warnings to the public: *No Salgan Despues De Las 8 pm*. (Do not go out after 8 p.m.) We were put under a cartel-dictated curfew, and most people listened. But this didn't mean that violence was confined to these hours.

My memories from this time are filled with guns. My parents tried to shelter my siblings and me as much as possible. In addition to being forbidden from listening to the narcocorridos and corridos on the radio, we also weren't allowed to watch even innocuous movies and games like Pokémon; all of those were too secular. We couldn't go to parties, and we were only allowed to have certain kinds of friends and wear certain kinds of clothes. But when you live in a place like Sinaloa, it is impossible to escape the narco culture all around you.

I've heard more shootings than I've seen fireworks. I've had to flatten myself on the floor of my Sunday school classroom as a debt was settled on the street outside. One afternoon as I was leaving school, I saw kids running back inside the school building instead of out. Gunmen in two cars were shooting at each other just feet from our classrooms. Time freezes during these moments: for four minutes, every pop signals the possible end of someone or something. And then, like hitting the "play" button on a video recorder, everything returns to normal.

I was in seventh grade when Cindy's closest friend, Gaby, invited us to have lunch at her house. Our parents were hesitant to let us go, but they eventually relented. We were seldom allowed to visit at our friends' houses at all, and their fears were usually well-founded. Only a couple days after our visit, Gaby's dad, a politician who had said openly that he was going to end the drug war in Sinaloa, was shot in his driveway in front of Gaby.

By the time I was a teenager, I was like most of my neighbors: I had normalized my near-constant anxiety. I would jump at loud noises from the TV, at a car engine roaring down the street, at the clatter of pans in the kitchen. Whenever I heard an individual speaking loudly in a store, I would flinch, assuming that a robbery was taking place. If these responses sound like the traumas of a battle-weary soldier, it's because they are.[3]

In those years, my parents were making plenty of money with their supermarkets, tortillerías, and other businesses. But the dangers of our changing city meant that they never felt free to live anything but a careful and timid life. We dreamed of moving somewhere else—we began developing plans to pack it all up and head to Los Cabos. But life never allowed that to happen.

SANTIAGO

When I was twelve and my sister was fourteen, she began to like a boy named Santiago. He was kind of like the Justin Bieber of our school—the young, *cute* era of Justin Bieber. He was tall with killer blond hair. His look and personality were as smooth as butter on a hot tortilla. Cindy was head over heels for him. She would write poems and letters to him. I would watch, mildly embarrassed for my sister but also happy for her. Whenever I liked somebody, I kept it to myself. I didn't want to reveal myself to people. I still don't. Cindy, on the other hand, would show the world as she pursued someone she admired.

Cindy and Santiago dated on and off again for years. Although their relationship ebbed and flowed, he was a constant fixture in our house. His mom lived and worked in the US, so he lived with his grandparents and found a close family in our household. He might have liked Cindy, but he loved our family. My parents adored him too—he was kind with my brother, who looked up to him in turn, and his laugh would echo through our house. It felt like I suddenly had an older brother who I adored.

On a particularly hot day during the first summer that Santiago was becoming a part of our family, he invited Cindy and me to go the beach at Isla Cortés with a few of his friends. Isla Cortés was a twenty-minute drive from our home and was one of my favorite places growing up. It was a serene beach with warm water that invited you to spend all day there.

When we got to Isla Cortés, we went to a popular seafood restaurant right next to the beach. When we pulled up to the restaurant, we saw a fancy white Cadillac parked in front that Santiago recognized as his friends'. They were a group of four, all brothers and cousins: Jorge, Joel, Noé, and José. As we joined these new boys over a meal of ceviche and *tacos de camarón*, we instantly connected with them.

On our drive back home, Santiago's tone momentarily shifted. "Listen," he said, "don't ask those guys questions about where they live or anything about their parents. This is serious." Santiago shared more information during our drive. When El Cártel de Juárez had still been running our town, Santiago had gone to the private school where all the rich kids went. This was where he'd met and befriended the boys we'd just met, who were, in fact, Amado Carrillo Fuentes's children and nephews. Though those boys now lived in other parts of Mexico, they and Santiago remained an inseparable group of friends. For Santiago, it was normal to be friends with the children of the most dangerous criminal family—just as long as you were careful not to bring up the wrong set of questions, everything would be cool.

Soon, Cindy and I became friends with Santiago's friends, the very individuals our parents had tried to keep us away from. I wasn't oblivious to who these kids' parents were. But I saw only a group of guys who were as sweet and gentle as Santiago, and I lacked the experience or worldly knowledge (covered in secular media and narcocorridos I was not allowed to listen to) to believe otherwise. Sheltered from the world for so long, Cindy and I didn't think about the potential consequences of our time with the Carrillo boys. I didn't have a sense of danger, and I had no idea what kinds of consequences our friendship might have.

Every time Santiago and the Carrillo boys came to visit, we would go out with them. We went to the beach, to restaurants, and sometimes to their family homes. Their aunt's house was enormous. It reminded me of when I had visited San Francisco the year before and seen the modern castles dotting the streets there. It turned out that the aunt loved the architectural style of the US West Coast so much that she'd had the design replicated for her own home in Mexico.

We always felt safe around this family. But there were strange moments. I remember lounging in the living room, chatting just as if we were still cracking shellfish at Isla Cortés. As we were talking about our day, Cindy grabbed a pillow wedged in the couch. When she pulled on it, a handgun flew out of the couch, rattling on the floor. Jorge picked it up like nothing had happened, and the day rolled on. Cindy and I exchanged a silent glance but didn't discuss the moment until later, when we were alone.

Our parents didn't ask many questions when we were with Santiago. They trusted him. *We* trusted him.

Our family was well-off, but our parents didn't want us to become spoiled. When Cindy started to act up in middle school, my parents took us out of the private school we were attending, and we received the rest of our education in the local public school. When Cindy and I got to high school, where classes were offered in morning and evening shifts, we went to evening school so we could help with AC and the family businesses during the day.

The supermarket that was closest to our house had these huge inviting glass windows and doors. It made for a bright space, but the daily morning task of raising the metal security gates that covered them was taxing. My dad did not care about that. He always said, "You have Cindy, you have Alix. You ladies both can do it together." He could be so annoying sometimes.

One morning, around 6:45, we had just finished with the windows and were getting ready for the employees to start arriving when our dad's brown Honda Odyssey pulled into the parking lot. He usually took his daughters' summer work hours as an opportunity to relax or handle various obligations at some of his other stores. Why would he be here now?

As he walked into the store, I saw an unfamiliar look on his face. It was anger. The number of times I'd ever seen him angry was so seldom, I can name them individually. And now, he was angrier than I'd ever seen him. Meeting him at the door, I asked what he was doing here. He said, "Grab your sister and go to the office."

We gathered in the office, and he slammed the door behind us. Then he said, "One of our employees, Margarita, called me this morning because she saw you both hanging out with certain kids." He was yelling. It was one of the only times he'd ever raised his voice at us. "She was concerned that you were in danger. I need to know if this is true."

We hadn't told our parents who Santiago's friends were, but we hadn't lied to them about them either. Yes, we both said, we were hanging out with the Carrillo boys. Cindy added, "What's the problem?"

"What do you mean, 'What's the problem?'" he mimicked. Didn't we know who their parents were? Hadn't he shown us how to live the right way? My dad gave us the lecture of a lifetime. He pounded the wall in anger.

Unfortunately, this lecture came too late. For the last few years, we'd been building memories with our friends—during every school break, every holiday, and on the weekends. Cindy and I thought we were capable of looking out for each other. It had never occurred to us that these boys' backgrounds would be a real issue, or that our parents would be that mad about it. We looked back at our dad, perplexed. How could anything about these boys possibly make our dad wake up early to yell at us, let alone work himself into such a state? It was like looking into an alternate universe. We told him that these were our friends, that they treated us with love. They weren't criminals—they spent their time doing what normal kids do (albeit with fancier cars and in lavish houses). The oldest boy was just seventeen. "We love these guys like they are our cousins," we said.

Our dad laid out the implications of these friendships from his perspective, as a respected businessman, as a Christian deeply involved with his church, as a father. What the optics were. That two teenage girls running around with four boys sparked other kinds of rumors of impropriety. He said, "You ladies could end up marrying one of these kids and become a narco's wife."

Today, I imagine being a parent in Sinaloa. I imagine how hard it would be to control and protect teenage daughters. I imagine how it must have felt to raise those daughters in the church and in God's love, only to find out that they've befriended the children of some of the biggest criminals in the world. My dad's anger transmuted into fear, disappointment, regret.

At the time, Cindy and I thought he was exaggerating the danger. Dads could be so dramatic! We never missed curfew, we didn't curse, and we did absolutely everything our parents asked of us. When we hung out with our friends on a Saturday night, we still showed up to open the store at 6 a.m., and we still got to church by 1 p.m. We were good, boring kids.

Cindy was always ready to fight back with our parents, and I usually hid behind her temper. I never wanted to disrespect my mother and father. I'd been raised to know that God would be mad at me if I did that. But that morning, I had had it. "We are perfect kids," I said. "How could you even be mad or question us?"

Disappointment streamed from my father's eyes. "You just don't get it," he said. "You are so immature, and it is my fault. But this is the last time I hear that you are hanging out with these kids."

We responded, "Okay, Dad." But this was the crucial and only moment of rebellion in my Mexican childhood. I was so naive. I wish I could go back and not disappoint my dad, but I can't change the past. The fact is that we continued to spend time with these friends, and we've felt the repercussions of that decision to this day.

A few weeks later, I was talking with a girl at school about how bad the shootings had gotten, a typical topic in Sinaloa. I was criticizing the organized crime that was at the root of the violence when the girl stopped me and said, "Well, aren't your parents part of Cártel de Juárez? Aren't your parents part of this whole thing that you want to blame?"

I was floored by her statement. What could she possibly mean?

She said she was just repeating what she had heard. For a few years now, she said, people had been saying that my parents were a part of the system that helped launder the cartel's money. That the reason my family spent so much time in the church was just to build up a good image and hide our illicit actions from the government. Many people in Mexico let *narcotraficantes* use their businesses and official records to move money in and out of the drug world. And since people had been seeing Cindy and me with the Carrillo boys, they'd concluded that our parents' money must be coming from the cartel.

I couldn't believe what this girl was telling me. I assumed this was random, small-time gossip, and I tried to keep it to myself. But inevitably, these rumors eventually reached my parents. Then there was another meeting in the grocery store office. This time, though, my dad wasn't angry, just sad. He said, "I have worked really hard to have a family that loves God, a family that was not involved with any of these crimes. I don't like this, and this is why your mom and I have been trying to move this family somewhere else." The problem was that much of our money was invested all over Sinaloa—in supermarkets, tortillerías, houses, and other stores.

I finally realized how much our friendships with the Carrillo boys were damaging my family's reputation. People thought that our testimony as Christians was a joke. For our parents, it was one of the most demoralizing aspects of the situation.

ESCOLTA YEARS

As a young child, I suffered from chronic asthma and feelings of self-doubt. When I entered ninth grade, though, the asthma started to subside and my confidence started to grow. It seemed like everybody already knew me and liked me. Many of Cindy's friends included me in their group. I was constantly getting asked out by the boys in my class and throughout the city. I rejected them all—I had game back then. I was elected class president both freshmen and senior years and was often invited to speak as the school's representative at local functions. On Mondays, I helped lead my classmates in *La Escolta de la Bandera*, a ceremony honoring the Mexican flag. The honor roll students at each school carry the flag for their local community. My parents deemed extracurriculars like cheerleading and theater, though, to be out of the question. Those were *del diablo*—from the devil! I did find ways to act later on in my life; it became a passion and a survival skill for me.

High school was also where I met my best friend, Lia. When we first met, I was bowled over by how funny she was. It was from her that I learned that bad words could be hilarious. My parents never let me use or even hear bad words, so I'd thought only awful people cursed. But Lia would drop the foulest words in the funniest way possible.

While Lia was beautiful and smart, her family wasn't rich. Her dad was a construction worker, and her mom was a supermarket cashier. They lived in a rougher part of town. That was enough of a strike against her to be mocked and ignored by many of the other girls at school. I learned about discrimination and class differences because of my friendship with Lia. I started noticing that people didn't invite her to the same things I got invited to (even if my parents wouldn't let me go). I saw that these people didn't actually like me because of who I was, they just acknowledged me because I was a part of their wealthier society. I once apologized to Lia about this dynamic: "I don't know why some of these girls are so mean to you. I'm really sorry."

Lia just looked at me, perplexed. "You think I give a shit? Who wants to hang out with those boring bitches?"

I thought that was just so cool. In fact, my understanding of "cool" changed because of Lia. While people thought *I* was confident, it was Lia who unwaveringly and authentically believed in herself.

Because my parents didn't want Cindy and me venturing out to parties or getting into trouble, they threw pizza parties at our house and invited our friends over. My house became a popular place for kids to hang out. This was when Lia started sleeping over once or twice a week. Our friendship was laughter and love. We never fought and, looking back, it's probably the most successful relationship I've ever had. I wouldn't have survived in Sinaloa without Lia supporting me. Eventually, though, the city would take her away too.

THE RED CHEVROLET

I was used to men talking and catcalling me. Girls get sexualized as early as ten or eleven, and it's just seen as a part of what we have to deal with.[4] A lot of my friends became involved with guys who worked for the cartels, and they would try to set me up with their boyfriends' friends: "Hey, Sergio's cousin wants your number. He wants to talk to you about . . . " You basically had to say, *I appreciate that you think I'm good-looking, but please don't kill me!* in the nicest way possible. This was when I started invoking my imaginary boyfriend.

Most days, after school, I would walk to my parents' nearby supermarket to do my homework until my parents could pick me up. It wasn't a long walk, but with my heavy backpack, it always felt arduous. One Friday, when I was fourteen, Lia was walking to the store with me. Trudging along, we talked about the snacks we would select when we made it to the store. A real perk of your family owning a grocery store was getting to eat plenty of junk food and so I would load up on sugar as a kid. As my mind settled on a pack of Chips Ahoy! cookies, I heard the rumble of a vehicle behind us. Lia and I turned around. We saw a red Chevrolet truck with fully tinted windows idling behind us. I wondered if the driver was lost. As we continued to walk, it became clear that the truck was slowly following us.

The street was empty except for us and the truck. These were pre-iPhone days, and neither of our cell phones had any credit on them. After several minutes of being followed, I turned around to see if I could make out who was in the truck. Maybe a classmate playing a prank. The truck pulled up next to us, and a man—maybe in his late twenties or thirties, it's hard to tell when you're a teenage girl—rolled down the window. "Hey, beautiful. Where are you going?" he asked.

Absolutely terrified but trying not to let my voice shake, I replied in a calm, airy tone. "Oh, we're just on our way to meet my parents right now! They're just waiting for us a few blocks over."

"Well, you girls seem tired. You want a ride?"

Lia squeezed my arm in fear. As tired as my legs were, I knew not to get in this dude's truck. The problem is, there's no safe way to respond when you're a girl. If you say yes, who knows what danger awaits inside that vehicle. And if you say no, you risk offending this man and inviting violence. But I stuck to my upbeat tone. "Thanks for the offer! I'm sorry—my dad is waiting for us and we have to go."

Walking faster, we finally got to the supermarket. Even as we were shaking in fear, I didn't tell my parents what had happened. This kind of encounter just came with the territory of being a girl.

A few days later, Lia and I were walking to a stationery store, getting some markers for a history project. As we crossed a street, I saw the red truck again, parked a few shops down the road. On the way out of the stationery store, we saw the same man as before, leaning against the truck. "Hello, beautiful," he called. "I've been looking all over for you for the past few days. I just want you to know that I'm around."

I told him that our teacher was waiting for us. The man asked, "Do you want me to talk to your teacher and tell them that you need more time?"

Even as I almost peed my pants, I was still polite. "No, no, no," I said. "My friend is also waiting for me."

I was terrified. That day, after school, I didn't have anyone to walk to the supermarket with me. I didn't see the man when I stepped outside, so I power walked toward the store with my heavy-ass backpack, trying to get there as quickly as possible. I was two blocks away from the supermarket when I saw the Chevrolet.

He pulled up to me, and this time, he didn't seem so nice when he spoke. "This is my third time trying to ask you out and I'm getting tired of it," he said. "I've been seeing you for weeks. I've been looking for you ever since I saw you at Sushi Factory." I hadn't been to that restaurant in weeks. This dude had been silently stalking me all that time. "You seem like a very sweet, innocent girl," he said. "And beautiful."

I felt paralyzed. If I tried to run, I wouldn't be fast enough. It was after 7 p.m., and if I screamed, nobody would be there to help me. I couldn't get to my phone or call anyone fast enough either. So I tried the only tactic that had worked in the past: playing nice and giving a phone number. I politely said, "Hey, thank you, but my dad is waiting for me. I would love it if we could go out sometime. I'll give you my number." The dude said he would take me in his truck. I kept saying no. But politely, like the dumb girl he saw me as. That act might have saved my life. I gave him my actual phone number, in case he called it to check.

He said, "Okay. I live in Culiacán. I'm going to call you tonight and let you know when I can come and pick you up. We can go eat whatever you want or we can go shopping. If you want to go shopping, money's not an issue for me." The man *looked* rich, and there might have been plenty of girls who would be happy to be trophy wives for wealthy men like him. But I wasn't one of them.

I watched the man finally drive off, and then I ran to the supermarket as fast as I could. Santiago and Cindy were there, and I started crying as soon as I saw them, running into their arms. This man had been stalking me for weeks and I hadn't realized how dangerous it was or that I needed to tell anyone. *He followed me here. He's going to call me. I don't know what to do.*

Santiago, the older brother I wanted to have, said he would take care of it. I didn't know what that meant. Santiago was just sixteen years old, but it was calming simply to have someone say that to me.

Sure enough, the man did call me the next day, something I had been anticipating and dreading all night. But when I picked up the phone, his tone was different. "Hi, beautiful," he said. "I wanted to call you, because I made a promise with you that I was going to call. . . . I want you to let Jorge and your people know that I'm not going to be calling you or following you again. Just tell them that I called to let you know." And then he hung up.

When he mentioned Jorge, I understood. Santiago *had* taken care of it. Santiago had talked with his childhood friends. My friends. And those friends had talked to their parents. And those parents had figured out which man with a red Chevrolet truck lived in Culiacán. And they'd put an end to his stalking. Santiago would tell me later that, to ensure our safety, the Carrillo boys had put the word out that Cindy and I were not to be bothered anymore. This gave us protection that most people in the city couldn't dream of attaining, but the cost was my dad lying awake at night, unable to sleep as he imagined the threats that would come to his little girls.

In 2008, several years after the incident with the man with the red Chevrolet truck, the violence in Sinaloa hit an all-time high. I could describe it as being *like* a war zone, but that does similes a disservice. Sinaloa simply *was* (and remains) a war zone. There was a massacre at the boulevard that left more than a dozen people dead. Three of my classmates and their parents were killed in different massacres throughout the city. Every night brought the booms of gunfire, terrifying and familiar. The Carrillo family's hold on Sinaloa was continuing to be violently contested, and Santiago began to feel that he knew too many of their secrets. He started fearing for his own safety, and ours. One night, over dinner, he told my parents, "I don't think the girls are safe anymore."

Sweet Santiago, your warning came too late.

AMERICAN COSTS

The hard part about telling this story is that I'm recounting it while living in the very country whose unceasing appetite for drugs has kept the cartels in power.[5] The fentanyl that currently plagues US communities, for example, is controlled entirely by two cartels—Sinaloa Cartel and Jalisco Cartel. These cartels, as one headline notes, "wiped out" the competition.[6] I saw the ravages of these cartels through my own brother's experiences while we were living in the Bay Area. He was a teenager then, and in an attempt to numb himself to the difficulties of life without his parents, he dabbled with hard drugs. It is likely that the drugs AC began buying originated in Mexico, making their way through California's Central Valley before being distributed through East Palo Alto.[7]

America's demand for drugs is why I lost so many friends. It is why my family ended up in debt to dangerous men. It is why I had to flee to the United States.

The US allows recognized war refugees to legally work here and enjoy freedom of movement. However, it doesn't recognize the cartel wars as a formal conflict, and so people like my family and me, fleeing that violence, are not eligible for legal protection. I learned this when I consulted with an American lawyer in an attempt to attain refugee status, leaving me with nothing but a hefty bill for the lawyer's time.

I HATE GOODBYES

One day in 2009, in my first year of college, Santiago got in a fight and was severely beaten. I still don't know exactly who attacked him, or why, but his body and his injuries served as a warning to others around him. I think that, because he was friends with the wrong people, the rival cartels saw a target on his back. He knew then that he could no longer live safely in Sinaloa.

Santiago, Cindy, and I all were enrolled at the same university. One day, as he was dropping us off from our classes, he told us that he was going to miss school the next week. He had something to take care of. A week later, we received an email—not even a phone call—in which he said he had to move to Canada. His mom, still working in the US, thought it would be easier for Santiago to get legal asylum there.

He's still there to this day. I have not seen him again. He never said goodbye.

Shortly before my dad would fall into his coma, Lia moved into our family's house so that she could be closer to her job. She was working nearby at Bodega Aurrerá, something like a Mexican Walmart. The four-minute drive from our house was much easier than a nearly hour-long commute from hers. While she was stocking shelves one day, a former teacher spotted her and commented that she'd always known Lia wouldn't do anything good with her life. Later, reflecting on the cruelty, Lia vented, "How the fuck am I supposed to achieve anything different if there is nothing to do in this stupid town? My parents cannot pay for college—all I have is work."

Lia was living with us when we fell into debt, and she witnessed the disarray we found ourselves in. It got to a point where my parents were struggling to even buy food, and there were times when Lia would come home with bags full of groceries for us. I was so moved by this kindness, by my confident and selfless best friend and her love for us. It still blows my mind.

A few weeks before my father would go into the hospital, Lia called me from work and casually said, "Hey, I'm going to be back at home for a few days, and then I'll reach back out to you." I thought she was hiding something from me. Was she going out with a guy and afraid to tell me? What was going on? I was still raw from Santiago's sudden departure.

Lia had this Kawasaki motorcycle. It was so loud. It was a running joke. You could always hear Lia approaching long before she ever arrived. A week after that phone call, as I was cleaning our porch, I heard the familiar rumble from blocks away. My friend was back! As she walked into the house, I peppered her with questions: Where have you been? Don't you know I missed you? Is there a guy?

But she cut off my questions, saying, "I need to tell you something."

There is a boulevard in Sinaloa where people hang out and drink in the evenings. People—rich kids, poor kids, everybody—just pull up, blast music, be seen. Well, everybody except for Cindy and me. We were still not allowed out after 8 p.m., which is when things really got started.

One night at the boulevard, Lia began talking with a group of girls her age. They were passing around some tequila. Another person had some snacks. Another some fresh candy. As Lia was talking to these girls she had just met, leaning into their car, a sports car filled with guys pulled up right in front of them. Nobody paid that much attention. People always cruised down the boulevard like that.

Then the sports car's windows rolled down. Two of the men inside opened fire on the car of girls and on the entire crowd. They were firing such a large caliber of ammunition, and at such close range, that Lia was splattered with pieces of bodies, skin, and muscle. "I threw myself onto the ground and I think I had so much blood on me that the guys thought I was dead," she told me.

People ran and screamed. One of the gunmen's main targets was still alive and had run out of the car. The sports car did a U-turn, and that's when Lia was certain they would notice her blinking eyes and kill her.

But Lia lay there, shivering in other people's blood and guts, for who knows how long. When the sports car left and she finally stood up, she couldn't stop vomiting.

The boulevard was close enough that I had heard the gunfire from my house that night. I'd seen photos of the massacre on the front pages of the *Noreste* and the *El Sol de Sinaloa*. Fifteen people had been killed.

But this wasn't the "something" that Lia had to tell me. It was this: "I started my application to get a visa to go to the United States," she said. "I'm tired of living in this town. I'm tired of being poor. And now I'm also scared that there is someone out there looking to kill me." Then Lia said that, because of the debt my family was in, she didn't feel safe staying at our house anymore. She was going to leave. Soon.

I asked her for one favor. I said, "Don't say goodbye to me. I don't think my stomach can handle it."

Lia's plan was to temporarily stay with a friend in Mexicali until her visa was approved. "If I can, I'll come back and get you . . . but either way, I'm leaving this place in seven days."

A few weeks later, my dad would fall into his coma and pass away. I was struggling with suicidal thoughts and depression. I needed somebody around me who could give me stability. It could have been my dad, but he was gone. It could have been Santiago, but he was gone. Lia stayed with me for a short period during this time. However, I knew soon she would be gone too.

I was nearly catatonic during this period. What was the point? I'd dropped out of college, my dad was gone, and my best friends were being pushed out of our hometown. I was eating breakfast in the kitchen one morning when I heard the Kawasaki engine outside. Lia entered the house. I knew what this meant. She waved at me from the other room, and I waved back as if I was going to see her in a few days, as if this moment wasn't what I knew it was. Cindy said that for weeks afterward, I would wake up crying and having panic attacks, trying to talk to Lia.[8]

A month and a half after Lia left, and two months after my dad died, AC and I headed to Georgia. Fleeing an invisible war that still affects innocent victims today.

CHAPTER 4

THE COST OF
BORDER CROSSING

My childhood was filled with vacations all over the US. My favorite trips were the ones to California: Disneyland, San Diego, San Francisco. When you come to this country with cash to spend, you are welcomed with open arms. Our family trips were filled with room service and fancy restaurants. During those trips, I imagined that living in the United States would be a dream.

There were always uphill battles, though, to obtaining our tourist visas beforehand. Our family trip to Disneyland required lengthy drives to the Mexican consulate in Hermosillo Sonora to submit our paperwork and undergo background checks, which included getting our fingerprints taken. It seemed like every time we went, a document was missing or incorrect, and we would have to make the journey an additional time. Once, when I was twelve, after standing in line for three hours, we were denied—my ears weren't visible in my passport photos.

Of course, visiting as a tourist and actually building a life here are completely different experiences. They, in fact, require you to be different kinds of people.

When AC and I fled to Georgia, I told him that we would be staying temporarily until we could return safely to Mexico. It was a lie I told to myself too. I came to the United States pretending it would be another extended vacation. But the Georgia towns in which we stayed looked nothing like the hotel resorts with poolside service that we'd enjoyed at the Happiest Place on Earth. I don't remember if the passport picture of the twenty-year-old version of me showed my ears or not. I do know that my tourist visa—the one that I eventually overstayed and has kept me trapped in this country—allowed me to live in a country where dangerous individuals seeking payment for my father's debts wouldn't come for me.

BORDERLANDS

There are more *kinds* of borders in the world than there ever could be walls and fences to enforce them: borders between those who belong in this country and those that don't; borders between the living and the dead, between the sacred and the profane, between the you that is seen and the you that is private; borders that dictate what is expressible and what must remain unspoken.

Some borders are meant to be crossed, brokered, even broken. There is a border between you and me, one that I am trying to breach so you can see me beyond the drawn-out lines of good-intentioned white empathy. And while I've crossed many in my life, there is really only one that this country cares about.[1]

What you consider "the border" between the US and Mexico is not just the wall and fences and *stuff* that divide the land on one side from that on the other. As the late David Graeber described it, "There's all these imaginary lines drawn around the world with not so imaginary weapons protecting them."[2] Those imaginary lines only hold power because of the collective narratives of control that are instilled *everywhere* in this country. One of America's most blatant anti-immigrant laws, Arizona Senate Bill 1070, for example, empowers law enforcement officers to attempt to determine an individual's immigration status when pulled over or detained. Such practices maintain the power of the border hundreds of miles away from its actual location. I witness the representation of the border and its policing in my daily life.

Two hundred and fifty years ago, a bunch of white British subjects signed a new nation into existence. As Roxanne Dunbar-Ortiz reminds us, these individuals were not the "nation of immigrants" that the blockbuster hip-hop musical *Hamilton* depicts.[3] They were, however, imaginative in how they created a new nation in a land already inhabited by Indigenous societies. We don't tend to think of the American Declaration of Independence as a form of imaginative writing. The truth, though, is that it started as a collectively authored piece of fiction. It conjured a society that had not previously existed. Before the Declaration, there were colonies that, under duress, were ruled by the British monarchy. After the Declaration, there were "Free and Independent States" that fifty-six US delegates decided would "have full Power to levy War, conclude Peace, contract Alliances, establish Commerce, and to do all other Acts and Things which Independent States may of right do." These sentences would be no more than fantastical daydreaming if it weren't for the action backing them up. It was the soldiers willing to put their lives on the line who transformed the document into a real enactment of a new governed body. The act of imagination that went into creating these United States was abetted by violence.

Which brings us to borders. It bears reminding that borders only exist because of a collective acceptance that they are needed. However, just because these lines are not physically real does not mean that they do not impact my life. Quite the opposite: borders govern every aspect of how I live. The border is what created the distance and safety from the danger that threatened me in Sinaloa. However, the border also insists that I must either return to my hometown and accept the debt and threat of violence that await me there, or remain here and face an even more dire financial insecurity—and the threat of capture and deportation.

The policing of the US-Mexico border has escalated in recent years, reflecting the US government's increasing desire to cast an image of authoritative control.[4] Because of this, the border has been hyper-militarized: in the physical wall that racist politicians love to vocally call for, in the increase of Border Patrol officers (now the largest police force in the

United States),[5] and in the cultural tools of surveillance and unease imposed on immigrants, from English-only policies in schools to recent legislation in Florida that outlaws transporting undocumented individuals into the state.

Sociologist Angela García explains that such intersecting efforts collectively "build a deep perception of threat within the everyday lives and routines of undocumented Mexican residents."[6] To be clear, it's not just the laws and their enforcement that make life difficult for immigrants—as Alex Kotlowitz explains, it is also the anti-immigrant hostility that is intended to "mak[e] life miserable for illegal immigrants in the hope that they'll have no choice but to return to their countries of origin."[7]

Borders also manifest in our language practices. Linguistic anthropologist Jonathan Rosa studies this phenomenon, which he terms raciolinguistics.[8] Describing this work, he told me:

> Raciolinguistics is a framework for understanding that borders have been drawn around languages and language varieties, around racial and ethnic categories, and around forms of political belonging such as citizenship. For example, what we call "Spanish" is not a single variety of language that corresponds to a single population or territory. There are *many* Spanishes, as well as many geographies and populations for which different Spanishes are important. So we must reject this idea that these borders are facts about the world. I've always seen languages as a space for rethinking interconnections among geographies, populations, and cultural practices.

Rosa's discussion points to the possibilities rejecting the kinds of linguistic borders that enclose my life and that make my Spanish-speaking tongue a foreigner in this country. One surprising border, for instance, relates to my name here in the US. With my grandfather's German last name, I am often asked if I am actually Mexican because it doesn't sound "typically" Mexican. Language closes off what counts as being Mexican and sounding authentic. Before I even open my mouth, my identity and my voice are often judged, overlooked, and doubted by the name I carry.

UNPACKING

I remember the day I packed my single bag before moving to the US. I was still in shock that it was really happening. But I also thought the change in location might light a path out of my depression, provide a way for me to save up money, and offer me some respite from my mother, whose own depression and ways of coping had made it painful to share space with her.

Packing became a game of tricking myself into believing that I'd be back in Mexico soon. I left behind my most valued possessions—my family pictures, my laptop, my favorite clothes, my books—and took only a carry-on suitcase. I needed to feel like I was going away for a weekend jaunt, that everything would soon be "fixed." I could not fathom the alternative.

I was scared to talk to AC about the trip. I was especially scared that he would ask about the future, but he never did. He had heard the conversations about how bad things were for us in Mexico; no one ever told him that we were entering a new stage of life altogether.

It was the first time in my life that I had to lead on my own. Cindy was no longer there to speak up for or protect me. In those first months in Georgia, I wasn't thinking about when I would be able to finish college or pursue a career. The most important thing was keeping AC safe. Since I knew so many friends with family in the US, I assumed that anybody could easily find work in the country. I had not yet learned that a tourist visa legally prohibited me from being hired. I knew nothing about the difficulties people faced without Social Security numbers. I just knew that my brother needed support and that providing for him was all that mattered. When we arrived in Georgia, I enrolled in English classes, hoping they would help me land a job.

The family friend who took us in was named Andrea Lulu. She lived in Gainesville, Georgia, about an hour outside of Atlanta. At the time, she'd been in the US for seven years. We stayed with her for eight months, and she was as sweet as I remembered her from my childhood. In her early forties, she maintained a youthful vigor even as she was raising four boys who ran, played, laughed, and screamed nonstop around the house. Her oldest was nine—the same age as AC—and her youngest she still held at her hip. As I helped Andrea Lulu in the kitchen, she would fill my heart with stories about having gone to school with my dad when they were kids. She had a plethora of pictures of him that I'd never seen before, and as much as they reminded me that I missed him terribly, they also did much to keep me focused in those days. If Andrea Lulu's children had been the only source of chaos in the house, AC and I would have found true sanctuary there. But she also had a husband, and he was the source of a new looming darkness for us.

Julio was a former architect from Tijuana. Though I never learned the specifics of the circumstances that had brought him to Gainesville, I knew that he had applied for legal asylum in the US. When AC and I were staying in his house, he was still waiting, now on an expired tourist visa, technically undocumented. I saw that his experiences in Mexico and with the US immigration system were making him bitter toward the two new interlopers in his house.

Andrea Lulu seemed to be afraid of her husband and unable to speak up for herself. I remember the first of many times he entered the house in the afternoons, found that dinner was not ready, and spat, "I cannot believe I live with two good-for-nothing women." Many of my friends believe that divorce is a sin, but I know that God would never pin someone to a situation of unhappiness. I wish Andrea Lulu had been strong enough to leave Julio. When I see the unhappiness in her eyes in photos on social media today, I still wish that for her.

Although he was terrifying at home, Julio was beloved in the community. I went with Andrea Lulu's family to an Apostolic church, where they were the epicenter of activity. This church is also where I met some of my closest friends during our time in Georgia. In the little spare time I had, I would socialize or swim with them at a nearby lake. However, if I came home too late in the evening, Julio would be waiting for me. "Only sluts are outside of the house after nine," he would say. While I learned to tolerate his disgusting misogyny, I could not handle the way he verbally and physically abused my brother. My primary scars from this period come from the unrelenting ways in which AC was bullied by this adult, the opposite of a father figure in the exact moment AC needed one most.

One time, AC and I were in the kitchen eating cereal when Julio came in. He looked at us and said, "This is the last time I see you eating my cereal or milk from this fridge. I get this for my kids, not for you." My hands were shaking as I watched AC, scared and unable to process what just happened. Months earlier, he had been a pampered and joyful kid. Now his food was being threatened by our chosen kin.

Things started escalating. If one of Julio's sons blamed AC for hitting him with a soccer ball, Julio would pull my brother roughly by his shoulder, twist his body to face his, and say, *This is my house. Don't mess with my boys.*

I started sleeping with a pair of scissors under my pillow. I needed to feel like I could protect AC or myself if need be. This new version of me emerged at the same time that I saw AC become a shell of himself, afraid to play at home. Even in these early months in the country, I was already afraid to seek any social services or legal aid. I knew we weren't supposed to be here, and I thought only bad things would happen if I contacted any authority. I waited months before even hinting in my phone calls with Cindy that things were difficult.

I also felt I needed to put on a brave face for AC, and asking for help seemed like the opposite of that. When my dad had been in the hospital, I had reassured him that I was going to be there for AC.

Andrea Lulu tried to stand up to her husband when she saw him bullying my brother, but since she, too, was undocumented, she felt constrained in how much she could do. One day, when she and I were in the house talking we heard all five of the boys shuffle in from the yard and grab Capri-Sun juices from the kitchen. That's when I heard AC yelp a quick "I'm sorry," on the brink of tears. Julio was again berating AC: "I didn't buy this juice for you. Put it back."

Andrea Lulu pushed back, incredulous at her husband's behavior: "You didn't buy that juice *at all*, Julio. It came from food stamps to feed our family." She and her husband began to argue. "C'mon, AC," I said. "I have a Snickers bar in my room. I want to show you something." I guided AC away just as I heard Julio throw the still operating rice cooker across the kitchen with a deafening crash. At that time, I didn't have the money to buy even small luxuries like candy, but every time I went to English classes or a store that offered candy in a small jar, I'd take a piece for moments like these. I tried to build a sanctuary for us out of sugar and reassurances of an uncertain future.

What did it cost me to be brave, though? I'd been thrust into the role of a single mom, I did not yet speak the language in my new country, and I was relying on the short patience of an abuser for our survival. I watched my brother get his breakfast taken away as Julio said that "Milk is very expensive. So if you want to eat cereal, eat it without milk." I am still working through the humiliation and harm that Julio caused. It still pains my heart to think that I should have done a better job. The eight months we lived there felt like a decade.

Our time there started to draw to a close when Cindy arrived. After hiding in Mexico and doing as much as she could to help my mom, her fear of the cartels and a yearning to reconnect with her siblings sent her north. Cindy came to join us in Georgia just as Andrea Lulu's house felt like it was collapsing in on us. There was nothing left of the old me by the time we were reunited.

ENGLISH LEARNER ANGUISH

I did everything I could to try to make a reality for AC that didn't look like the hell I felt we were living through. I don't think he knew the meals or sleep that Cindy and I sacrificed over the years to make sure that he had soccer uniforms and that his league fees were paid. To this day, I carry guilt that while I had a "good," privileged childhood with the full presence of my parents, I could never offer my brother the same. Just as I couldn't find resources for myself, I did not find pathways to get AC the help he needed. What he needed was his mom and dad.

His anxieties manifested in all sorts of ways. One chilly winter night in Georgia, when AC was ten, I woke up to the sound of our front door opening and saw him sleepwalking out toward the snow-covered street. I chased after him, finally able to wake him up on the curb outside the house. Sobbing and disoriented, we walked back inside, our feet numbed by the icy ground. After that, we began blockading the front door with furniture at night.

There were also problems at school, where AC was getting teased and bullied for not knowing English. My own still developing English skills meant I wasn't always sure about the kinds of language support his school was providing.[9] I'd grown up watching American TV shows like *Lizzie McGuire* and *Hannah Montana*, but the dialogue had usually been dubbed over in Spanish, and I hadn't understood whatever original English remained. In Georgia, I didn't make much progress in my adult English classes, since my time was so limited.

I ended up learning much of my vocabulary from *Friends, Sex and the City*, and rap music. They were icons of American pop culture I'd enjoyed while still in Mexico, and they became crucial instructors once I arrived in the US. The rest of my English I learned alongside AC, trying to help him adapt. His vocabulary struggled to catch up with the complexities of growing up in a new country. What are the proper English words for missing your mother and being afraid of the man who does not let you eat safely in the house that is not your home?

We had only been in this country for a matter of weeks and AC was crying himself to sleep every night because of what was happening at school. I had enough. I promised AC that we weren't going to sleep that night until his English was in a better place. We stayed up until 2 a.m. working our way through his school books, as well as some children's books I'd picked up at a garage sale. We practiced common words that he would encounter, drilling the phrases he might hear or have to respond to at school.

It took AC six months to be able to converse smoothly in English. Much of the bullying stopped when classmates realized he was a soccer whiz, and he formed a friend group around sports. Nevertheless, my brother's linguistic journey came with an official designation from his public school. When he first entered school, he had been given a language assessment battery and been deemed an English learner (EL), a label that fundamentally alters how students are treated in schools.

Educational research often speaks of the "hidden curriculum" that unfolds in American schools, the implicit lessons about race and gender that are taught between the lines of the textbooks in the ways different students are treated. The EL label limits the classes a student can take and often follows them throughout their entire academic career. Teachers and administrators are told which students in their classooms are ELs, ideally to provide them with better individual supports. Instead, these students are often singled out by adults and peers alike. Instead of celebrating that AC was becoming bilingual, he was given a label that held him back. When transnational youth enter US school systems, we are treated as if the brilliance of our tongues is a bad thing, a threat to the Eurocentric values of school.

Ramón Martínez, an associate professor at Stanford University's Graduate School of Education, pointed to the hypocrisy of language education in US schools: "Monolingualism is the unmarked norm, but it's not the norm worldwide. On Earth, it's not normal."[10] The majority of individuals in the world speak more than one language.[11] American exceptionalism fails to acknowledge this and instead prizes English fluency above all.

When AC and I later moved from Georgia to California, the EL label followed him. It limited his access to classes that could have prepared him for college[12] and never allowed his full brilliance to come out. As an adolescent still coming to terms with the world, he had to deal with the EL label pulling him down socially, academically, and emotionally. I am amazed that AC didn't drown.

UNHOUSED

When Cindy finally came to the US, she joined us at Andrea Lulu's, but we knew we all had to move as soon as possible. Living with Julio was dangerous.

Looking back, it was Cindy's bravery that guided AC and me out of that nightmare. If she was ever scared in that house, she never showed it. Instead, she helped confront Julio, and she focused our efforts on finding consistent work and saving up enough money to lease our own place. While I attended my adult English classes and looked after AC, Cindy cleaned houses and looked for any other work opportunities we could both take on.

Despite our efforts to save up for our own place, we quickly realized that it was a financial impossibility. I began researching shelters near us instead, figuring out which ones would take all of us together. At the last minute, as we were figuring out the math of what possessions we could carry to the shelter with us, a friend at church said we could stay with them for a week or two. For the very first time, I started understanding what it meant to not have a home, or food, or a place to sleep.

For the next six months, we rotated from one friend's house to another, trying to stay in close proximity to AC's school. At home in Mexico, we'd each had a private bedroom with an attached bathroom; now, the three of us were sharing a single bed. And yet we could not have been more grateful for the kindness of the families that hosted us. We never tried to overstay our welcome, usually moving from one place to another every few weeks. If it wasn't for the love of many good people, we wouldn't have survived. We briefly lived off the tiny amount of money Cindy had brought with her from Mexico until that, too, ran out. For weeks, our diet was Jack in the Box tacos. When AC asked for fries too, Cindy and I shared one portion of tacos so that he could have fries. Since work was inconsistent, there were days where we couldn't afford to buy even these cheap flavorless meals for all of us, and on those days, we would get food only for AC. Cindy and I would hide the fact that we didn't eat.

Eventually, we met Yolanda and Caesar. They had two kids around AC's age, and they told us they had a room for rent. "We know that you're going through a hard time," they told us. They offered this room for $100 a month, framing their kindness as a business transaction in order to protect our pride. It was just enough for us to feel like we were living on more than charity. It gave us a sense of ourselves in a moment when we needed our strength. We took the room.

I have never in my life felt so happy with so little. I finally felt a sense of security. I started building back my strength and reflecting how this country had toughened me up. I was still a scared kid raising a younger scared kid.

We stayed at Yolanda and Caesar's for eight months. Cindy and I found a job at a radio station (more on that later). Incredibly, Caesar would drive us daily to that job in Norcross, forty minutes away. Sergio, who worked with us at the radio station, suggested moving in with his family in Norcross so that we wouldn't have to commute so long. It would mean switching schools for AC, but in that moment, such a change was appealing. Although his English had improved, he was still not comfortable with the language and still struggling at school. So, after sitting with the invitation for a week, we agreed to move in with Sergio.

I remember the afternoons in Sergio's house, surrounded by his sister and mother. AC and I used the family's computer to complete his homework, going through English activities together and then looking at cartoons that he liked. These were times of calm and healing. Some of my happiest memories with AC come from this period, taking goofy pictures on a webcam to send to our family. I think Sergio's mom saw something of herself in the struggle we were facing. She told us her own stories of acclimating to the United States, a nostalgia folded in with the assimilation this country exerts on you.

At the time, I didn't know that my family was part of a trend. Even though we were technically still on tourist visas, we reflected the growing number of undocumented individuals who are also unhoused and ineligible for federal or local services. Who can access various programs varies widely from city to city, and from one year to the next. Many federal programs remain inaccessible to undocumented immigrants, and fear of deportation is a major barrier. Whenever the US economy takes a dip—whether from a housing crash or a global pandemic—the people who suffer first are those who are most vulnerable. That's us, the "shadow" population of immigrants.[13]

In the absence of social services, Yolanda's and Sergio's families were the only reason we survived. Their love and support were why AC wasn't fully consumed by the awfulness of our situation. I knew not everyone is lucky enough to find such generous friends. Seeing the sheer number of individuals experiencing homelessness in the US was shocking, especially compared to the relatively small visible population of unhoused people in Mexico. I started imagining that when I got a little bit of money, I would create a nonprofit to help people experiencing homelessness. I was tired of seeing people living on the streets of America, tired of how people on corners asking for money were ignored, tired of how this country refuses to treat them with dignity. Once my life was in a more solid situation, I was going to help people experiencing homelessness like my family had. I was going to do it on *this side* of the border. This was also a time when I came into the full strength of my own resilience. I don't care what life throws at me now. My time hustling in Georgia assures me that I'll be able to overcome it.

AN OVERSTAYED WELCOME

Despite stereotypes to the contrary, most undocumented immigrants enter the country legally. Overstaying a tourist visa is one of the most common ways individuals end up undocumented in the US, and my experience is part of this data.

In those first couple of years in America, my siblings and I would fly to the US consulate in Tijuana twice a year. There we would renew our legal permission to visit the US as tourists for the standard period of time the government allowed—six months. We would then return to the US. Tijuana, nearly a thousand miles from Sinaloa, seemed like a less dangerous place to do this than our home state, and we stayed for just a few days each time. We would drain our savings to book the cheapest flight, stay with local family, and go to the doctor and the dentist.

After going through this routine for nearly two years, the tone of the questions at the consulate became more pointed. The officials started asking for the address of where we were staying in the US, whether we were really on vacation, and why we were getting tourist visas so many times. The person assigned to process our paperwork could clearly see that we were, in fact, living in the US. I think it was a moment of compassion on their part that allowed us to walk out with fresh visas that day. But it was also the day that I realized that this attempt at doing things the "right way" wasn't going to work anymore. It was the last time we renewed our visas. When it comes to surviving in a country that sees you either as a source of tourist commerce or as an animal, there is never a right way to survive.

Looking back, I can see that this idea that we had—"Oh, we can just travel back and forth and keep asking for permission"—was stupid and risky. Reports of individuals like us being detained and deported were showing up in the news. And living here on a tourist visa was not really any better than being undocumented. I was not able to work legally nor access healthcare or higher education. In most college systems, financial aid is not available for undocumented individuals. Still, it was mentally devastating to let our visas expire. When I'd had a visa, even though it hadn't been the right one, I hadn't felt like I could get deported as easily. A tourist visa did not carry the mental anxiety of *being illegal*.

WHITENESS IN PASSING

For those of you who drive to work, consider your daily commute: flicking a blinker, making your morning-podcast-fueled turns, hopping on the freeway. You probably expend a minimal amount of emotional energy on this part of your day. For me, however, my commute is filled with fear. When I'm on the road, any little thing could start my deportation process. An accident could happen, or a cop could pull me over. A flat tire might draw the "aid" of the highway patrol.

Even when I am simply *being* in public, my life feels exposed and dangerous. It's a static hum of harm that buzzes constantly whenever I am out. This threat in the US feels different from the public bloodshed and violence I witnessed in Mexico. But it feels just as predatory. This is where the real costs of borders come into focus. The paralysis of knowing that my mere presence is a crime. The border follows me like a shadow made of sand, weighing me down.

Immigration checkpoints operate not only along the border itself but up to one hundred miles inland. They are a particularly vicious tool that many of us navigate regularly. There are permanent checkpoints, like the long-standing structure at San Clemente that I pass through to visit a close friend in Orange County, and there are also temporary checkpoints, fashioned from orange traffic cones so that police can funnel cars. They are staffed by law officials—often individuals from Border Patrol or local law enforcement—requesting identification from drivers and passengers in every passing car. They often operate in areas inhabited by communities of color. In Los Angeles, where I currently live, friends circulate social media posts to alert each other to new temporary checkpoints that have been set up so that we can plan to avoid them. José Luis Cano Jr., an assistant professor at the University of Texas Rio Grande Valley, studies the role of border checkpoints in the US and explains how checkpoints expand the force of borders and also function as tools of surveillance.[14] As Cano explains, "The checkpoint is a law enforcement strategy to mitigate the movement of people and their vehicles."

Cano's work speaks to how each checkpoint "impedes infrastructure" by clogging traffic and creating unnecessary detours.[15] His scholarship considers how these checkpoints functionally slow down the activities of every person in the surrounding area. What unfolds depends on the prerogative of the officer on duty. "Maybe they won't even ask you to roll down the window. They might just be like, 'You look white, go through.' Or 'You look a little bit different, roll down your window,'" Cano says. For me, this means putting on my friendliest smile and maintaining a calm demeanor, even when I am internally terrified each time I hand my identification to a legal authority. Every time I make plans to drive to a new restaurant or enter an unfamiliar part of the city, I take into account how close I might come to a temporary checkpoint and at what point I might need to show my ID or speak to an authority who might be listening for my Mexican accent. On a daily basis, I am mapping the world into zones that are distinctly unsafe and those that are.

Angela García has shown that undocumented Mexican immigrants will change their hairstyles, adapt new gaits and postures when walking down the street, and in one instance, pack a white dress shirt to wear on the drive home from hours of hard physical toil so as to look less like the day laborer they actually are.[16]

These are Clark Kent–like performances of white American values. They are a sacrifice of self, taken up in the name of safety.

There is an uncomfortable truth that I've been dancing around throughout this chapter: I often do not feel safe in large gatherings of other Mexicans and Latinos. This is not because of the people themselves. I love the comfort of being around other Latinos. I am, however, terrified of the predators they might attract. If I go to a popular taco truck and a lot of Mexicans are there, I may feel unsafe. I know US Immigration and Customs Enforcement (ICE) might be paying attention to these social hot spots. I've learned that I cannot live in a Mexican American community. The US has traumatized me such that living among my own people is too triggering. Consider the reality of being thrown into fear by my own kin. This is perhaps one of the most pervasive qualities that America has instilled in non-white people since its inception.

I am incredibly proud of my Mexican heritage, and I also keep it hidden away in my day-to-day actions. I long to live among my people, yet the idea also fills me with fear. In our necessary efforts to present a whiter image to live in this country, we lose camaraderie, solidarity, and family. In trying to seem American enough to go unnoticed on the street—through appearance and behavior—I excise aspects of my humanity.

A HOUSE ON THE OTHER SIDE OF A BORDER

A few years after my siblings and I arrived in America, my mom called. I could hear in her voice that she had just suffered a loss. I put my phone on speaker so that my siblings and I could all hear. She said, "I need you all to know that two hours ago the bank came to get the house." My mother was hiding in another Mexican state at the time; a neighbor had informed her of the house's repossession. "I am fine, but it's no longer ours, and I could not go to take anything from there."

Pictures of the event made it in the local newspaper. With no warning, the police came to help the bank seize the property. One moment, you know there is a house with all of your family's belongings, and the next, you no longer have a place to call home.

Over the phone, our mother's voice sounded as if she could be just down the street from us. But, of course, she was hundreds of miles away. We were separated by borders of intimacy, of legality, of experiences with abuse and exploitation.

In the months before that call, my mother had sometimes been able to have friends check in on our house. There had been a heavy question in my heart that I had never summoned the strength to ask her out loud. I didn't have it in me to hear the answer. The only object in that house I thought about regularly was my dad's piano, the piano I can still hear at night. What had happened to it? On the day that my mom called us to say our house had been taken away, it hit me: The piano too was no more. It was not there. My dad is not there. My friends are not there. What remains on the other side of the border is no longer a home or a place to "go back" to. Only memories and threats and debt are left.

CHAPTER 5

THE COST OF EMPLOYMENT

Nearly a decade ago, I was living in Palo Alto and working one of my first nannying jobs. I had settled into a routine of taking my charges to a local donut shop in the morning. We got to know the shop owner, who was always kind and talkative, as well as the other four workers who staffed the shop—and appeared white to me. One day, I pushed the stroller into the shop and noticed that there were just two people at the counter instead of the usual four. I didn't recognize either of them. I asked the owner if he was short-staffed that day. I'll never forget his response.

He said no, he wasn't short-staffed. "I started hiring *smarter,*" he said. "Your people are twice as productive. . . . I only need two of them to get the same job done and you never hear them complain. They are the most reliable workers I've ever had."

I smiled as I processed what he said. Even as he complimented "my people," he was also flaunting his desire to overwork his staff. When I see thriving businesses throughout this country, I often wonder what costs—personal, emotional, physical, spiritual—are extracted from "my people's" hard and cheap labor.

Immigrants remain the backbone of this country, yet we also remain forgotten and invisible.[1] I am still amazed at how employers squeeze superhuman amounts of labor from a person's need to survive and chalk it up to a "strong work ethic." America romanticizes a hustle culture that saps the energy from workers who dream of brighter futures. This is the true cost of American conveniences, and I see and feel it every day. This country will take everything it can from us, while we barely get our needs met. After all, if I don't like my work conditions, where else would I be able to turn?

Friends have asked me why I don't just get one of the many fake Social Security numbers on offer in the underground market to access better work opportunities. Of course, there would be serious consequences if I got caught, which is more and more likely as tools like E-Verify become more widely used. (E-Verify uses a web-based database to confirm the validity of an applicant's work status, allowing companies to quickly weed out those of us that might not have official permission to work in this country.) But, more importantly, I don't want to go down a dishonest path. My mother reminded me one day, as I vented my frustration with the lack of opportunities around me, that I didn't *choose* to be undocumented. However, if I bought a Social Security number that was fake or that belonged to someone else, I would be choosing to commit both a fraud and a sin. It's one thing to carry a label that I didn't ask for. It's another to deliberately commit a crime.

I will serve you in a restaurant, care for your kids, clean your house. When you see me as labor, it means you don't see me as a person. I am simply your food being prepared, your children being tended to, your home being maintained. And then, when that need is fulfilled, I disappear from your mind. Capitalist labor strips all of us of the effects of empathy. That's a collective loss. As I share several of my journeys through the under-the-table labor economy in this country, I share details of harassment, of physical injury, and of wage theft incurred by "my people"—immigrants, writ large.

MAÑANA Y SIEMPRE

From working in my parents' stores growing up, I learned how businesses operated and how to work hard. I never thought that working in the US would be as challenging as it's proven to be. Nothing prepared me for the unending, unique ways I've been made to feel worthless while on the job. Working under the table comes with the assumption that I don't deserve to be *at* the table.

So when my siblings and I first arrived here, none of us spoke English. Cindy and I had taken our required English classes in high school, but as anyone who's taken similar classes in the US can attest, those lessons don't stick unless you're actually immersed in the language every day. After acing my classes, I promptly forgot the vocabulary. By the time I arrived in the US, I could count on one hand the English phrases I knew: *How are you? How can I help you? Please. Thank you.* I didn't know basic numbers yet. But I was desperate to find work as soon as I arrived. I had a kid to feed, a mother back in Mexico who I wanted to support, and plans to nestle away savings to cushion my siblings and me as we figured out where our lives were headed.

Surprisingly, the first job I found in the US (and the first time I was employed by a business not owned by my parents) was creative, fulfilling, and affirming. When I was living with Andrea Lulu in Georgia, she was helping her church organize a large all-day event for the Latino community in Gainesville and needed someone to introduce people throughout the day. I had done some radio announcing for my church in Sinaloa, and I agreed to help host the event. I joked and ad-libbed on the mic throughout the day. I remember that, as dark as my life felt during that period, it felt nice to have people laugh at my jokes and to speak Spanish for a community.

At the end of the event, a man approached Cindy and me, saying he might have a work opportunity for us. He had been searching for people to host a Spanish-language youth-oriented Christian radio program, *Mañana y Siempre* (Tomorrow and Forever), but none of the candidates he'd auditioned so far had worked out. These days, with the explosion of podcasts, there is an abundance of youth-focused Christian programming, but at the time, I remember having reservations about working on a show that was trying to shove Christian culture down people's throats. Nevertheless, Cindy and I took the invitation seriously. We showed up for the interview dressed like a million bucks.

After talking with him for an afternoon, we got the job! The guy seemed trustworthy, and of course, he was a Christian like us. He slotted us onto the radio schedule for the next week, and our program would air weekly after that. We figured minor details like pay rates could all be taken care of later. In the meantime, he offered to pay us in cash, telling us how convenient it would be. In retrospect, the untracked payments allowed him to keep our underpaid cheap labor off the books. We were still so ignorant about money and US compensation.

For nearly a year, Cindy and I produced every aspect of the radio program. *Mañana y Siempre* was more than Christian content. We interviewed up-and-coming musical artists. We brought on doctors to discuss physical health for young people. We interviewed a psychologist to discuss mental health. I led a segment on fashion. Through it all, Cindy and I got to be ourselves and to craft a wholesome experience for young people—Christian or not. I loved it. It felt like a hobby but we put in full-time work hours, sometimes showing up to the studio at 7 a.m. and not leaving until 7 p.m. For several months, the radio program was also simultaneously filmed for broadcast on local television.

One time, while at a restaurant eating sushi, a young girl came up to my table and asked if I was Alix. "Yeah, hi. Do I know you?" I asked uncertainly. The girl was starstruck—she said she loved my show. I couldn't believe it. This happened several times in my first year in America.

Besides the public recognition, the increasing number and variety of commercials that were airing during our show suggested that it was gaining popularity. And yet, despite the obvious signs the program was working for somebody, financially it wasn't working for *us*. Cindy and I were being paid very little.[2] We were, at this time, in the process of moving out of Andrea Lulu's house, trying to save as much money as possible. We spoke up about our need for fairer compensation and were always told—by multiple people in the radio station—that either there had not been an increase in revenue or that a raise was coming in the future. It was always *later, later, later.* But later was not soon enough, and eventually it got to the point where we didn't have enough money to buy new school shoes for AC. We had to resign, and it was devastating. I had been doing something creative where I got to speak Spanish. I cried during our last show. I remember Cindy supporting me. I felt a new kind of depression wrap on top of familial grief. I was scared about finding a new job. I thought about AC and about what my dad might say, and I thought about the basic financial securities that the radio station had refused to provide.

MANGO MARGARITAS

Cindy was the first to find another job. She spoke just as little English as I did, but her good-natured smile and blond hair meant she was able to start as part of a housecleaning crew. A friend from church was a part of the group and didn't mind paying Cindy in cash—another employment check avoided. She made just below minimum wage, $7.25 an hour in Georgia. For thirty-five to forty hours of exhausting work a week, Cindy earned about $200. It gave us enough money to feed ourselves and slowly save up for a security deposit for our own apartment. Soon, she also found a chain restaurant that was hiring, about a ten-minute drive from where we were living. Cindy hoped to quit the low-paying house-cleaning job, and we decided that we would both apply.

This was one of the first moments that I realized that my sister and I were not experiencing the same America. When we went to apply, we joined a handful of other individuals waiting in line to be interviewed. Cindy and I decided to stand separately and not say we came together. The manager was friendly as he talked to each person in line. When he got to me, I told him in my poor English that I was looking for a job. I was nervous, and I am sure it was hard to understand me. His friendliness evaporated instantly. He looked at me coldly and said, "We are not hiring." Then he moved past me.

Eventually, he got to my sister. It turned out that she had practiced her lines a little bit better than I had. No one expects a Mexican to be as light-skinned and blond as she is. The manager seemed to assume that she was from somewhere in Europe, and he spoke to her kindly. My poor English had disqualified me, but hers had not. He walked away to get her an application for employment.

Shortly after this, we interviewed at a Mexican restaurant, which hired us both as waitresses. To be put on payroll, Cindy and I needed to apply for our ITINs, which required showing our Mexican identifications and birth certificates, proof of current residence, our Mexican passports, and our current contact information. To work in this country as an "undocumented" individual actually requires an abundance of documentation.

Once we were hired, I thought to myself, *If it's a Mexican restaurant, there must be a lot of Mexican people. It will be nice to work with them.* I felt like I hit the jackpot. Maybe my lack of English wouldn't be such a deterrent after all. I was wrong.

Many of the repeat customers were consistently rude to me. When I asked my sister if she'd been having similar experiences with these customers, she said no. It was clear that these same people were extending patience and kindness to Cindy. How was it possible that two people doing the same job with the same minimal English proficiency were being treated so differently? Looking back, the reason is so obvious. Living and working alongside Cindy helped make something abundantly clear: America doesn't have a problem with undocumented people. It has a problem with *brown* undocumented people. It is people who look like me who are seen as the problem. The combination of race and language and economic insecurity are a recipe for self-doubt and struggle.[3] Even now, whenever Cindy and I talk about being undocumented, it is like we have been living in two different countries. Cindy says she never felt threatened. Never feared deportation when driving down the street for groceries. Never felt anxious on the freeway. She sees how the US has been different for each of us.

My memories of the months I worked at the Mexican restaurant are some of the darkest I have. Regardless of the positive attitude that I carried with me in that restaurant every day, customers treated me cruelly because I had a hard time understanding their orders. If someone had an order that differed from what was printed on the menu, I would usually have to ask a coworker for help. Something as simple as "hold the lettuce" or "put the cheese on the side" was hard for me to understand. Sometimes people would purposely make their orders hard for me to understand, speaking quickly or phrasing things in a convoluted way, finding easy justification to stiff me on the tip. There were judging looks, rude comments, demeaning come-ons. One customer wrote "Thanks for nothing" on the receipt where the tip is supposed to go. Every day, I experienced the unique cruelty of American judgment at my attempts to nourish my bilingual tongue.

As humiliating as those customer interactions were, they were only part of my daily ordeal. The restaurant managers also quizzed us on the menu to make sure we were always on top of what was being served. I was new and had a million things to worry about, and learning the menu wasn't easy. I was consistently penalized for getting the menu wrong, and would have to stay late doing extra chores. What was I going to do, quit? Not a chance. While the other servers left around 11 p.m., I would often have to stay and clean until 1 or 2 a.m. because I didn't know what type of tequila was in the mango margarita.

One night, I was scrubbing my way past 1:45 in the morning. Everyone had left except the "nice" manager, who offered to help me clean the fridge. He said, "Tu estás muy bonita para ser mesera." *You are too pretty to be a waitress.* I laughed. Then he said that if I wanted to make more money, I could.

I was still so naive and innocent. I took his offer at face value and asked him what I needed to do to get paid more. He said, "Well, you'd just have to be extra loving to me." I panicked and told him it was time for me to go. I grabbed my bag and fled with half of my assigned tasks unfinished.

The next morning, a torture began. Before our shift started, the same manager told the staff that I had left the previous night before finishing my work and so I would now be staying late for the rest of the week. "If you see Alix working, do not help her."

I quickly learned that a man's ego is as fragile as a glass cup. The "nice" manager started harassing me every time we were alone. He would whisper the things he wanted to do to me, threaten me, or remind me why I still had this job. "I want you waitressing because you are hot," he'd say, "but you are so slow and stupid." For seven months this dude found every opportunity to tell me that I was a stupid piece of meat. Over and over.

I was too scared and depressed to fight back. I couldn't risk not being able to pay rent. We'd already experienced homelessness by this point. I had no choice but to stay quiet.

Why didn't I report his behavior, or at least tell my siblings? Our lives were hard enough, and I couldn't bear to bring any more pain into our household. Cindy and I were barely keeping it together, grieving at night and trying to keep AC positive about a school that was crushing him. At the time, I still had a valid tourist visa, but I wasn't legally allowed to work. I didn't feel I could report the manager and risk someone checking my ID. Enduring an old angry man's insults and harassment of me was easier. For many women in the workplace, it still is. Such decisions reflect the realities of those of us living precariously within America's legal system. To me, police have always been a threat, not a source of protection. They are always in the pocket of someone with interests that are not my own. In Mexico, that was the cartels; in Georgia, it was a foreboding immigration system.

Most of the men who have been "nice" when I am at work just want something from me that I am unwilling to give. It feels shocking even today to acknowledge that, yes, people wanted to kill us in Mexico, but because of my gender, I am in a different, *consistent* kind of danger here in the United States. I would eventually learn to move through work environments coldly and unflinchingly, like sharp ice. During that early period in the US, though, that restaurant manager was one of far too many who got the nice version of me.

PLAYING MOM

I finally quit when I could no longer stomach the fear of working with the "nice" manager. For several months, I did not work. Cindy continued working at the Mexican restaurant, barely covering the rent for the apartment we'd successfully gotten on our own. She carried our family while I tried to find a job, but my limited English and my fear of another foul manager made the search unbearable. We were drowning as a family, I in my own personal maelstrom, afraid of the ghosts of my friends and family, afraid of the predators I'd encountered at work. Just as I felt myself hitting rock bottom, a family friend, Pastor Jesse Valdez, threw us a lifeline by offering to host us in the San Francisco Bay Area, where he and his family lived. His incredible act of kindness yanked us across the country to California, where his daughter, Christina, allowed the three of us to live with her as we resettled our lives.

I didn't know what kind of work I would find in California. It wasn't so much that I was ready to get back into the workplace—it was that there was no other alternative. Now, it's obvious to me that I'd been trained in the duties of being a nanny from the moment AC was born. As soon as our parents brought him home, I was taught how to hold him, feed him, bathe him, change his diapers and clothes, and put him down for naps.

Perhaps it was ingrained in the infectious laugh that baby AC rewarded me with, but I have wanted to be a mom for as long as I can remember. As a girl, I dreamed of raising a big family, of packing them all in a huge van and driving to the beach. My imagined future was sandy, noisy, joyful. It was this vision that helped me raise AC. He made parenting feel like a fun game rather than a sullen duty. Whatever made him happy was a joy to me. I'd work all day to make him smile.

And so, when Christina introduced me to another parishioner in her church who needed childcare, it felt like safe work fell into my lap. My new employer, Claudia, was kind and bilingual. She introduced me to the world of taking care of other people's children in a way that felt validating. Claudia agreed to pay me in cash. (Over the years, as I've gotten savvier about needing to be paid under the table, I communicate clearly with each family I work about being paid in cash only. Some families want to go through various payroll systems and agencies, such as Care.com. I've had to turn down more lucrative job opportunities in order to find employers comfortable with my payment needs.)

When I started working with Claudia's family, it felt like an extension of the joyful games AC and I used to play when he was younger. The majority of a nanny's day-to-day work is with a child or two, taking ownership of all aspects of their well-being until their parents finish their workdays. However, the determining factor in every nannying job I've had—both the affirmingly good and the indelibly bad—is the relationship I have with the adults. Some have made my work feel fulfilling, while others have belittled and exploited me. Claudia was an amazing first boss in the world of domestic labor. I fell in love with the job and thought of myself as a temporary surrogate for the family I would someday have myself. I never imagined that nannying would be a career or that, more than a decade later, I would still be doing it. Instead, it felt like I was the lucky recipient of this fantastic gig where I got to pretend to be a mom, play with babies, and make good money doing it. I didn't want to think about the fact that each day I took care of kids carried me further away from the professions—filmmaking and writing—that I was most passionate about.

When Claudia's children were old enough to go to public preschool, it was time for me to move on. This is a routine part of my job, moving to a new family about every two years as children age out of needing my care. The first family that I started working for, outside of the generous bubble of my church community, was in Berkeley. The family had two infants, and both parents were self-important professors. At that time, it was still hard for me to understand spoken English at a native pace, and looking back, I see some of the information I needed to function in their monolingual household was likely lost in our early conversations. They paid me very little, were rude to me, and saddled me with duties well beyond my job description. I hadn't been hired as their housekeeper, but those duties were folded into what they expected of me every day: clean their toilets, wash all of the family's laundry, cook for the whole family, and do it on top of my primary childcare duties. My workday was supposed to end at 4:30 p.m., but they often didn't let me leave until 4:45 or 5. I didn't know how to speak up about the lack of respect they showed me or their literal wage theft. I was struggling to cope with all this while still creating a loving environment for their kids.

One day, as I was straightening up their kitchen, one of the kids started playing with a can of whipped cream the parents had left out. I was under strict instructions to make sure the kids didn't eat sugar. I didn't realize the cap had popped off the can and that the kid was spraying a mess of whipped cream on the counter. At that moment, the mom came into the house and started belittling me. "Are you stupid?" she asked. "Don't you know my kids don't eat sugar?"

The abuse was constant. The parents would yell at me if the kids were not perfectly cleaned and dressed, rather than in the clothes or diapers that life finds us in from one moment to the next. They would "forget" to pay me despite daily reminders, sometimes for two or three weeks. With my developing English, I didn't know if another opportunity would arise so I silently bore the poor treatment. I was still in my early twenties, and I knew I was a bright spot for those kids, whom I still love. I've never understood how those parents could have treated me like that, in their household, while I was with their kids all day. The awkward negotiation to make sure a family pays me in cash instead of going through a payroll system that would flag my lack of a Social Security number means I am also vulnerable to labor abuse.

I endured eleven horrible months with this family. I thought this negative experience might be an outlier. But other nannying jobs revealed similar patterns. And even when families are supportive, the hours are often exhausting. One family needed my workday to run from 6 a.m. to 7 p.m. Others have needed support 8 a.m. to 8 p.m. Add to this the fact that nannies like me often do not get breaks. I am writing this paragraph in the ten minutes during which I've finally been able to sit down and eat a quick lunch. Nobody at an office job would ever accept working without a break for nearly eight hours. Likewise, nobody would be okay with their pay withheld for two weeks because an employer *forgets*. Such practices are illegal. But when you are undocumented, you have to put up with it.

Families have ebbed and flowed in terms of niceness toward me, but I have consistently received demands to do extra work. I am not your dog walker. I am not your house sitter. I am not your cleaner or your chef or your therapist. Over time, my confidence and English proficiency grew to the point that I started setting firm standards for my employers. If I saw the familiar patterns of a family mistreating me, I would give notice and stop working for them. My referrals and growing network of other nannies meant I could usually find new work quickly. But it took a lot of pain (and therapy) to understand that my work isn't some sort of favor that I'm doing for wealthier people. I am your employee, but we are a team. I began to take pride in my work and negotiate better. I became selective; interviewing with prospective families is as much for me as it is for them.

Outside of working for Claudia, one my first very positive nannying experiences was with a family where the mom, Sarah, spent my first week on the job working alongside me. I love her kid to this day; I'll call her Isabel. She was a six-month-old Cabbage Patch Kid of a baby when I started caring for her. She had a huge mop of hair and chunky cheeks that, in my memory, are always hugging a smile. One morning during that first week, Sarah suggested we all go on a walk. I pushed Isabel in a stroller while Sarah took the leash of the family bulldog. We talked about life, about dreams, about what I wanted to do in the time I wasn't working with her. It was the first time in any job that someone had asked me about my family and where I came from. After a few days, I felt comfortable enough to tell Sarah I was in the process of creating a nonprofit to support people experiencing homelessness and also taking classes in my spare time. Sarah listened and took my work seriously. It blew my mind that after years of nannying, this was the first time an employer wanted to get to know me personally. That this was the first time I felt *seen* as a human being in someone else's household.

That Friday, as I was gathering my things to leave, I told Sarah how much I'd enjoyed our conversations and how much they'd meant to me. Sarah looked at me incredulously. "Why *wouldn't* I get to know you? I am trusting you with the person I love the most. You are going to be at my house forty-five, fifty hours a week. How could I not want to get to know you better?" My treatment in other houses had me blind to the possibilities that this could be what working as a nanny with a caring family looked like.

I thought back to how my parents had treated their employees, and how they had taught me, too, to speak to them with dignity, love, and respect. It wasn't until that week with Sarah that I myself experienced this attitude from an employer. Something in me changed that day. If you've never spent your days feeling like a stranger in someone else's home as you change their children's diapers and sing them songs, Sarah's kindness might not seem like such a big revelation. But this was the first household in which I enjoyed not only the company of the babies I was caring for but the company of the parents too. I set my expectations to maintain that.

Not everybody has the luxury of a job that they enjoy. I didn't have that luxury for many years. And even nannying, though fun and fulfilling, is still a job I do to support my night and weekend work as a writer, filmmaker, and dreamer of better worlds. But for now, with the filter of accepting only humane treatment in place, it's time for a short training guide. Many Americans have an unrelenting fascination with seeing how the other half lives and works. TV shows like *Maid*[4] and *The Bear* have taken millions of readers and viewers behind the scenes of working-class jobs. And so, in the spirit of American voyeurism, and to further elucidate the hourly costs of taking care of someone else's family, let me break down the not-so-easy steps to being a nanny.

HOW TO MAKE SOMEONE ELSE'S CHILD YOUR OWN

When you're working with kids in any capacity—whether as a teacher, entertainer, doctor, or nanny—they are the most important thing in your world. Before I ever get to your house, I spend hours ensuring I bring the best version of Alix to care for your babies.

Most workday mornings, I wake up around 4:45 or 5 a.m. I do a brisk forty- to forty-five-minute workout and then enjoy a leisurely cup of coffee and breakfast. I need to be energized and enthusiastic, fresh and crisp, like lettuce. I know that the children are going to keep my brain and my body busy all day. I want to feel fulfilled and still have post-workout endorphins in my bloodstream when I arrive at work. I also find time in these early hours to pray and to mentally prepare for the stress of driving and traffic. I am never late.

I always wear dark clothes to work. I want to feel comfortable playing, getting dirty, going to the park, painting, crafting. And then there are the diaper blowouts, the drool, the spit-up, the vomit, the runny noses, the family pets that shed. When I nanny, I never look "nice." What's the point? Looking nice doesn't matter when you are with kids. What matters is having fun with them, centering their needs, making sure they know they are taken care of.

I make sure to wear walking shoes. My entire day is spent on my feet and knees: walking, chasing, dancing, sweeping, mopping, cooking, washing. Every act is focused on the well-being of the environment of the children I am caring for. Maybe I'll have thirty minutes to myself to steal some time to eat lunch and scroll through awaiting phone notifications, but otherwise I am on the move.

Over the first few weeks of working with a new family, my life metamorphoses to accommodate a new set of demands, parenting styles, and child-rearing preferences. Among the heterosexual couples that I've worked for, it is usually not the dad who shows me around the house; the invisible labor of nannies and parents alike is gendered. I keep on my phone a running list of reminders and timing and measurements (how many ounces of formula, how long a nap) to refer to throughout the day until your routines become mine, memorized in my arms and legs.

You will give me a house key, and you will show me where I should park. I will ask you essential questions to get started: Where is the milk or formula? Where are bottles washed? Diapers kept? Are there any particular feeding, napping, or changing regiments I should be aware of? As the days and weeks pass, I'll also need to know where your washer and dryer are and how to operate them, what quirks your dishwasher has, where food essentials are kept, and how to work the nuances of your family's bespoke stroller and car seat and humidifier and other accoutrements that are a part of your children's daily routines. I'll come to know your nicknames for your babies, your dogs and cats, and your spouse.

I will see your dirty laundry. I'll see your pipe left out from the previous night, still loaded with weed. I'll place my brown-bag lunch in your fridge next to last night's takeout. The imposition is initially uncomfortable, but it also helps me understand the environment I'll spend the next couple of years in, and it helps me get to know the children around whom I will center my love every day. I'll spend more of my day in your house than my own, and often, I'll spend more waking hours with your baby than you will.

One of the least appealing parts of being a nanny is that there is absolutely no job security. Even if I am a stellar nanny who markedly improves the well-being and happiness of a child and their family (and I am), once a child starts preschool or kindergarten, my services are no longer needed. The costs of searching for a new job every couple of years are never factored into the lost wages of nannies like me.

Every two to three years I am seeking new work, relying on referrals and luck. I'll need to carefully negotiate my rights as a worker, maintaining my filter of the families I want to work for while also conveying the need to be paid under the table. I've occasionally had dire stretches of unemployment in between jobs. When medical disaster strikes, my savings can plummet disastrously. Often, when I ask for referral letters, parents will write, "Oh, Alix, she is a part of our family." I'll take their kind words to help me get a job, but I am always struck that a family who treated me as a second-class citizen in their house imagines I share their blood. No thank you. As my English has improved, I've made better decisions about who I work with, and I've gotten more confident in my ability to negotiate. But always, in the back of my head, I am wary of the ways each family might exploit my good nature.

I need to be aware of the latest parenting styles. Some families will want you to be working on enrichment with their kids. Some parents, for example, ask me to speak Spanish with their children. Others want me to support phonics and English storytelling. "Gentle" parenting is an ongoing trend, and how one chooses to set boundaries for a developing mind will vary greatly from one family to the next. I've never believed in time-outs, but if that is your parenting style, I'll follow your lead. It is a reminder that your kids are not my own. When you hire me, you are not hiring an additional parent. A nanny helps guarantee you'll be productive in your own work and your children will have a great day. The peace that a good nanny brings to your life is a blessing.

Because you are paying me, you often assume I come from a humbler background than you. Unless you, like Sarah, get to know me, you won't be aware that I grew up with nannies too, that the houses I lived in were often bigger than yours. You see me as what this country has done to me rather than as the human being I am with your children.

Oh, there's the safety stuff, like protocols around choking hazards and CPR, and figuring out which families want me to tell them about the smallest scratches and which will ask me to use my own judgment.

There are the pictures I'll take throughout the day to share with parents. They live on my phone, a reminder of the small army of kids who are slightly better in this world because I came to love them.

Those are the teachable skills. The unteachables are many: How to genuinely love babies. How to have the patience for a child who refuses to adhere to a schedule dictated by regular working and napping hours. How the love of my own parents and my own nanny, Lupita, taught me the lessons of empathy and compassion I impress on your children each day. How to slip out of a family's life when these kids matriculate into preschool and kindergarten. How to put on a cheerful "So long!" when I leave the kids I love for the last time.

LABOR OF LOVE AND ESSENTIAL WORKERS

When the pandemic swallowed us up in the early months of 2020, the world suddenly felt a new kind of fear simply by going outside. *Will we be safe? Can we trust people near us not to put our lives in danger? What risks am I taking with my family's safety if I go to work, or to school, or to the grocery store?*

For undocumented individuals like me, though, these fears were sadly nothing new. As awful as the pandemic was, it was doubly awful for undocumented immigrants. Set aside the fact that deportations and detainments increased to record levels—under a Democrat presidential administration, no less.[5] Set aside the collective fears of illness, especially in the early days of the pandemic when it was unclear how COVID was transmitted, who should wear a mask, or if public transportation was a safe option. Set aside the immediate and devastating loss of work that immigrant communities in particular faced as waves of service work closed.[6] Set aside the widespread disinformation that targeted Spanish-speaking communities.[7] And set aside how mainstream news media regularly portrayed immigrants as a health threat. Even beyond all this, an obvious fact remains: while many Americans were able to shelter in place and take health precautions, undocumented labor persisted *as normal*.

So let me be blunt: I still showed up. In March 2020, when California governor Gavin Newsom issued a statewide shelter-in-place mandate, I was in the kitchen preparing lunch for nine-month-old twins.[8] The parents I was working with benefited from my presence as they worked in the back of the house, and they continued to pay me consistently. But they never had to get on the freeway. Eventually, their car battery died from lack of use. All of their groceries were delivered. I still showed up.

With my asthma flaring up and my anxiety spiking, I was struggling silently. I was highly vulnerable to the effects of COVID-19 and terrified of getting sick. And of course, on top of that, President Donald Trump was scapegoating undocumented communities.

For several months, many nannies I knew were provided a paid leave so that they could shelter in place. Cindy, who was also nannying at the time, stayed home for six months, getting paid. I wasn't offered this option, and I didn't ask for one. I could see that my employers needed me, and I did the best to care for the twins. I made a lot of sacrifices, and it cost me a new, heavy bout of depression and fear.

The pandemic has made it clear that this country doesn't function without the labor of people like me. Society keeps moving because I show up. The disregard this country has for essential workers like me is astonishing. From farmworkers to restaurant employees to domestic workers, many of the lifelines that kept our country operating were staffed by the undocumented community. We, of course, did not do this alone, but I nonetheless remain awestruck by this country's disdain for us. At the same time, I'm grateful that I have always valued people's labor the way I do; it's how my dad taught me, and in some way, the love I bring to your kids is a part of his legacy too. I don't think my dad ever imagined that I would become a nanny. But he prepared me to be the fullest person I can be.

We talk about taking on a big passion project as a "labor of love." When I am preparing a script, or when I created my nonprofit, those are big labors of love. But there's another way to define the term. It is the very meaning of my work, every day, as a nanny. I labor to love your children. I do it well. It is the ultimate form of *essential* labor. And it is invisible and exhausting work.

CHAPTER 6

THE COST OF LOVE

The phone call that almost killed me came from an unknown number one Saturday morning in 2017, while I was on a trip to Chicago.

"Is this Alix Dick?" the voice asked. Yes, I said, it was.

"This is Ravenswood Clinic. We have the results from your pregnancy test. It came back positive."

That call set in motion a series of events that turned my life upside down—along with my family relationships. But this isn't the story that you think it is.

You might wonder what love has to do with being undocumented. One answer is that, on the most basic level, love was the reason I came to the United States in the first place. I love my brother and will do anything to keep AC safe. But after I began my life here, I realized that my undocumented status was making it exceptionally difficult for me to find romantic love.

People usually forget that undocumented people have real lives. Most people imagine a faceless person doing hard labor—a nanny, a house cleaner. We've been portrayed this way for ages, the media focusing, for example, on the labor of seasonal farmworkers without acknowledging the basic human needs those workers have. I want you to understand that I have desires and dreams just like everybody else. One of those dreams has been to find someone to love and marry.[1]

When I was a child, everyone around me pursued the kind of Hollywood love story that only a lucky few actually found. The storybook romance ideal was sold to me by my parents. They'd met when they were kids. My mom was nine and my dad was seven. My dad's parents used to knock on doors in Sinaloa to share the message of Christ with people. You might think nobody would open their doors to them, and you would generally be right. But when they knocked on my grandma Amelia's door, she needed something to believe in. A stay-at-home mom with little support from an absent husband, she was lonely and depressed. So, when my future nana and tata showed up to her house, Amelia invited them inside for a *cafecito*.

Grandma Amelia had a big backyard with hulking trees and grassy spaces to play in. My nine-year-old mom was in the yard riding her brand new bike. She noticed a diminutive light-skinned, brown-haired boy watching her, wearing a white shirt with blue stripes. He'd been dragged along by his parents on this proselytizing trip. The boy then approached her and asked, "Can I ride your bike?"

"Of course not, little sucker," she said, "but I'll give you a ride." My mom was always the boss.

Meanwhile, inside the house, the adults were hitting it off. Grandma Amelia soon started attending Nana and Tata's church. She found a community and support that day, and my parents found in each other a best friend.

Despite my dad's childish pleas, my mom didn't want to be his girlfriend as a young kid. She made him wait until they were sixteen and fourteen. My parents were so proud of their childhood romance, and they were always telling and retelling the story to my siblings and me. Their relationship was one of their biggest accomplishments. No matter the challenges they faced, my parents always chose and relied on each other. Growing up, I saw how my parents worked together. They built wealth. They sustained a home for our family. I thought that my own life would be the same way, that a dude who would change my world would magically show up in my backyard. But all I've found is walking garbage, fake promises, and men who have less personality than a boiled potato.

Growing up, I used to think all marriages were like the one I saw at home. So why was I more scared of love than most girls I knew? Was it my deep fear of abandonment? Was it my trauma from familial heartbreak? Still, I believed in the idea that whenever the right man came my way, I would fall into his arms and write my own fairy tale. I wanted the little boy in the white-and-blue-striped shirt, asking to borrow my bike, an innocent love that leads to a lifetime of happiness.

It wasn't always like this. Finding boys who liked me and wanted to date me was never an issue. I had my first kiss when I was nine years old, with the son of a pastor in the back of church during Sunday school. He was the cutest little blond boy with blue eyes. He was my first little love for maybe six or seven years. We never kissed again—because God was watching! My sister and I knew from a young age that we would wait until we were married to have sex. She waited until she found Eduardo, the pianist in the church we attended in the Bay Area. He is kind and smart and can play just about any song you ask him to, like a human jukebox. He and Cindy have been happily married since 2017.

As with Santiago, Cindy was always the romantic one who fell easily in love. Me, on the other hand, I have always been hard to win over. I'm willing to pay a high price for what's real. And people like me don't get to date carelessly. I took pride in the fact that I never let men hold much influence over me.

Until that suddenly changed.

DARREN

In 2015, when I was living in East Palo Alto, life continued to be challenging. I was nannying, working many hours with nonprofit organizations that supported the immigrant community, and continuing to take care of AC. As always, money was tight; it often caused the relationship between me and Cindy to be on the brink of exploding. Amidst this hectic life, I got a follow request (I kept my profile private) on Instagram from an account I didn't recognize. Even though I figured it was spam, I apprehensively approved the request. The account started liking and responding to my posts. Gradually, I got to know the person behind the account, Darren.

Darren had seen a picture of me tagged on a mutual friend's Instagram page. The friend and I had recently hiked the Stanford Dish, a popular Silicon Valley trail near the university. At the time, I was extremely depressed. I felt like I couldn't find my way in the United States. AC was going through the gauntlet of his teenage years while also living with family loss, and Cindy and I didn't know how to support him. We were trying hard to make a safe home for him, but nothing we did ever felt like enough. Meanwhile, my mom was still in Mexico, hiding, trying to pay off our debt, dealing with her own fears, and battling depression.

I was twenty-five and incredibly naive. I had never used a dating app or gone on a real, grown-up date; I'd been too busy working, caring for AC, and trying to survive. Sure, I had dated back in high school, and I'd had some "situationships" in Atlanta and the Bay Area. Looking back, I can see that I met some good men who hoped to love me, but I wasn't healed enough from all the trauma I'd experienced to open my heart to them. I had seen much of the ugliness and hardship life had to offer. But I had not yet had my heart broken.

One of my favorite rappers at the time was Drake. Even though my English skills had substantially improved, I couldn't always understand all his lyrics. Still, I related to the things he rapped about: his voice, his insecurities, his openness. One day, I posted a selfie and captioned it with lyrics from Drake's song "Take Care." This post drove Darren straight to my DMs. "So, you like Drake?"

I threw back some sarcasm: "No, I just made that line up all by myself." My reply launched an exchange that lasted for hours, and then days, and then weeks.

Sometimes, to help me navigate the English-language conversation we were having, I Googled English phrases and slang. I didn't even know what "I'm falling for you" meant until he said it and I looked it up. Talking on Instagram felt easiest and safest. After a month, I finally let Darren call me on the phone, and we started texting as well. That's when we became closer, and my insecure self slowly started to let this stranger into my life. We often talked for hours. He asked me so many questions. He wanted to know about how I was raised and about my parents and my family. He asked me about how I saw the world. He wanted to know every detail about my life, and I surprised myself by opening up to him.

He seemed trustworthy. Nobody had ever been so interested in me. I was lonely, unseen, depressed, and suffocating in the closed-off world I was living in. Darren was a breath of fresh air.

Darren and I found more similarities between us the closer we got. We were both deeply involved with our churches. We were both drawn to the ocean; he loved to surf on weekends. He had been a professional football player. He was a lavish cook and would send me photos of his latest feasts. And goodness, he was funny! We would text inside jokes that would evolve and pull us closer throughout the day. It felt like everything I wanted in my fairy tale was on the other end of my text messages. It seemed like the only problem was that Darren lived in Chicago and I was in California. The three blinking dots on my screen belied the fact he was thousands of miles away.

After we'd been talking for four months, we were on a video call and he asked me to look in the mail. I found a letter from him: "Hey cookie girl, I think I'm falling for you. Will you come to Chicago?" I had told him earlier how much I liked getting mail. It felt like he knew everything I was longing for.

At the time, Cindy and I were in a rocky place. Co-parenting AC was causing tensions between us. We had very different views on how to raise him and were constantly arguing. In an effort to strengthen our relationship, I shared with Cindy the relationship that Darren and I had been cultivating. However, she didn't respond in the way I'd hoped. She told me it was a bad idea for me to date anybody long-distance; our precarious immigration status and our parenting duties made it too risky. Without even asking about him or about how I felt about Darren, she decided that she didn't like him. Despite that I was in my mid-twenties and Cindy was only eighteen months older, she still treated me like a little kid. She believed she needed to know absolutely everything about my life. So I compartmentalized: at home, I was AC's co-parent with Cindy, and on the phone I was a long-distance girlfriend to Darren. After weeks of him trying to convince me to visit him in Chicago, I relented.

Darren and I planned for a four-day visit in November. Although I lacked a US ID, I could still use my Mexican passport to fly within the US. So that he could book a first-class ticket for me, he asked me to send him pictures of all my IDs. I did as he asked, not knowing what a mistake this would be later on.

Cindy would never have allowed me to fly to another state to meet a complete stranger. So, I came up with a cover story: I was going to Los Angeles with my friend Angelica. However, I am not a good liar. I knew my face would betray me. So I texted her the fib and avoided her in the days before my trip. Because we weren't talking much during this period, it wasn't that hard.

Over FaceTime, Darren and I made plans for the visit. He picked the outfits he wanted me to wear. Even though we were barely making ends meet at home, I bought a handful of gifts for him, and in the weeks before the visit, I regularly mailed him cards. When the day came to fly, Darren got an Uber for me to get to the airport, since I didn't yet own a car. He paid for everything. I remember sitting in my spacious first-class seat, full of excitement and hope. I was finally going to meet my Prince Charming in person.

I was wearing what he'd requested: a short black dress with high-heeled boots and a long red coat. I had my long hair in curls and had put on the red lipstick he wanted me to wear. It was a frigid November evening when I landed. It was too cold for the outfit he'd asked me to wear, in retrospect, one of the first signs my fairy-tale vision might have been out of sync with reality.

Darren called me after I landed, telling me to go to the arrival area. I saw his car outside—a black Porsche Carrera—first, and then I saw him. He had flowers in his hand and was tall, strong, and dark. His head was cleanly shaven, his scalp shiny and smooth. He was like a cookie that had just come out of the oven. I left my suitcase at the curb and ran into his arms like the cheap movie I thought I was living in.

We held hands on the entire drive to his house. I kept touching his face as if I was making sure this wasn't a dream. Then my phone rang. It was Cindy, who had a feeling something was up. When I told Darren I had lied to her, he said I'd made a mistake and needed to fix it. I told Cindy the truth—from another state in another time zone—and she was angry. She said, "You're always doing stupid things, and when you need my help, I won't be there." However, in that moment, even Cindy's judgment couldn't take away my happiness.

Darren had just bought a loft in downtown Chicago. It was spacious, with huge windows and elegant decor that felt luxurious. I felt intimidated by the upscale setting. That night, he made us dinner—lasagna— and baked us gooey brownies, knowing I loved chocolate. I had been in Chicago for just a few hours and was already impressed by Darren's efforts to make me feel special.

Darren knew I was waiting to have sex until after I was married, and he supported my decision. He was the first man I'd dated that didn't judge me for it. Besides, he said, he wanted us to be married soon anyway. We went to church the next day. I met his pastor and his friends. He was respected and seemed to be part of a caring community. Everybody he introduced me to treated me well. Throughout the visit, Darren and I talked about our shared future. It felt like my fairy tale.

When I returned home to reality, I felt like the darkness of the last few years might finally be leading to a new dawn.

We continued to date long-distance for seven months after this first visit. We traveled often to see each other. We talked over FaceTime three times a day; he said he needed to *see* me. My phone pinged constantly with his texts. It seemed like every second of my life was filled with Darren, which was exciting until it wasn't. I was overwhelmed, but after a few weeks, I got used to his barrage of messages. But then Darren started making critical comments about my guy friends. He didn't like me spending time with other men.

Darren was my first "real" boyfriend, and I told myself his behavior was normal. I cut off friendships with anybody he didn't approve of. If he didn't like something about myself, I would change it. I had brown hair, but he told me he wanted it darker and shorter. I went to a hair salon right away. I was sure that Darren loved me and was helping me. So, when he demanded control of every move I made, I gave myself over to his will.

One day, my phone's battery died while I was at work, and I didn't have a charger with me. I knew Darren was texting me and I wasn't going to be able to respond. I called him as soon as I got home. He told me he was offended that I'd ignored his feelings. Hadn't I thought of him, being worried sick all day? Darren didn't talk to me for two days.

I thought that this kind of thing was normal. This man loved me. He thought something had happened to me. Darren needed time to cool off, and he was making me take time to reflect on my supposedly poor decisions.

Weeks later, Darren flew me to Los Angeles to visit me. He rented a car so he could drive us around and a house next to the beach so he could surf. We spent three days surfing, holding hands, and watching sunsets. Everything was perfect. On the last day of his visit, he took me to the Grove, a popular, swanky mall. I still got swept up in the glitter of Los Angeles in those days. Darren talked constantly about getting married, but I was still surprised when I found him leading me to a jewelry store in the mall.

We walked in, and a lady standing in front of a counter greeted me by name. She was expecting us and offered champagne. Since I don't drink, she gave me orange juice in a champagne flute instead. In that moment I was overcome with feelings—but not good ones. I was confused.

As I learned that I wear a size-five engagement ring, I felt the difference between talking about a future and actually committing to one. I saw a life of constant badgering texts, isolated from any friendships he didn't approve of. But I also saw a life of security with a man I knew was crazy about me. I inhaled deeply, trying to give myself time to think. I let Darren assume that I was overwhelmed by the moment, but it wasn't joy that was coursing through my body.

With pride and glee, Darren took pictures of every ring I tried on. Since I'd found myself in this situation, I wanted to look at all the options and enjoy the process. However, after a few rings, he became annoyed.

When I told the lady that one ring she'd pulled out wasn't my style, he complained loudly enough for others in the store to hear: "C'mon, Alix, anybody would kill for that ring. You are just being picky." My face flushed with embarrassment.

As we walked back to the rental car, Darren completely ignored me. I was used to his sulky behavior by now. I walked alongside him as if everything was fine. He called his mom, who had always been kind to me, and put his phone on speaker. This was a rule that Darren had instituted: when either of us was on the phone and we were in the same room or nearby, we had to put the call on speakerphone. It was one of his constant forms of control over me that I had unthinkingly accepted. And so, as we walked, I listened to Darren and his mom talk about me. "So," her familiar voice lilted, "how did the appointment go?"

Darren looked at me for the first time on the entire walk back before answering. "Well, it turns out Alix is a very hard person to impress." I felt a familiar shame flood my cheeks.

After he hung up, I tried to calm myself down. I asked him why he was acting like this. He said that I had the wrong attitude. I found a part of myself fighting to breathe and push back on this fairy-tale fantasy. Maybe we were rushing into buying an engagement ring, I said. As he peeled out of the parking lot, Darren shifted into a high gear and sped down the streets of Los Angeles. We nearly rear-ended another car as he weaved erratically through traffic. I apologized to him again and again. I just wanted the kind Darren of an hour earlier to return.

MARRIAGE AND GREEN CARDS

When it comes to fixing an immigration status, the options are very limited. People often think one of the surest paths is to marry a US citizen. But it's not as simple as that. Marrying a US citizen can start you on the pathway toward citizenship, but it is a long process, one that is often not assured.

In 2016, when Trump was first elected, two of my friends offered to marry me so that I could stop worrying. The news was regularly saying that Trump would deport all undocumented people when he took office.

My anxiety was constant. I would drive anxious. I avoided going out at night because I was afraid of looking suspicious. When I went grocery shopping, I feared that a police officer would stop me.

Undocumented life was always unnerving, but it became so much scarier when Trump was first elected. I don't believe that anti-immigration sentiments started with him, but I do think he emboldened people to hate what they don't understand.

Even more than before, I felt like I was in danger doing normal tasks. One day, my friends and I drove to go hiking in the Santa Cruz Mountains. My bladder is tiny; it seems like I can't even look at water without needing to use the restroom. So, as soon as we arrived, I rushed to the bathroom.

When I got out, I saw a police truck, different than the ones around the Bay Area. I didn't get a good look at the lettering, but I was certain it said *ICE*. I was terrified. I ran back inside the restroom, hid, and called my friends. "Please go read what type of police vehicle that is," I pleaded.

One of my friends went to look. He texted me that it was just a park ranger. I was safe. I came out of the bathroom and my friends met me with worried looks on their faces. While we were hiking, I explained to them why I was feeling the way I did. None of them had ever experienced that fear, even though all of them were immigrants themselves, two Filipino, one Indian, and the other Dutch.

On the way home, we stopped at a Safeway to get snacks. My friend Daniel, a US citizen, walked through the store with me. He said, "I don't know what it is like to be you. But I know my parents sacrificed a lot for me to be here. My way to pay for this life could be to marry you. But not for real. We are both single and like the beach. I wouldn't charge you," he joked, "but I would like a roommate to share cooking and laughter with." I was touched by his offer, and I could tell he was serious. He gave me a few days to think it over.

I couldn't believe the kindness my friend was extending. But I soon realized that I couldn't go through with it. I believe marriage is sacred. Besides, if something ever went wrong and hurt Daniel, I would never be able to forgive myself.

I called and told him that I appreciated his heart, but I would not be marrying him. I'm glad I didn't as a few months later, he met the love of his life.

Laura E. Enriquez, a sociologist in the Chicano/Latino studies department at UC Irvine, has written about immigration, college student mental health, and romantic decision-making in US families.[2] Her surveys, interviews, and ongoing analyses of undocumented and mixed-status relationships challenge the popular stereotype that undocumented individuals actively seek partners who can "fix" their status. Nearly every individual that Enriquez talked to "cited love as a necessary requirement for marriage and concluded that they would not marry someone simply to legalize their immigration status." Yes, my status affects how I have lived in this country, but it does not dictate my wedding vows.

WHEN YOU KNOW, YOU KNOW

I think back to the late-night conversations I used to have with girlfriends about marriage. We all thought that a moment of finality would help us cross this adult threshold, thinking that "when you know, you know." But I didn't "know" if I wanted to marry Darren. I only knew that danger was preying on my tomorrows.

Darren knew that my tourist visa would be expiring soon. I had told him about my last trip to Mexico, when I'd realized I would not be able to renew it again. In front of me, he called a lawyer friend and asked if his marrying me would help me get a green card. The lawyer said the process would take time, but it was a common way to remain legally in the United States. I didn't feel bad about it. I truly believed he wanted to help me, not seeing the ways this could lead to Darren having more control over me.

I thought that perhaps my fear of getting married so quickly was due to other issues, not because my gut was telling me not to do this. I didn't trust my instincts. I knew that this period was a honeymoon from my sadness, and I needed to do everything possible not to let Darren's dangerous streak take over my life.

After the ring-shopping incident, I went home and he flew back to Chicago. We resumed our long-distance relationship. Darren reverted back to his usual loving but overbearing self. Now, though, his constant text messages were filled with links to wedding decor, venues, and reception ideas. He already was an excited bridezilla—and he hadn't even proposed to me yet. I worried that expressing my doubts would trigger his rage, so I replied to his texts with enthusiastic emojis, going with the flow. Darren was at least making me feel valued. At home, Cindy and I were fighting every day about AC. I was working three jobs. In addition to being a nanny, I was working with a nonprofit focused on immigrant rights and with a local health clinic supporting Black and brown communities in East Palo Alto. The recent passage of AB 60 in California had allowed individuals in the state to obtain driver's licenses regardless of their immigration status. And so, even though I did not yet own a car, I was teaching classes in English and Spanish to help undocumented individuals pass the driving test. Darren's marriage fantasies were the only thing I had that I could look forward to. Beyond that, I had little will to live. At the same time, I felt guilty for not being more excited about marrying him. Isn't this what every girl wants? Isn't this what I wanted? This dude was crazy about me and he loved God. He didn't judge me for my hardships and was prepared to support me and my goals. Shouldn't that be enough?

My guilt triggered daily panic attacks in which I felt like I was suffocating. My hands would sweat and I would lose the ability to concentrate.

I started being afraid of my phone. I didn't have the time or emotional energy to be in contact with Darren every second. But I was also terrified that if I didn't respond to his calls and texts quickly enough, he would get mad. I didn't know what would set him off.

Every time I tried to erect boundaries around our relationship, he shamed me. Didn't I realize how unappreciated he always felt? If I tried to pull away, he put more pressure on me to help plan the wedding. He started asking me what my dream marriage proposal looked like, and I would try to laugh it off or tell him I wasn't sure. "Oh, whatever comes from your heart, sweetie!" In reality, I didn't even want a proposal anymore. I wanted a break. I needed peace. Darren was exhausting.

By August, we were making plans for me to visit him again in Chicago. My heart wasn't in it. I thought about how giddy I'd been when I saw him for the first time last November. Now, the fairy-tale dream had faded, leaving me with nothing but anxiety. Was he going to propose? God, I hoped not. I wanted the kind man he used to be, not this new version. Would he calm down once we got engaged?

The day of my flight, my friend Vicky texted me, asking me to call so she could tell me about a dream she'd had the night before. I was rushing to work and figured I'd call her later. I went on with my day, caring for kids, making them smile, feeding them, and filling their lives with happiness. After work, Darren sent an Uber to take me to the airport. On my way, Vicky texted me again: "Hey honey, I had a nightmare about you last night. You were in a muddy lake drowning. I tried to hold your hand, but it was a stranger's hand in mine. I was praying for you all night. Is everything okay? Hit me back. I love you."

People don't always believe that dreams mean anything. People don't always believe that God is sending us help and tries gently to protect us. But as I read that text, I thought to myself: "That's how I feel. I feel like I'm drowning." But by then, I was at the airport, and I didn't respond.

I landed in Chicago and Darren was excited to see me, but by now, the city and this man had lost their luster. In the few weeks since I'd last been at his house, everything felt different somehow. I couldn't put my finger on it, but his house even smelled different. What did my girlfriends always say? *When you know, you know.* My gut was telling me that another woman had been here. But that couldn't be right. This dude was blowing up my phone every hour . . . How would he even have time to cheat? He had pictures of me all over his Instagram and Facebook. I knew all his friends. It wasn't possible.

He cooked dinner as I decompressed from the flight and from my daily life with Cindy. A shampoo commercial came on the TV. As soon as I saw it, I stood up and went to look at the shower drain. I have no idea what pulled my body in that direction, but sure enough, I found a clump of unfamiliar short black hair. I rarely get mad, but when I do, I become like the Hulk. I gathered it in my fist and flew into the kitchen.

I started screaming, "Whose hair is this? Why does this house smell like another woman?"

Darren looked at me calmly. He said that the hair was his sister's, Marilyn's. I didn't believe a word he was saying. I yelled and cried and demanded the truth.

My screams were loud enough that one of the condo security officers knocked on the door and asked us to lower our voices. I couldn't believe I'd become the woman who makes a scene. Once again, I felt ashamed of myself. My tears stopped, and then Darren started crying. I went to pack up my suitcase; I no longer wanted to stay. Then he went to the closet and pulled out a tiny jewelry box, which held one of the engagement rings I had seen and liked three months ago. He'd been planning to propose the next day but wanted to show the ring to me now, so I knew he was serious.

Darren used his wealth to control my emotions. Through tears, he told me that there was no way he would spend this kind of money on a ring and be cheating at the same time.

I calmed down. I asked him to put the ring away and to call Marilyn. After a few minutes, she came on speakerphone and confirmed Darren's story. Sure, she had taken a shower at his place. Perhaps some of her hair had found its way into his drain. I knew that her hair was brown, not black, but somehow, I ignored that fact. I went to bed confused, disoriented, and scared.

The next morning, as Darren was making his signature cinnamon French toast, my phone rang. It was a private number. I answered the call and put it on speaker.

"Is this Alix Dick?" the voice from an unknown number asked.

"Yes, it is."

"This is Ravenswood Clinic. We have the results from your pregnancy test. It came back positive."

A few days before coming to Chicago, I had gotten a physical at a clinic. I was interviewing for a new babysitting job and the family had asked me about my health. A checkup at that clinic always included a pregnancy test. It didn't matter that I wasn't sexually active, the test was part of the process.

Darren stood in the kitchen looking at me.

I stared at my phone, dumbfounded. "I'm sorry," I replied hesitantly. "I believe you are mistaken."

The man's voice on the other end said, "Is this Alix Dick?"

I said yes.

"The information we have here is correct. Have a great day." The man hung up.

For about thirty seconds, the only sound was the sizzle of egg-soaked bread in the skillet. I looked at Darren, who was shaking.

I spoke slowly, as if to a cornered animal: "Baby, that's impossible. There is obviously a mistake."

Darren's broad chest rose and fell, looking like he was about to hyperventilate.

"You think I'm an idiot?" He charged toward me and screamed into my face. "You have to be fucking kidding me. You blame me for cheating when you are a lying piece of shit?"

I started crying with terror. I kept repeating that it was impossible for me to be pregnant. That there was no way. The more I talked, though, the angrier he got.

He took the bowl with eggs and milk and threw it at the wall. He threw and smashed every object in the room as I stood there shaking.

All I wanted to do was get out, but he was between me and the exit. As he continued to call me a fucking cheater, I finally snapped back to reality. I found my tongue and told him he was only calling me a cheater to drown out his own conscience. "You know damn well Marilyn didn't take a shower here. The only cheater here is you."

He seized my arms and threw me onto the sofa. He put his whole body on top of me and grabbed my mouth with his hand. "Repeat what you just said."

I panicked and my asthma kicked in. I couldn't speak and I couldn't breathe. I was desperate for air, crying, and trying to escape.

I somehow kicked him enough to get him off me and ran toward the door. But Darren grabbed my leg and my body slammed to the floor.

Darren held me down and screamed in my ear. He hit me as he yelled, "I did cheat on you!"

I fought with all of my strength to get up. His assault and tirade continued. "You know why? Because you deserve it. You never appreciate all the money and gifts I get you!"

His fingers dug into my arms as he dragged me back to the floor. "You are ungrateful!"

The bruises on my arms and neck and waist would be there for days. In the moment, I could only see myself trying to inch my body closer to the door.

"Nobody would ever want a girl like you! Nobody would ever believe your bullshit about waiting until marriage! I cheated on you because you deserve it!"

I don't know how long he attacked me and held me prisoner under his weight as I fought and screamed and begged for help. At some point, I dissociated. I knew I was going to be raped or killed. I couldn't breathe; I didn't have enough air to fight back.

As I lay there, my cheek to the carpet, I could hear my dad's voice reciting Psalm 23: *The Lord is my shepherd, I shall not want.*

I was too weak to scream, so I prayed. *Lord, forgive me for all the times I didn't listen to your warnings. Forgive me for ignoring your voice. I don't want to die in this way. I don't want Cindy to be traumatized by me. I don't want to hurt AC. Please save me. Please hear me. Please save me.*

I know that God heard me that day. The security officer from the night before pounded on the door.

Darren squeezed my mouth with his hand. "If you say anything, I swear, I will kill you."

Darren opened the door and I got up, shaking. My arms were bruised. My face was red from the lack of air. The security guard saw all this but did not acknowledge it. He only said the neighbor had called. I still cannot believe the willingness of men to look past violence.

"Ah man, I'm so sorry," Darren said. "Yeah, we were arguing, but everything is fine now." The officer told him to go get some fresh air. Darren grabbed his keys and left.

I didn't know how long he'd be gone. I raced through the house. I grabbed a pair of scissors and a knife. I put them in my purse. I splashed cold water on my face. I looked in the mirror and saw scratches and bruises all over my body. I looked on the floor and saw handfuls of my hair scattered everywhere.

I needed to leave, but Darren controlled everything. I didn't have money for a return flight. Hell, I didn't even know how to get to the airport. But the first step was to get out the door. I packed all my stuff in three minutes. I was rushing to the elevator when Darren came up beside me, smoking a cigar.

He spoke softly. "Let's go back to the condo, cookie. Everything is fine. I'll make you breakfast. Everything is fine."

The hardest part of this story for me to tell you is this: after all he'd done to me, *I still did what he said.* I went back inside the apartment.

I cried and asked him to take me home, to just get me an Uber.

He started crying, too. He said he'd never actually cheated on me, that he'd made it all up. I pretended to believe him. I knew what he was capable of, so I needed to placate him for now until I could find a way to leave.

He drove us to a CVS and bought four pregnancy tests. They all came up negative, of course. But he still wanted me to go to a clinic to get a pregnancy test there. I said I would do this if he took me to the airport and bought me a new ticket back to California first. I would go to a clinic when I got home.

The hours passed. Darren made us food, but I was in a state of shock and couldn't eat. We went to bed like nothing had happened, but I hid the pair of scissors in my pajamas.

I didn't sleep that night. I had found the earliest flight home and would need to leave for the airport at 4 a.m. The hour finally arrived. Darren drove me to the airport, telling me the whole way there how much he loved me. I felt like I was going to throw up. I was disgusted by this man, but I'd swallowed my hate for him, and he'd bought it. I'd been acting for a long time, and this had been a performance to save my very life.

UNTALLIED VICTIMS

Domestic violence in the US, regardless of immigration status, remains a silent pandemic in and of itself. Any given year in the past decade saw between 1.2 and 1.8 million victims of domestic abuse. Women, particularly between the ages of eighteen and thirty-four (the ages I've been in the US), are the most frequent victims of intimate partner violence.[3] One in four women has experienced physical and sexual violence from a partner. Over half of all women murdered in the US are killed by a current or former romantic partner. That's the grim reality for *all* women in this country.

Estimates of the rates of domestic violence involving at least one undocumented partner are difficult to research. But some estimates suggest that intimate partner violence rates among Latina immigrants—undocumented or not—are twice as high as the overall US rates. One survey found that 78 percent of immigrant survivors of domestic violence were hesitant to contact authorities or organizations with proximity to the federal government.[4] A clear picture of the specific experiences of undocumented partners in this country is lacking. The policies of many sanctuary cities in the US separate police and ICE interactions, in part to encourage victims of domestic violence to come forward. However, the fear of law enforcement remains strong for many of us.

It is likely that most accounts of domestic violence involving undocumented immigrants go unreported. Likewise, many undocumented immigrants are isolated from family and friend networks, with few sources of support to get out of violent relationships. Coercion and threats targeting our undocumented status only add to these concerns. For example, when I tried to break up with Darren, he wielded my undocumented status to try to keep me emotionally and physically under his control. Laura Enriquez writes that cultural expectations about Latinas and our role in society only added to the feeling of being stuck in life-threatening relationships. In the case of one of her research participants, she writes, "multiple forms of inequality enabled the abuse."[5] For me, it was the fear of deportation, isolation from a family network, the demands on me as a "good" Christian Mexican. These all meant I let Darren's words and fists control me.

There are more than 3 million undocumented women in this country, and we make up a substantial portion of the victims of domestic violence. When I tell you that I never told my family, my friends, or the police about this abuse as it was happening, it was because of the shame and fear that I felt about my undocumented status.

JUDGMENT

When I got back to the bay, I took an Uber to the clinic. I had Darren on FaceTime the entire time I was there. I told the receptionist I needed to speak to the doctor that had called me the day before. The receptionist checked her computer and said there was no record of them having called me about my pregnancy test. "The pregnancy tests are complete immediately, and yours was negative," she explained.

I was so confused and scared. Then who had called me? I was shaking. The receptionist saw the fear in my face as I told Darren I would call him again when I got home. When I hung up, the receptionist tapped my shoulder and said, "Hey, are you okay? Do you need help?"

I almost broke down in front of her. Finally I said, "I'm stressed."

She asked, "Is he mistreating you? Do you need assistance?" For the first time, I understood that I had experienced domestic violence, that I'd been manipulated and hurt for a long time. I told her yes, he'd been mistreating me, but I was okay now. I touched her shoulder in gratitude and left. If she'd only known all the bruises hiding under my long-sleeved shirt.

Had Darren somehow set up the call just to make my life miserable and gain control over me? Could it have come from the girl he'd been cheating with? How could she have known the name of the clinic I'd gone to, or even that a pregnancy test was part of a physical? Nothing made sense. Hours and days passed. I couldn't eat. All I did was lay down in bed and cry. I had days left from taking a week off work to spend with Darren. He continued to call me, and for reasons I don't understand, I picked up his calls. He was angry and still doubted my story about the pregnancy test call: "Look, nobody calls from a hospital by mistake."

I decided to call the police. Was I going to report Darren's abuse? No, I was going to tell them about the strange pregnancy test call I'd received. You might wonder why I would contact the police about a mysterious phone call but not about the man who had pummeled me nearly to death on the floor of his home. If you've never been abused and emotionally controlled, I can only say that you don't know what it is to feel such corrosive fear in your bones. Even though we were in different states, I was still afraid of upsetting Darren. My brain wasn't working logically.

I called the Menlo Park police. The detective I spoke with asked if I thought the call might have been a prank.

"A prank?" Nobody would do that to me. Plus, nobody had seen me go to that clinic appointment. The detective explained that this wasn't like in the movies. He didn't have the ability to trace the call and find out who it was.

The next day, Cindy and I were taking AC to soccer practice. Cindy had no idea what I had just gone through, and she was still bitter that I had lied to her about Darren. She hated every time I went to Chicago. We were squabbling co-parents with too much on our plates.

We dropped AC off. The air was thick, the two of us were silent, and I could hardly breathe. Cindy finally broke the tension and said, "I heard the guys were doing prank calls the other day." I couldn't believe her words. "Edgar"—a friend of ours—"said he did a prank on you that might have seemed too realistic." I asked her if it was about thinking I was pregnant. She looked at me very angrily and said, "Why would you think you are pregnant?"

When Cindy mentioned "the guys," I suddenly remembered that Edgar had been outside the clinic just before my appointment. He'd waved goodbye to me as I'd gone inside.

Edgar had made the call. I had nearly been murdered because of a stupid joke.

I didn't have anything to prove to Cindy, or anyone else. All I wanted was peace. I started crying. I was shaking and couldn't stop. I couldn't believe my own sister was judging me for something she didn't understand. It felt unreal. I was so lonely and hurt. My sister watched me crying. There was only disappointment in her eyes. I asked Edgar to meet me a few days later.

Edgar and I met at a Starbucks. We sat down and I asked, "First of all, how the hell did you know I went for a physical?"

He was proud and smug. "Does it matter?"

I said, "I almost got killed because of your stupid joke."

"I did you a favor. Everybody knew that guy is bad for you. So, you're welcome."

Edgar never apologized. I found out later that he liked me and had been trying to sabotage my relationship. Pathetic.

Nonetheless, talking to Edgar did give me a bit of clarity. I thought about how my Christian expectations about true love and the lack of experience I had due to my undocumented status had dragged me into this miserable situation with Darren. I had not wanted to commit to having the young family of his dreams. Even before his fists crushed any chance of our sharing a future, I'd known I didn't want to marry this man.

I began to keep Darren at a distance. In response, the first thing he did was threaten me. Because Darren had pictures of all my IDs to book my travel, he said he could easily turn my information over to ICE.

After months of him trying to get me back, I blocked Darren on my phone and on my social media accounts. Then he started texting me from his friends' phones. He messaged me to say he was flying to San Francisco to see me and make things right. As with the engagement ring he'd pulled out the night before he battered me, now he sent me a picture of his plane ticket so I could see just how serious he was. But he didn't realize that I too was serious. I knew he was up for a promotion, and he'd introduced me to his boss. I told him I would call that boss and tell him how Darren had abused me.

When he realized I truly would never agree to see him again, he texted me a picture of my IDs, repeating his earlier threat: "Maybe I should show this to ICE hahaha." Cruel threats like this are a common abuse tactic in mixed-status relationships. It was terrifying. My final tourist visa had just run out. I was officially undocumented, and there were real, immediate consequences. Any little mistake could lead to tragedy. Darren's threat momentarily got to me. Could I make a life with this monster work, if it meant I could stay in the US and keep AC safe? But I also knew Darren's anger knew no limits; this man could kill me. I had fled Mexico to escape violence, only to find it again in this country.

Sadly, Darren taught me the basic facts about love in America. Because of my undocumented status, I lost a period of my life when I should have been learning how to love and be loved in healthy ways. Instead, I learned that people like me will always be in danger. We feel so threatened by being exposed that marriage seems like a way out.

One day, I'd had enough of his threats. I decided to call Darren on Zoom.

He answered, sounding worried. "What's wrong?"

I wasn't my old self. I'll never be able to recover the naive, cheerful Alix that first messaged with Darren so many months earlier. But I still willed my voice not to shake when I told him he was dead to me and never to talk to me again. He started crying like one of the toddlers I was then caring for. He said he'd always known I didn't love him. All I cared about was his money.

I never asked why he'd hit me. I never told him how the twelve months of our relationship had completely changed my view of the world and my view of men. I didn't tell him that I would never be the same. I never saw his face again. The book of fairy tales had closed.

CHAPTER 7

THE COST OF FAITH

When I reflect on my life, I see how all the things I used to cherish about my home in Sinaloa are gone now. My dad isn't there. My mom now lives near Cindy in the Bay Area. AC lives in Spain. We are still so close, it weighs on me that I only see him via FaceTime.

Given all this, what do I have left to look back upon, or forward to?

I am scared of experiencing more loss. I've shed so many parts of my life in Mexico, in Georgia, even here in California. My career aspirations. My friends. My time working toward college degrees in both Mexico and the US. My house. My first car. The notebooks full of novels and scripts that I wrote as a kid. My childhood home full of my belongings. Over and over again, I've lost things that are foundational to a healthy life and I have had to start over again.

And yet, I love who I am now—how, through a stubborn will to survive and a desire to love this world, even at its cruelest, I have re-constituted myself. I've learned to fight for me and for my brother. I still wrestle with nightmares and panic attacks. But when I see the person I am now, I am so proud.

And so, I want to use an intentional phrase about this journey: it is *by the grace of God* that I am here, and that *we* are here. I used to be broken. Suicidal, lonely, bitter. Angry about the things I'd lost. But there was a strength that wrestled my grief out of my limbs. That strength is the hand of a God that I have come to know. He has given me a second chance. Whether or not your own beliefs share similar biblical roots, my life remains bound up in yours.

I used to take my faith for granted. But in an American society whose politics and values are steeped in theological hypocrisy, my unrelenting faith in a Christian god feels so costly. Sharing details of my Christian identity means that some readers might make assumptions about my values or my political commitments. So, in this chapter, I will tell you about the costs of evangelical American Christians who are happy to turn their backs on people like me. But, first, I need to tell you about when I witnessed my own death sentence at six years old.

BREATHING WITH GOD

I have chronic asthma. I've lived with it since I was a kid. Some of my earliest memories are of being left in the hospital overnight so that doctors could keep an eye on my breathing. My parents stayed with me as late as they could, but they weren't allowed to stay the whole night. This is where some of my fears of abandonment and my distaste for goodbyes come from. I often shared my hospital room with other sick kids. Many of them are no longer with us today. I also sat for days in a room with a nebulizer affixed to my face, sounding like an alien as I fought to breathe. Dr. Flores, the specialist my family came to know well after months of hospital stays, often came into my room, listening, assessing, prodding at me and walking away with my parents to discuss my condition elsewhere on the hospital floor. On one such day, after the doctor and my parents trailed out, I realized my dad had taken my backpack with him, stuffed with toys and markers. Like a tiny ghost, barefoot, with my nebulizer in place, I tracked my way down the hall to where I knew Dr. Flores's office was.

Something told me to wait outside the doorway, which was slightly ajar. I heard the sniffles of quiet sobs from my mom and dad as the doctor told them how grave my condition was. I remember Dr. Flores saying, "She's dying," and the declarative finality with which he said it. These stays in the hospital, he said, would prolong my life for only so long.

My parents looked defeated. They didn't say anything to me, but their faces alone confirmed the truth that I wasn't supposed to have heard. My parents, my grandparents, my aunts and uncles, all of them knew about the doctor's prognosis. But my abuelita didn't give in to defeat. She told the rest of the family to pray for a miracle. She reminded me of the picture book she'd given me when I was younger, *Jesus Is Your Friend*. I decided to take my grandma's suggestion seriously.

The first time I took my grandmother's advice and knelt to pray was a few weeks later, after another appointment with Dr. Flores. I listened as he explained how my lungs *still* didn't work normally. He warned my family that I could die any day. Afterward, I knelt down on the dark hospital floor. I was wearing one of those ugly hospital gowns, and I was extremely cold. I started talking to God. Something in me knew that I was not alone in that room. I couldn't explain it, but the book my abuelita had given me said that when even little kids prayed to God, God heard them.

I had watched some of the other kids in the hospital die, and my mind was flooded with the knowledge that someday—perhaps soon—that would be me. I'd seen loss eat away at those kids' families, and it was devastating. I was young, but I understood grief better than most adults.

During my stays in the hospital, I'd met an eight-year-old girl, Alondra, also a patient there. She had the coolest toys and the purest and most giving heart. For months and months, we were best friends. Eventually she lost her beautiful long brown hair, and a cheerful bald Alondra replaced the girl I'd been playing with. I didn't understand that the lifelong friendship I dreamed of having with her wasn't going to happen. Instead, one day my family brought me to the hospital after I had an asthma attack, and Alondra's parents told us that their daughter had passed away just hours before we'd arrived. I was rocked with the pain of loss. I heard the grief that was swallowing up her parents as my mom and dad held them. Inflicting that pain on my family became my biggest fear. I started to pray for healing because I wanted to protect my family. I begged God to let me breathe. I knew that he could hear me. Somehow, I always felt him near.

Reluctantly, my family also started to pray. With the exception of my abuelita, we hadn't been an especially religious family before this period.

Occasionally we went to church, but we didn't attend regularly or pray consistently until my grandmother pushed us to do so. We prayed together as well as individually, and I started finding my own relationship with God. Once, during a particularly bad asthma attack, as my dad prepared for the thirty-minute race to the hospital, my mom had us all pause: "We're going to pray before we leave." My dad was exasperated but obliged. The faith in my house started because of me. Every time I had an asthma attack, we prayed.

When I was eight, the severe asthma attacks stopped. Some people might not see that as a miracle, but I know in my core it was. It was my prayers, my grandparents' prayers, my mom and dad's prayers. I still carry an inhaler (when I can access one in the US), but I have never been hospitalized because of my asthma again.

My parents' gratitude for my recovery eventually drove us into the church. Participating in the church became a part of my parents' identity, a safe space for my family. My dad played the piano during service, while my mom led the women's ministry. I started leading Bible school for kids and later became involved with the worship team.

This isn't to say that all of my experiences in the church have been uniformly positive. For many years I thought that churchgoers were all pure, all generous, all *good*. But the thing is, people don't go to church because they are perfect. People go to church to be redeemed, to be healed, to get better. In this way, they are like hospitals.

This isn't to excuse the harm that certain church leaders have caused, particularly in the US, where right-wing evangelicalism is all too strong. Some of the people involved with churches are terrible, and their values don't represent my own. And some of the fundamental values espoused by evangelical American Christians are abjectly racist, perpetuating harm and xenophobia against people like me.

ANTI-IMMIGRANT EVANGELICALS

These days, I make a clear distinction between my relationship with God and my relationship with the church.[1] When I was a child, this was not so much the case; the two relationships were closely bound together.

And, when my siblings and I fled to the US, it was the church community that sheltered us in Atlanta and that brought us to California. It was the church community that helped me find some of my first jobs here, at the radio station and as a nanny.

However, true to the title of this book (and chapter), there have been substantial costs associated with my faith. That's what I want to tell you about.

The longer I live in the US, the more I see the language of Christianity weaponized by right-wing values and used to enact xenophobic policies, from family and child separations at the border to Trump's infamous Muslim ban in 2017. It is not so much that individual passages from the Bible encourage this kind of harm. Rather, the transformation of the evangelical movement in the US into a strongly nativist voting bloc has tied Christianity to beliefs that harm me. These Christian values are used to advocate against immigrant rights, even though this "nation of immigrants" did not exist until centuries after the Bible was written. These harmful practices do not reflect Christianity. It is long past time that we separate those practices from the values of Christ as I've come to know him: openness, acceptance, a duty to welcome outsiders.

Judaism, Islam, and Christianity—the Abrahamic religions—all center stories of migration within their sacred texts. In Christian and Jewish scripture, God calls on Abraham to move to unknown lands: *The LORD had said to Abram, "Go from your country, your people and your father's household to the land I will show you."*[2] In the New Testament, we read of how King Herod, in an attempt to purge the infant-messiah, ordered the execution of all male children under two throughout Bethlehem, forcing the Holy Family to flee to Egypt. In addition to Jesus's own migration, numerous Old Testament verses command people to extend hospitality to foreigners, like Exodus 22: *Do not mistreat or oppress a foreigner, for you were foreigners in Egypt* and Leviticus 19: *When a foreigner lives with you in your land, don't take advantage of him. Treat the foreigner the same as a native. Love him like one of your own. Remember that you were once foreigners in Egypt.*

Alongside these commands to provide hospitality, the Bible also shows Jesus as merciful, compassionate, inclusive. His belief in second chances flew in the face of existing laws and social systems. However, even though the documented life of Jesus is nothing less than an account of a radical brown rebel who was killed for his convictions, today's white evangelical leaders hold an altogether different interpretation of what it means to be Christian.

Anthea Butler, in her clear-eyed book *White Evangelical Racism: The Politics of Morality in America*, tracks how the meaning of "evangelical" has shifted in the US context. Where it had once meant a belief in literal interpretations of the Bible and supporting broad Christian worship, the term came to refer to a primarily white movement that has been deeply tied to right-wing politics since the mid-twentieth century.[3] Despite its interdenominational nature, evangelical Christians are often unified as a political and voting bloc.

Butler explains, "Race and racism have always been foundational parts of evangelicalism in America, fueling its educational, political, social, and cultural mores." American evangelicalism has fully embraced Donald Trump across multiple presidential election cycles. The movement has become synonymous with *white* evangelicalism and white supremacy. Their biblical interpretations endorse a kind of "Americanism," and much of it is fueled by political and cultural brokers. Kristin Kobes Du Mez's *Jesus and John Wayne: How White Evangelicals Corrupted a Faith and Fractured a Nation* traces how evangelical churches have come to center authoritarian values and leadership. This evangelical worldview has filtered into mainstream political rhetoric and news reports. Across multiple twentieth-century wars, the media pushed the message "that America was a Christian nation, that the military was a force for good, and that the strength of the nation depended on a properly ordered, patriarchal home."[4]

Of course, it's not just in the contemporary US that whiteness has become tied to Christianity. Renaissance paintings by artists like da Vinci, Giotto, and van Eyck show Jesus as a white man, even though multiple historical records indicate that Jesus would have had a darker complexion. The whitened image of Jesus, the same depiction that I saw throughout the churches I attended in Mexico, helps convey the assumption that Christian values are tied to the same white ideologies that colonized Indigenous land and enslaved Black individuals. These ideologies are still at work today. A study led by researcher Steven Roberts in the US found that individuals who identified God as a white man were more likely to see white men as authority figures and white people as "particularly boss-like."[5]

At the churches I attended in Georgia and California, I heard fellow worshippers—not always white themselves—use Bible passages out of context to support perspectives that actively harm me and other immigrants in this country. This form of "proof texting" is common in Christian communities.[6] They would say, for example, that God made authorities and, therefore, their laws should be respected. They would also say that stricter immigration laws existed to protect Christian Americans and were part of God's will. Evangelicals often read popular media sources in a similar way. Francesca Tripodi's research explores how conservative Christians use "scriptural inference" to interpret media sources like Fox News.[7] Tripodi suggests that these practices are how individuals learn to endorse and espouse the racist rhetoric of conservative ecosystems.

A REFLECTION IN WASHINGTON

In 2017, I flew to Washington, DC, to join an organized march for immigrant rights, in particular to support the Dream Act. I was there alongside many of the prominent activist networks that I've had the opportunity to connect with over the years. The feeling was one of family and friendship; we were united in our efforts to protect Dreamers. Our demonstration was also meant to advocate to allow at least some members of the undocumented community to resist the racist policies we often encounter in our day-to-day lives.

We marched to the Capitol and held a sit-in inside the lobby. Although we all risked being arrested, to me, the need to demonstrate alongside my immigrant and undocumented family felt more important. Counter-demonstrators were there as well. They held signs denouncing "illegals" and calling on the government to "defend" the border. I noticed that many of the counterprotestors were dressed in the familiar conservative clothing of the churches I had attended: long skirts, straight long hair, plain fabrics. I had worn similar clothing growing up. These counter-demonstrators were Christians, fighting for values that were completely opposite from the ones that had motivated me to fly across the country. I felt betrayed by my fellow Christians. At the same time, I heard the other immigrant-rights protestors around me making fun of the "religious weirdos" on the other side. "Look at these idiots," they said.

Both sides of this fight were jeering at different parts of me. I was both the unwanted "illegal alien" and the simple-minded "religious nut." There was no space for nuance on the protest line. Back home in California, I realized my church friends and my organizer friends were distinct groups. They never interacted and weren't even aware of one another.

I think about how Jesus immigrated in his youth. Born in Bethlehem, on what is today the West Bank of Palestine, he had to flee to Egypt for his survival. And, despite modern depictions smoothing down his passion into a soft-spoken savant, he was also a radical. He was someone who would fight for people like me.[8] Instead, America's been brainwashed to worship the image of a white dude with blue eyes who supposedly came to save good Republicans. That moment in DC revealed clearly to me who Christianity in America is often for, and it was one of the first times I felt heartbroken by the acts of Christians.

BLUE RIBBON

My Christianity requires me to welcome and support my neighbors. This is why I take my marginalization as an undocumented woman so personally. Humanity does not have to be this way.

Christians can offer much more than the "thoughts and prayers" that they so often express anytime they bear witness to a tragedy in this world. I don't believe God wants us to idly sit by and simply *pray away* the hardship of others. You have to work if you want something changed. My faith exists alongside my labor.

In 2017, I was nannying by day, working with various immigrant rights organizations on weekends, and looking for opportunities to start the nonprofit I'd long dreamed of. Even as I was spending much of my time providing for AC, I felt a greater calling to help those around me. When I was younger, I'd thought that I would follow in my father's footsteps by becoming a lawyer, plans delayed by my immigration. Now, years into making this country my home, I was identifying alternative pathways to support those around me that didn't require advanced college degrees that I still cannot attain here. A friend from church introduced me to someone I'll call Elizabeth. Elizabeth was a tall, gorgeous, accomplished woman who had graduated from Stanford. She and I went to different churches in the Bay Area. She had previous experience volunteering in the kind of organization I wanted to start, and she had a deep network that we could connect with. We hit it off and started sketching out the nonprofit that became Blue Ribbon.[9]

When I create something, it is never alone. I try to build a team that can make a positive difference alongside me. When it came time to create Blue Ribbon, I knew I wanted my team to treat the individuals in our work not as projects but as other human beings. My vision for Blue Ribbon came from a deeply personal place. Not many of my friends know that I've been homeless, that I've spent weeks and months in the living rooms and spare rooms of other families. I've seen plenty of church outreach efforts that offer Band-Aids to ongoing challenges. They fail to address the root issues of inequality. Instead, I wanted to offer unhoused people more than just the temporary support that I'd seen so many church outreach projects distribute. Blue Ribbon was designed to help integrate unhoused individuals back into society, to restore the feeling of dignity they may have lost.

I assessed where outreach could support people most effectively. Every weekend, our team drove to various locations within a few hours of the Bay Area: Sacramento or Fresno or Bakersfield or Stockton. Sometimes we would just stay in San Francisco.

I created a program in which we developed relationships with people experiencing homelessness over a period of at least six weeks. We identified organizations and resources available in their neighborhoods and brokered partnerships with those orgs on behalf of the people we'd met. We advocated for them and helped them connect to local groups that could eventually provide them with permanent housing if they so chose. We found them medical clinics and dentists, programs related to drug dependency, support related to foster care. We found resources available in their cities and worked to give them the feelings of confidence they needed to take tentative steps forward. The area in which I felt we were most successful was helping those looking for jobs find stable employment.

Policy debates about how to support the needs of the unhoused focus on economic decisions rather than on individuals and their humanity. Blue Ribbon recognized that people labeled homeless have been removed and *othered* by society. Building on my own sense of being an outsider, I focused Blue Ribbon on making individuals feel welcomed by society again.

There was Dianna Rogers. I met her one day as she was asking for help outside of a Cheesecake Factory. It was a blustery Friday night, and I am never off the clock when it comes to my calling so I sat down next to her and asked if she wanted me to get her some dinner. She instead asked if I could get her some water and bandages. I went to the CVS across the street and used the remaining eighteen dollars in my purse to purchase her requested items, along with some bread, jerky, and protein bars. I told Dianna about Blue Ribbon and asked if she might see me for coffee and chat about ways that I could provide ongoing help. We agreed to meet the next day.

I spent four hours that Saturday learning about Dianna's life. About how she'd been an accountant and had owned a home in the neighborhood. Her husband had started cheating on her after she was diagnosed with cancer. That led her to a maelstrom of alcohol abuse that swallowed up her marriage, her home, and her job. The Dianna I met was brilliant and cancer-free but also awash in debt and alcohol dependency. She felt that she had nothing left but her faith and her stubbornness to try to survive. She had been experiencing homelessness for seven years.

As she told me about her life, I saw how her story reflected my own. In her memory, her life had once been perfect, but then tragedy struck and took it all away. Dianna was trying to find her way back to feeling normal and recover the sense of self-confidence that she once had.

I didn't find Dianna a job. She did that herself. Instead, I committed to stand alongside her at every step of her journey. Like many of the people I worked with through Blue Ribbon, it was Dianna who made the calls, attended the interviews, and found her first job after years of not feeling like she could. Likewise, I worked with her to find temporary housing and a therapist to talk to. Our conversations continued to be life-changing for both of us. I got her a phone and we stayed in contact. The last time I heard from her, she was working at a community college.

Sometimes we go out into the world trying to do something good in the lives of the people around us but, in the process, our own lives are transformed. What stays with me most about Blue Ribbon is the ways in which I was changed by the Diannas I got to meet. To me, the most successful part of the program I created was seeing these individuals feel like they got their humanity back.

As Dianna's story suggests, this was individualized work. It often looked like saying to someone, "Hey, I'm going to get you a prepaid phone to use. I am going to connect you with some local restaurants that are looking for jobs. There is an organization we work with that provides showers and so, next week, when I am here, I'll have some clothes and we can set up a time for you to go on an interview. I'm going to go with you and I'm going to wait outside so someone is there for you when you are done." It sounds simple, and I did nearly that exact same process many times. It provided figurative and sometimes literal hand-holding. It boosted the confidence of individuals who had internalized the lies this country sold them about their lack of worth. We saw people find purpose again, a reason to live. It was just a couple years earlier that I'd lost my own feelings of identity, dignity, and self-worth. Really, this was about putting myself—my own experiences, my own heart—into this work. That's where I saw results happen.

Our efforts didn't always work out. Not everyone wanted our help, and not everyone could stay alongside us on our weeks-long process. My availability was dependent on my own need to work and survive, and I lost touch with a few people along the way as a result.

Even though Blue Ribbon was a project I led alongside Elizabeth and other Christians, I was very intentional about not making this a church-focused project. *Remember, don't tell them we're Christians*, I would remind our team at the beginning of our work in a new city. We

did this not out of shame or subterfuge, but because the love of God is
inherently a selfless love. I knew God loved the unhoused people we
were connecting with. I was there to remind them of that through our
actions, and I wanted our work to stand as its own gospel; we were not
there to preach or convert. Still, nearly every weekend, at least one of
the unhoused people I'd met would ask to pray with me. These quiet
moments in parks and parking lots are some of my most cherished memories of Blue Ribbon. It was a calling to support and welcome society's
outsiders. Outsiders, just like me.

Well, just like me except for the fact that the vast majority of the folks
we helped were white. They all had valid Social Security numbers and
were eligible to work in this country. One of my biggest desires was to
meet Mexicans and immigrants like me. People who didn't speak English
fluently, just as I hadn't in my first years in the US.

I was incredibly busy during the Blue Ribbon years. I was nannying
for a family, traveling to Los Angeles for other immigrant rights work
and filmmaking projects, participating in my church, and taking college
courses on general law in the hopes of completing a degree and eventually enrolling in law school, all while still raising AC. Despite all this,
I prioritized growing this program because I knew it worked and was
the strongest expression of my Christian faith. I spent years growing our
volunteer base. I had patrons who wanted to make large cash donations.
I paid for the legal filing to make Blue Ribbon an official nonprofit entity.
However, since my tourist visa was expiring, we filed everything under
Elizabeth's name. I thought I had every reason to trust Elizabeth. We'd
connected through church friends, and I assumed our intentions with
this work were equally pure.

One afternoon, one of the parents I was nannying for showed me an
article on his phone. "Hey," he said, "isn't this the nonprofit you have been
talking about?" He showed me a full profile of Blue Ribbon in the local
newspaper, which spotlighted the organization's "founder and leader,"
Elizabeth. There was no mention of me anywhere. I couldn't believe it. Elizabeth had taken my vision and my words and claimed them as her own.

My concern was not about getting credit for this work, but about the breach of trust between Elizabeth and me. She had been coordinating interviews with the journalist for weeks without telling me, without consideration for the reputation of Blue Ribbon at large. Elizabeth's quotes emphasized the organization's connection to our church, undermining my desire to focus on helping people rather than preaching to them.

I'd spent plenty of my own money to recruit volunteers. I hosted receptions at coffee shops to share Blue Ribbon with interested young people. These gatherings were successful, but Elizabeth, even with her financial privilege, was never willing to chip in for these events. I footed the bill time and time again.

Despite Elizabeth's overall *American-ness* and privilege, people gravitated toward me rather than her, not just on the streets but in our partnership and planning meetings. I started to see that, somehow, Elizabeth was jealous of this small, good thing I had in my life. I think she started to think that the two of us were in competition with one another.

Signs of this competitiveness had been present months before the news article about Blue Ribbon was published. One day, Elizabeth and I carpooled to a meeting with a woman named Susan, the executive director of a food bank in San Francisco. Susan and I had a lot in common and—as usual—I spoke openly about my personal connection to Blue Ribbon's mission. At the end of our lengthy meeting, Susan not only confirmed her commitment to an ongoing collaboration with the food bank but also went one step further. She offered to pay my personal rent for the next three months. "You should be doing this work full-time," she said. "It's clear this is the work you are called to do."

Her words felt so affirming. I was committed to this work while also believing I could juggle the other commitments that I had and declined the offer. I warmly embraced Susan as I thanked her. Elizabeth stared at her phone during the exchange and then completely ignored me on our way back. Her parents paid her rent and the lease on her Mercedes, but somehow her jealousy of me was strong enough to warrant the silent treatment.

Elizabeth's resentment meant that she got meaner and meaner to me. If I made a minor mistake—a grammatical error or scheduling oversight—she spoke down to me, targeting my insecurities about my English and lack of a college degree: "I thought you had experience." "I thought you knew what you were doing."

When I tried to talk with Elizabeth about the way she was treating me, she became evasive and dodged my questions. I asked her directly about the newspaper profile and she said she hadn't mentioned me in her interview because of my immigration status. All my trust in her disappeared. I was worried that she might turn my information over to immigration officials, or get me caught up in some sort of financial scheme. Eventually, I realized I needed to distance myself from her, even if it meant walking away from an organization I had nurtured. There would always be other pathways to doing the work of God.

I told Elizabeth that we needed to part ways, and she told me she would continue to run Blue Ribbon. I watched—through Instagram posts and texts with friends—as the program fell apart in a matter of weeks. It broke my heart, but I am less upset with Elizabeth than I am at myself. I hadn't known how to stand up for myself. After that experience, I became much more cautious when collaborating with others. We need to be on the same page not only about our vision, but our values, our hearts.

Blue Ribbon was a reminder that even so-called Christians do not always love their neighbors—especially neighbors who speak English with an accent. I have seen many of my fellow Christians for what they are. I have seen young women, claiming to be committed to modesty and purity culture, judge other women for their clothing choices, and I've seen more "provocatively" dressed friends exhibit authentic Christian values. I have heard Christians mock followers of other faiths. I've seen people with graduate degrees and intergenerational wealth and white privilege stall out in life, and I've seen friends who came to this country with nothing but the abundance of God's love absolutely flourish.

Coming out of the height of the pandemic, my faith was tested time and time again. When I moved to Los Angeles, I needed to find a new family to work with. Ongoing health challenges weighed on me constantly. As so much debt—from white evangelical values and from the trust I'd put in churches—continued to take its toll, I needed to be reminded of the goodness around me. I created a miracle jar. Anytime I saw God's work, I'd write it on a strip of paper and put it in the jar, a collection of reminders for the moments I needed them.

Recently, I was overcome by yet another medical bill related to health challenges I'll share in chapter 9. I was crying on the phone with my mom when she said, "Can I remind you of something?" I rolled my eyes. *She's going to give me some Bible verse or recite some uplifting meme.* Nope. Instead, she started recounting my hospital stays as a child. "Do you remember when they finally let you go from the hospital when you were a kid? Do you know what Dr. Flores told me? I want you to keep it in your head."

I was equal parts annoyed and crying as I tried to remember this story. "What did Dr. Flores say?"

"Dr. Flores said, 'The fact that this girl is alive at seven years old. . . . Wow. I want you to know that this girl is special. Your daughter's been breathing and feeling like hell for years and somehow, she is here with us right now.'" My mom reminded me that little me had been a warrior, and I can be one as an adult too. Many of the kids that I saw growing up at the hospital died. I don't take the gift of life lightly. It's why I fight for justice today.

For the miracle jar, I wrote down the fact that I was breathing well, even given all of the physical pain I'd been experiencing.

A beautiful conversation with my mom and my improved breathing: I opened the jar to add my two new miracles and found it already full.

There is an abundance of goodness and miracles around us. We have to work to see them, and we have to work to create them. Miracles and change come from the time and energy that we invest. These are the miracles I keep for myself when no one is watching. I share them with God, and now I share them with you.

CHAPTER 8

THE COST OF
MENTAL HEALTH

I've always felt at peace in the ocean. Even as her waters roil and her waves slap the earth, her consistency and strength are a calming force in my life. From the Sinaloan shores of my childhood to the crowded beaches in Los Angeles, I find my heart and body being pulled toward the water.

My asthma has often prevented me from paddling out as a surfer. So instead I've spent countless hours riding boogie boards, weightless and flying, one cresting wave after another. A day at the beach—wave riding, paddling, floating—leaves my body sated. With my energy joyfully drained into the dimpled mirror of the ocean, I am renewed for days and weeks.

The seasons of depression that I've gone through are irregular. I never know when they will storm into my life or for how long.[1] They didn't start with my arrival in the US or grief I experienced or violence I witnessed in Sinaloa. Instead, they go back to my childhood. As a child, I suffered from a heavy feeling that the word "sad" doesn't even begin to represent. My depression has its own wave that I've had to learn to float upon. I sometimes lacked the strength to do things that others could do normally. I went for days avoiding my closest friends, not eating, not getting out of bed. By the time I arrived in Georgia, I was already familiar with some of the layers of my depression—the foamy slosh I was born with, and the murky depths of violence and threat that the tides of life had pulled in. I already knew that I was sometimes suicidal. I knew I needed support and I looked for clinics and therapy and whatever resources might be available. I never found anything that I could afford.

Sometimes I think of my life as acts of a film. A movie, at different points in its arc, may contain both a happy ending and a tragic one. A director will choose which moment to end on.[2] If I end my story now, I won't hurt anymore. But also, if I end my story now, I won't see the joy awaiting me on the other side of this cresting wave.

The difference between swimming and drowning is also time. Every leap into the ocean is a momentary lapse into drowning until your senses awaken and you take control.

The extreme costs of my mental health have been a constant presence in every chapter of this book. Every moment of shame or abuse or exploitation weaves a new layer of trauma. I believe that anything is possible when you swim through life. Radical imagination and possibility are always right next to the floating debris of the modern atrocities thrown upon the undocumented community. However, treading water is not something we are built to do for long periods of time. Depression hits differently when you're already exhausted by the waves of a cruel society.

THE COBRA

Sometimes there are snakes in the water.

My relationship with Darren broke my heart for many reasons, but mostly because I never defended myself. I blamed myself for the spirals of violence and fear that I'd gone through. Then my anger turned deeper. And with it came deep shame. I sensed Darren's predatory spirit in the men I occasionally chanced to date. No one felt different until I met Tariq.

My friend Adrian, a producer and musician, was throwing a release party for his new record at his Los Angeles studio, and I agreed to help set up. I helped put out snacks, grabbed decorating supplies, and made that studio beautiful.

Later, when the party was in full swing, I was exhausted and ready to leave. As I was getting my stuff and saying my goodbyes, Adrian asked me to do one more favor on my way out, show his friend Tariq where to park nearby. As I walked out looking for a car, I saw a bearded man in a red jacket, wearing black shades in the early evening.

"Are you Tariq?" I asked.

"Sorry, no. My name is Elliot," he said as he waved and walked inside.

I waited for Tariq to arrive. And waited. After ten minutes, I texted Adrian: *Sorry, Tariq never came, I'm out.*

Adrian wrote back immediately. *What are you talking about? He's inside.*

I realized Tariq had played a joke on me. Even though I was about to go, there was no way I was leaving without saying anything to this man. I went back inside, saw the red jacket, and tapped its wearer on the shoulder. "You think you are funny, don't you?"

He smiled and extended his hand. "I'm Tariq, the guy you are looking for."

I couldn't help but laugh. This dude was definitely a jerk and a little full of himself. I didn't think I was impressed, but he stayed on my mind long after I left the party.

Days later, I got a random DM from Tariq. He apologized for making me wait and kicked off a series of messages that went back and forth for weeks. Considering how Darren had swept me away on the phone, I didn't want to give Tariq my phone number just yet.

The first time we finally talked on the phone, Tariq opened up to me about his own insecurities and his own tricks for hiding them. His playful deceptiveness and dark glasses were the costume that helped him live in the world. We talked about God, trauma, music, and the seemingly million things we had in common. He said that Adrian talked about me so much that he felt like he already knew me. He later said he'd fallen in love with the idea of me before we'd even talked.

It was after one of these soul-opening conversations that Tariq asked me on a date. Five dates, actually.

I had told him I was still recovering from the psychological harm I'd endured with Darren. I didn't feel like I could speak about the physical abuse I experienced, but he knew how painful and traumatizing that relationship had been. So, Tariq offered to let me get to know him in person through five mini-dates. If I wasn't interested in continuing to see him after that, he would feel like I at least had given him a chance. For each date, he would drive up to the bay from Los Angeles, and then I could decide if he deserved a chance to get to know me on a deeper level.

I was smitten.

What better place than Sausalito for a first date? He picked an elegant restaurant near the ocean. We sat next to the water. I shared her calming presence, and Tariq and I enjoyed eggs Benedict.

Tariq had been, on the phone, funny and charming, qualities that were amplified ten times in person. He was still corny, but now we had inside jokes to share, and the kind of anticipatory spark that felt like a flame was igniting in slow motion. We spent the whole day zipping across the bay. At each stop, a morsel or a joke. In his car, we listened to a playlist of songs that we'd shared with each other.

On the weekends that followed, he would drive up to the bay after work on Friday and plan an outing for us. He showed up with flowers and, generally, did the most to win my heart. At first, it didn't feel safe for him to know how much I liked him, but he was patient.

One Sunday, after weeks of dates, I planned a picnic spread for us. We went to Dolores Park. I laid out flowers alongside the fruit and sandwiches. The mood was laid back and charming. Most of our conversations ended with playful roasting. He was hilarious, and we found ways to clown on the differences in our taste, leaving us giggling like little kids. As I was jokingly talking trash about a musician he liked, he lifted his hand in mock protest, saying, "Don't say that or I'll slap you!"

He was trying to be funny, but I flinched violently at the sight of his hand. I was flooded with past memories. Our playful moment ended.

We were quiet, and I did the brave thing. I told him more about my past trauma. I went deep, and he followed me. He seemed to understand. After two hours of unpacking the threat that might have pulled us under, I felt seen and understood. We kissed for the first time. I finally felt safe in the arms of a man. Until I wasn't.

The first six months of dating Tariq were sweet as honey. He continued to drive up from Los Angeles to see me every weekend. Our relationship felt magical. He planned dates, brought me flowers, sang me songs, made me the coolest playlists. He wrote a song for me—"The Girl with the Red Lipstick"—and played it on his piano. He was sweet and flirtatious.

As our relationship started to feel more serious, Tariq regularly talked about marriage. Christians, especially those who are waiting to have sex until after getting married, often feel a cultural pressure to settle and marry quickly. I wasn't fully emotionally available. But Tariq seemed like the right person to think about the future with. He was hardworking, generous, funny, loved God, and shared so many of my interests.

Tariq was incredibly close with his mom. He'd never known his father, and she was the most important person in his life. So, when his mom was diagnosed with a severe illness, he rearranged his entire life to take care of her. He began to spend much of his money flying back and forth to visit her in Washington State. He missed work and lost wages. Her medical treatments frightened her, and she was lonely.

Tariq started to treat me poorly during this period. Everything made him upset. He was bitter, sad, and irritated with me. He berated me for the smallest thing. I know firsthand what family turmoil can do to a person, but I assumed that he, like my family members and me, would emerge on the other side with his sense of self still intact.

I tried to be everything to him, but it was never enough. At one point, he threw in my face the fact that I didn't feel safe flying to LA because of my immigration status and so he was doing most of the traveling in our long-distance relationship. I blamed myself for the pain I was caus- ing him. We danced an on-again-off-again tango for months. We came together when he beckoned and broke up when he was hurt. Back then, I didn't understand that Tariq and I were in a codependent relationship. I didn't even know what codependency was.

For a little while during this period, I considered marrying Tariq. Even when I was his verbal punching bag, cussing me out every time he was stressed, I still felt that he loved me. But I was yearning for the Tariq I'd known before his own unworked trauma took its turn on me. I wanted a Tariq that didn't exist. This period made me realize, with even more clarity, the mental hardship of undocumented dating. The men I dated used my status to try to pressure me into marriage. Tariq made it clear that, in his mind, we would be happily married and living together in Washington, near his mom, if I just came to my senses. Every time he brought this up, I would tell him that I needed more time. Tariq, and other men over the years, have implied that I should "put up" with their careless behavior because they were offering me a solution to my undocumented status. If I wanted to, I could be married already. But I'd rather suffer as an undocumented person than be in a bad marriage.

Tariq's mom eventually recovered, and he was back in LA more regularly. I thought the sweet and playful Tariq would return—the one who'd serenaded me and made me laugh with his corny jokes. But Tariq continued to verbally abuse me, and now he was nearby more often to do so. I'd thought that the stress of his mother's illness had been why he'd become a monster, now it became clear that a monster is just what Tariq was.

During one of his visits with me in San Francisco, as we were walking through Chinatown, we ran into my friend, Todd. I hadn't seen him in years and greeted him with a kiss on the cheek. Tariq wasn't pleased. On our way back home, he started screaming at me for it. I never talked back. His words would send me into a tailspin for days.

Once, I spilled a few drops off coffee on his leather car seat and he exploded in rage. His words cycled around me constantly. *Wow, Alix, you sure are friendly with your guy friends. Wow, Alix, how are you so clumsy? Wow, Alix, how can you be so stupid?*

Eventually, I fought back. I changed into someone who mirrored his behavior. This is when I started referring to him with my friends as the Cobra. Everything he struck out at became poisoned. Including me.

Whenever he yelled at me, I yelled louder. Still healing from my time with Darren, I was genuinely afraid Tariq would one day hit me. I thought that if I could be as verbally violent as he was, I would be physically safe. We had explosive knockout verbal wars every time we saw each other. Violence has never been in my nature, but finding the fight inside me was the only thing that made me feel safe. I'd spent too long recoiling from the tongues and fists of men, and so now I stood up to Tariq.

I thought this aggressive version of myself would cause him to miss the old me—just like I missed the old him. Instead, the relationship became even more obsessive and codependent. I was locked in a living hell with Tariq, trying to make things so nasty that we'd be forced to hit the "reset" button and go back to the start. Meanwhile, Tariq was exorcising his own depression, taking out his pain on me. We were using each other for opposite purposes, and I didn't know how to stop it.

Our relationship finally sputtered out over plates of seafood in San Francisco one afternoon. Although he had promised, earlier, to never yell or lose his temper in front of me again, he began going down that same path. Our waiter remembered me from when I had dined at the restaurant with friends weeks earlier. He even remembered my name: "Hey, Alix-with-an-i!" That small exchange set Tariq on fire. He wanted to know why other men knew my name, why I was so friendly with other men, why I had to talk to any man who wasn't him. He could not see that I simply wanted to be kind and polite to the people around me. It is in my nature. His jealousy ruined my appetite once again. He wanted me to be the illusion of who Tariq thought I was, a timid and submissive receptacle for his pain, and that did not match the reality of who this country had made me. We spat bitterness back and forth over our rapidly cooling dishes. Tears flowed from my eyes and Tariq stood up and said: "You know what, I can't do this. I need to get some air." He used his promise to keep his temper in check as an excuse to walk out of the restaurant. I didn't know then that it was the last time I would see him in person. I waited for nearly an hour, but he never returned and didn't reply to my increasingly worried calls and texts. I ended up having to take an Uber back to my house. I didn't hear from him until later that night, when he texted me that he was driving back home to Los Angeles. Knowing he had given up on us that day, I didn't feel like our relationship could go on any longer, and so I broke up with him that night over the phone. I'd had abandonment issues already, but Tariq instilled a deeper fear in me that I could lose the people around me at any moment.

Just a few weeks later, Tariq posted a picture of himself with a beautiful woman I had never seen before. He was smiling—the old Tariq glistened in that picture. A few more clicks and it became obvious this girl wasn't new in his life. He'd been seeing both of us at the same time. When I confronted him about her over the phone, he said he had fallen in love with me for who I was at the beginning of our relationship but hated the new version of me—that is, the version of me that he had made me into. Tariq and this other woman married not long after. I was brokenhearted but felt like I'd been thrown a life preserver at the same time. For days, I wondered if I should talk to Tariq's wife to warn her, but I never felt brave enough. I only wish her well and pray that she never experiences the abuse that I did.

DROWNING

It should be no surprise that the limited research on immigrant mental health consistently shows lasting effects of fear, precarity, and toxic stress.[3] Uncertainty, unemployment, the constant messaging that society doesn't want you—all of these churn hostile waters. This stress is compounded by the personal traumas that have brought us to the US. With few resources, fewer people to trust when it comes to seeking help, and a support network often cut off by borders, the mental health challenges of the undocumented community are as overlooked as they are substantial. Although undocumented youth may be able to access mental health services in K–12 and college settings, the adults among us carry unwieldy burdens of layered distress with no way to unload it.

My own nest of depression, unresolved grief, and abuse at the hands of far too many men in the US threatened to overwhelm me. I'm not proud of it, but I need you to know I almost drowned. I tried.

SECOND CHANCE

After Tariq and I broke up, it felt more difficult to stay afloat with each passing day. AC was sixteen, and he went from seeing me as a best friend to someone he resented and hid things from. He needed his mom, a role Cindy and I could never fill for him.

AC coped with his anger by smoking weed, doing other drugs, and sometimes not coming home until the early hours of the morning. Seeing my sweet brother transform into a ball of anger nearly consumed me. We fought often, and afterward, I would sit there feeling like there was nothing left for me to lose. This country had taken everything. I had lost my dad and my friends in Sinaloa. I had lost my hopes of becoming a lawyer anytime soon. I had lost Darren. I had lost Tariq, and I spent far too much time looking at his wife's social media posts and thinking that this beautiful woman was everything that I was not. I was nearly $35,000 in debt from trying to go to college in between my jobs. And now I was losing AC. It felt like the harder I tried to progress personally and professionally in this country, the more I felt like I was drowning.

One night, I was up waiting for AC to come home. I was so angry with my life, and I was starting to hate the new version of my brother. Around 3 a.m., AC shuffled in, reeking of weed. He looked surprised to see me, asking why I was still up.

"Do you think that it's okay for you to come home at this time? You're sixteen, and I've been crying and praying to God that nothing happened to you."

We started fighting. I unloaded all of my anguish on my stoned brother, as if that would make my situation better. *You are so messy. You don't care about what Cindy and I have sacrificed for you.* I started saying things I didn't really mean. I told him that he was the reason my life was ruined; he was the reason that I couldn't live a normal life, that I regretted having brought him to the United States.

He shot back that he'd never asked me to bring him here, never asked me to be his mom, that—you know what—I was just a sister trying to be something she's not. We yelled at each other. I started tossing all of the dishes that AC had left around the house into the sink, trying to prove my point. Finally, AC just shrugged. "You know what? I don't give a shit."

He headed toward the front door. I moved to intercept him. And that's when he jumped off of our second-floor balcony. I saw him fall and I heard the thud of his feet on the ground. I was in shock. Even as I called for him, he took off running.

I was up all night, calling AC's phone and waiting for him to return. The next morning, in one of the few times in my nannying career, I called in sick. I blamed myself for everything that had happened. I was unable to conjure hope. I could not see a future for myself.

A few weeks earlier, a friend of mine who knew I was struggling had offered me a bottle of her antidepressants to see if they might help. I'd given them a go for a couple of weeks but then got worried about becoming dependent on them when I had no way to get more. That morning, I did something that I'd never planned on doing. Cindy had gone to work, and I was alone at the house. Breathing hurt, being alive hurt. I couldn't imagine that anything could make being alive okay. In that instant, my depression and suicidal thoughts took over. I took the pills—maybe the whole bottle?—because I was looking for a way to stop feeling a pain that seemed unbearable.

As it happens, Cindy came home early that day, and that was what saved my life. I remember only flashes of the next twenty-four hours. Cindy screaming. Carrying me to a car with a neighbor. The sounds of ambulances and medical equipment.

I remember the rough grasp of two nurses as they threw my body into a bed that felt like a rickety metal cage. A doctor saying they needed to pump my stomach quickly, that my sister didn't know how long ago I'd taken the pills. Being fully conscious of what they were saying, trying to answer their questions but my body not responding. As they wondered aloud if they'd gotten to me in time, a wave of understanding hit me. It doesn't matter how strong we think we are, we are not the owners of our lives. I felt so ashamed for trying to make a decision that belongs to God.

As a tube was inched down my esophagus, the sounds around me blurred into my memories of the hospital I slept in as a child, fighting my asthma. How the doctors back then came up to my family when I was on the mend, telling them that there was something special about seven-year-old me. "One day Alix is going to speak about the miracle that is her life." Twenty years ago, God had given me a second chance and here I was, wanting to die. I started praying. *God, take all the things that you don't like about me. Take them away. I just need a second chance to show AC that I can be a good sister. That it doesn't matter what life throws at me, I'm going to trust you and I am not going to forget the things that you have done for me.*

When I opened my eyes, hours later, Cindy was sitting in a chair. My pastor was next to her. "Oh, hello there," he said kindly, as if nothing happened. Cindy gave my hand a squeeze, and it was as if the past night's terrors were washed away. I was drowsy and nauseous, the smell of the hospital reminded me that, even as a child, I'd never liked spending time in places like these. I'd been cleared to go home, and Cindy and the pastor ushered me out, walking and talking normally, as if this was just your typical stroll through the lobby of a hospital. I was embarrassed, confused, wondering if AC knew what happened and if he might ball up even more resentment toward me.

When we got home, my hunger awoke within me. We walked in unsteadily together, my appetite and me. AC was in the kitchen, the energetic and clear-eyed version of himself that I didn't see as often. "Hey," he said lightly. "I'm making some food, if you're hungry." My brother cooked with the same kind of tenderness as when I used to cook for my dad. He was making *pollo con crema* and some rice. We never apologized and never told each other how scared we'd each been that the other would drown. We didn't have the words to express how this country and our lives in it had turned us into monstrous versions of ourselves. That meal was like a prayer, though. From them on, we started trying to fight for each other instead of with each other. I started actively seeking support to navigate the challenges of my life.

A year later, we were figuring out a more harmonious way for us to live and support one another. However, around the same time, due to an event that AC may share the details about someday, he was left with no choice but to leave the United States immediately. At only seventeen, he moved to Spain by himself. It destroyed our family all over again. His expired US visa meant he would not be able to reenter this country anytime soon. I dropped him off at the airport, not knowing the next time we would see each other again. I tried to avoid saying goodbye, just like I had with Lia, all those years ago. But AC did not let that happen: "I don't know when I'll get to hug you again. Please don't let me leave without it."

I remember I was struggling to breathe as his arms wrapped around me. While our relationship is stronger and more beautiful than ever, I am still learning how to live without him.

FLOATING

Do you remember opening your eyes underwater for the first time? Submersed, you inhabited a quieter, deeper world, and the weight of the water pressed coolly on your pupils. Limbs and sunlight pulled into a new focus, just for a moment before you bobbed up for breath. But this kind of seeing, this unlocking another world, is always temporary.

I'd known I needed help long before my body tried to drown. It took too long for me to find a therapist. I'd asked at clinics to no avail. I'd attended counseling sessions at my church that never seemed to help. Those sessions might have been a good fit for individuals who were having occasional relationship difficulties or momentary anxiety, but they were not the kind of full-fledged counseling that someone with depression needed.

I'd downloaded apps like BetterHelp, but they require a Social Security number to even create an account.[4] During my Blue Ribbon years, I'd talked with social workers who would promise to connect me with friends or services. I waited for months, and nothing ever happened.

One day, I broke down when I was talking with a pastor friend on the phone, after he'd asked me about the Cobra. "I don't think you realized that perhaps you were in a codependent relationship," he said. I told him I'd been looking for help for too long and I no longer knew where to turn. That evening, he called me back and put me in contact with a psychologist he knew: "He's a good friend of mine and I told him about you. He is very expensive, but maybe we can work something out."

A week later, I had my first appointment with my therapist, Martin. He cut his rates for me, and I've paid $150 for each of our weekly sessions, far below his actual rate. In particularly dire financial periods, he has cut his rates to $50. Each week, we talk virtually, and he's slowly helped me see the world of trauma I was swimming in. He helped define the effects of my traumas as what has only recently been understood as complex-PTSD (C-PTSD).[5] He helped me name my depression and identify the signs of what can trigger and flood me in my daily life.

At first, though, I didn't like therapy. Martin's job is naturally invasive, and opening up has never been easy or relaxing for me. It's often the hardest part of my day. These sessions are like those moments of seeing the world underwater. I have to come up for air at the end of our sessions, but I am often left with the reminder that things can look different from below, from within. For the first time, therapy let me see how I needed to take care of myself. I took a break from prioritizing anyone else's needs over my own. As I made a financial investment in my mental well-being, nothing mattered more than putting the pieces of my heart back together. It took me three years before I was ready to start dating again.

As I learned more about C-PTSD, I learned that my memory loss is likely a result of my trauma. That goes for my working memory—constantly losing my keys or missing day-to-day obligations—as well as the long-term recollections locked away in my brain. My brain has blocked a lot of memories. I almost feel like it's just trying to protect me from the past. But it doesn't block just bad memories; it also blocks the good ones. Entire seasons of my life, like the period where we lived at Sergio's house, were locked away until I started working on this book. My mental health has cost me remembering key moments of happiness.

BALANCE

A few years into therapy, I could feel the muscles of my mind strengthening. With my therapist's help and a lot of hard work, I was fully over my relationship with the Cobra. I had never felt more relieved. It was 2019 and everything seemed bright. I was *doing* this. I was healing the bruises of so much internal pain. I was seeing a future unfold before me. I was surviving when that simple fact had never felt like a certainty. I was proud of myself.

And then the pandemic swallowed us whole and brought a new set of fears. I had no medical safety net, and my asthma made me particularly vulnerable to the effects of COVID-19. The people with whom I was in physical proximity shrank to the family I nannied for, my sister, and her husband. Everyone else became a box on Zoom or FaceTime.

How loud is the ocean? You have to not-so-slightly raise your voice when you're in the ocean if you want to be heard by other people. This is why the beach privileges solitude. I learned during the pandemic to appreciate the dialogue between my own thoughts and the ebbing tide.

One day, during the worst of those opening months of the pandemic, I drove the two and a half hours to Big Sur by myself. It was a huge accomplishment for me. Long-distance drives have always terrified me because of the idea of being pulled over or followed. Couple that fear with the new threat of COVID-19, and it was a journey that felt cathartic. I was proud of myself for completing and even enjoying a simple drive to the ocean. When I arrived, I didn't get out of the car. I was afraid to walk alone, afraid to encounter someone who might be sick. The view of the ocean was amazing. Sitting in the car, hearing her waves crash, oblivious to the rest of the world, felt reassuring. It felt like I was my only friend in that moment. I was enough.

SWIMMING

Sometimes, when I visit the ocean on one of her quieter days, I see my image reflected back at me on the rippling waves. A me and not-me out in the sea. I float on my back, gaze into the sky, and think about what I might have in common with the Alix peering back at me from the water. I reflect on the words of the late rapper Mac Miller: *I was drowning, but now I'm swimming.* I fear so many of the people around me, but I have so much in common with them too. We are all glimmered fictions waiting to be understood.[6] And so, one day, I held still in the water and simply felt. I felt the trauma of unresolved pain I have never, even in therapy, allowed myself to process. I slowed down enough that, when I sat down to write this chapter, some of my long-buried emotions finally caught up with me.

Recently, I left work early one day, something I rarely do, knowing it will inconvenience the family I work with. But I was too fatigued to persist. I parked outside of a café. I didn't even have the energy to go inside to get anything. I just needed to pause. I was confronting my history and I wept. I may have escaped a codependent relationship with the Cobra, but I am also exhausted from loving a country that will never love me back. I am missing AC so much my stomach aches.

Up until recently, my coping mechanism for mental pain was to just carry on. To numb myself through constant movement and exhaustion. Today, I get by knowing how life has shown me things can always get worse. I remember the many moments in my past when I didn't think I was going to make it through. Knowing I am here now is a form of coping. This moment, too, is one I'll overcome. I don't understand this life and its aggressiveness. It is "the foam of an imperfect dream" and I want to be back in a place that doesn't exist.[7] Even in this painful moment, I know the tide will turn, that there are better moments waiting for me on the waters.

When I went into the hospital with a belly full of someone else's pills after fighting with AC, it felt like two things were happening at once: what the world saw as the attending physicians saving me and what I saw—the conversation I had, underwater, with God. When my sister and pastor took me home, they knew about the pills and that my stomach had been pumped, but they didn't know that when I was unconscious I was making a deal with God. And that deal is what I'm holding up now. It doesn't matter how turbulent the seas get, I'm going to show people that there is always something waiting for us on the other side and that it is worth fighting for.

It wasn't so much that God gave me another chance that day. It was that I reinterpreted the hardships of this country and my life. All the things I hated—my lack of English, my lack of resources, my lack of excuses, my lack of "intelligence"—became the reason I need to share my story. Speaking to and learning for and with *everybody else* has kept me alive. When you're out in the ocean, you are a part of her. There are a countless number of us that will face the currents and storms I have weathered. I write this chapter so that they might find energy coasting in my wake.

I don't get to the beach as often as I'd like these days. Life is like that. But I know she's there, waiting for me, ready to cradle me, and hold me up. We've had our strife in the past, but the ocean forgives.

CHAPTER 9

THE COST OF HEALTHCARE

Early one Friday morning in the spring of 2022, I get in my car while the sky is still gray. The directions I received the night before take me forty minutes south as I follow the turn-by-turn steps on my phone. I take an exit somewhere in the middle of Orange County, then park in front of a nondescript strip mall and walk through the doors of a hair salon.

My instructions tell me to say a password to the receptionist. Then I am guided to a door that looks like a storage closet. I open it, and like in a children's story, I walk *through* the closet and into a larger room on the other side. Then I find myself facing the impossible: in this utility closet that's not a utility closet is a standard dental chair.

For the next three hours, I sit in this chair while a stranger—who may or may not have formal dental training—examines my mouth. He administers anesthesia, extracts a tooth, and performs several root canals. Through it all, a television plays telenovela reruns to distract me from the pain and to drown out the sound of the dental work for the unsuspecting salon patrons on the other side of the wall. I pay nearly $2,000 in cash for the services I've received.

By the end of the procedure, I have missed a day of work, endured far more pain than this maybe dentist had told me to expect, and nearly drained my savings. As my swollen mouth and I make our way back home, I think about the absurdity of my situation. In an era where the world's accumulation of knowledge is instantly accessible on a device that fits in your pocket, I am forced to seek illicit medical triage in the back of a beauty salon. This isn't the first time the US healthcare system has tried to kill me. Today was but an additional line item in my debts of survival.

AMERICAN HEARING LOSS

When you are undocumented, you learn that even your own body cannot be trusted. Internal signals of illness may leave you waylaid and bedridden. Your body takes you out of your regular work and social responsibilities, and now you are hurting doubly or triply. (Over time, you will lose count of all the ways you've been sabotaged by yourself.) Your finances, mental stability, personal relationships: everything falters when your body lets you down.

My hearing was one of the first things this country took from me. My left ear no longer works. Back in my early months of living in America—while I was working at the hellish Mexican restaurant, raising AC, and learning English—I got sick.

At the time, we were usually able to address our dentistry needs during our visa runs to Mexico. However, because I wasn't able to see a dentist regularly in the US, I ignored my teeth until they started to hurt. One of my molars became infected. The infection took over my mouth and swelled in my cheek. I would sometimes have fevers, and blisters would pock my mouth for weeks. The cheapest dentist I could find in our area needed $1,500 to fix one of my molars. I did not have that kind of money, nor the support system you might normally rely on in these kinds of situations: family who could help financially, dental insurance, the ability to take out a loan or run up a credit card. Without a Social Security number, you can't even get a credit score.

The dentist warned me that without care, I would likely lose several of my teeth and the infection could move to other parts of my body, including my brain. With no other options, I started taking homemade remedies, like garlic, tinctures, and rubs. But nothing worked. And then it got really bad. For eight months, my mouth alternated between states of numbness and throbbing agony. Sometimes I couldn't sleep because of the pain.

My entire face swelled up. It became a bloated badge of my inability to get the medical care my body demanded. One night, I woke up to blood pooling down my neck. My ear was bleeding—the infection in my mouth had spread to my ear. I perceived sounds in distorted echoes, as if I was underwater. To this day, my hearing has not recovered. I often find myself apologizing at work and in semi-crowded restaurants with friends: "I'm sorry, what did you say?" It is an apology for having tried to survive in America.

The people who imagine that undocumented immigrants come here to leech off American resources do not realize the compounded costs of living that we endure. Bipartisan legislation has been enacted based on the false premise that immigrants want illicit access to luxurious medical treatment. About thirty years ago, California's Proposition 187 denied undocumented individuals in the state the right to access public benefits, though it was later overturned by the courts. In 2019, President Trump issued an executive order to suspend US entry of immigrants who cannot demonstrate proof of healthcare coverage. He railed: "Immigrants who enter this country should not further saddle our healthcare system, and subsequently American taxpayers, with higher costs."[1]

Despite all this, I've tried my best to maintain my health. I've found local programs that offset the costs of routine checkups, physicals, and dental cleanings, and I've saved up for minor surgeries. Recent California legislation provides health insurance for all undocumented individuals to receive primary care, though in my experience follow-up for special-ized care has been lacking. One of the steps in my application process included showing proof of income and sharing my US tax records. Like with many immigration policies, the contexts of healthcare access are constantly changing. In the times when I've been in most dire need of medical support, however, the available resources have been insufficient. And each time I've moved, I've had to search for local resources, clinics, and health advocates all over again. In my first year in Los Angeles, I found nothing.

The Kaiser Family Foundation has reported on how undocumented immigrants are more likely to confront barriers to healthcare than citi-zens or legal residents.[2] Legal and financial barriers delay needed care, leading to substantially worse health outcomes for our community. It's funny how quickly healthcare options vanish when you are asked to provide a Social Security number. Establishing resources through the Affordable Care Act, for instance, requires tracking people via Social Security numbers. And with constant changes to statewide policies, it often feels nearly impossible to keep track of which programs and policies currently exist.

In the months leading up to that underground dentist visit, I refused to listen to my body's warning signs—the feeling that something was off in my mouth, stomach, and lungs. I wasn't oblivious; I was responding to how I'd seen my labor and my body interpreted as dehumanized labor in this country.

"COMPASSIONATE" CARE

The knowledge that my life only matters as a body for labor feeds on my heart like a parasite. It chews at my feelings of self-worth, self-esteem, and hope. It feasts on my financial insecurity. It whispers that it's not okay to miss work. It reminds me that I can't afford the healthcare I need. Instead, I carefully watch my diet and brush my teeth after every meal. I do regular maintenance in hopes of forestalling a major tune-up.

The domestic, agricultural, and industrial labor that my undocumented community provides comes at the cost of our wellness. We are on the front lines of the US's most dangerous and unhealthy workplaces. After 9/11, undocumented immigrants were tasked with cleaning up the debris of the World Trade Center, as Karla Cornejo Villavicencio showed in her book *The Undocumented Americans*. Undocumented labor has also been used to restore cities in the wake of climate disasters, as reported by Sarah Stillman.[3] And every year, pesticide poisoning and excessive heat afflict the agricultural workers in this country.

The COVID-19 pandemic pulled this reality into sharp relief. Undocumented individuals were among some of the first casualties of the pandemic back in 2020, and we continue to experience some of the highest rates of COVID infection and death.[4] If we are also members of other vulnerable groups, such as individuals experiencing homelessness or chronic health conditions, our risk increases. For me, an undocumented individual with chronic breathing issues, the pandemic was particularly terrifying. Not knowing when I would be able to get my inhaler refilled (I could not afford the out-of-pocket expenses to see a doctor who could write the prescription) only added to my unease. I needed to constantly monitor the health risks around me while also continuing to assess my environment for deportation risks. The double bind of healthcare and legal danger made my life in this country suffocating.

Even before the pandemic, undocumented immigrants faced unhealthy living conditions in this country. We avoid hospitals as sites of state surveillance, and we can't access most forms of subsidized healthcare offered through legislation like the Affordable Care Act. Even in sanctuary cities, where we may be legally able to get medical treatment, we often cannot afford the medical bills or the time away from contingent work.

Christopher Moriates, chief of hospital medicine for the VA Greater Los Angeles Healthcare System and a professor of clinical medicine at UCLA, describes how, in states like Texas, uninsured and undocumented individuals may only be granted care when their condition has become critical. Emergency dialysis is one such example. "It's called *compassionate dialysis*, but there is nothing compassionate about it," Moriates explains. When individuals get critically sick, hospitals will provide them with emergency dialysis and then send them home with instructions to only return when their condition is once again critical. At that point, treatment is "more costly and . . . way more dangerous."[5] Infuriatingly, these barriers to healthcare do not even cut costs for hospitals or the healthcare system. Patients are not charged for this limited care, so the costs are footed by the hospital and by the broader national healthcare system. Continually placing financial stress on our hospitals and denying consistent, desperately needed care to undocumented individuals is financially imprudent—and morally bankrupt.

This model is all too prevalent in undocumented medical care. After learning about the hearing damage I'd suffered due to my tooth infection, Moriates said my experience was common: "We admit people to the hospital with serious tooth infections who did not have dental care. These patients now require serious treatment—IVs and antibiotics—because they couldn't see a dentist to begin with."

Moriates is also the executive director of Costs of Care, a nonprofit organization focused on creating pathways for more affordable and equitable access to healthcare in the US. Moriates points to ways doctors can support our physical needs, despite a political system of willful bureaucracy. Moriates helps demonstrate a value-based approach to healthcare that guides individuals "who care for patients [to] optimize healthcare outcomes while also taking direct and specific responsibility for costs and patient experiences."[6]

TOUGH COOKIE

In the weeks before I ended up in the back of the salon, I felt a familiar pain and ignored it. It was a dull ache underneath my tooth, accompanied by my numbing denial that it would get worse. I couldn't afford for it to get worse, and so I ignored it.

On Monday, I took some Tylenol and hoped the pain would stop. On Tuesday, I popped a few more Tylenol and powered through. On Wednesday the pain got worse, but I took some more Tylenol and told myself: "Maybe it will just go away." On Thursday, I was eating lunch with the twins I was nannying when I bit into my sandwich and pain seared across my nerves. It bloomed into life, rooted deep into my gums, petaling across my mouth.

I found a dentist that was only a few blocks from where I was working. Somehow, I got an appointment within an hour. I took this as a hopeful sign.

I left work early for the first time in months and happily filled out a new patient form. The bright pain in my mouth blinded me to the questions I was filling out; I ignored the spaces where I was asked to provide a Social Security number. I knew I didn't have dental insurance, and I definitely knew I didn't have $5,000 or $6,000 to pay in cash. But I kept telling myself that I was a human being and they'd give me the care I needed.

They took X-rays, and the dentist pulled them up on a computer screen. He said, "I'm pretty sure that you're in a lot of pain right now."

That was for sure—I was dizzy and seeing stars. He continued, "Right now, you need to get an extraction. And then, you need two root canals, and crowns." He paused, then said, "I usually don't do two root canals at the same time, because it's a lot, and that's on top of the extraction."

What he didn't know is that I'm a tough cookie. I wanted to get this operation over with and I knew my opportunities to do it—given the cost, the time off from work, and finding a dentist who would see me—were limited. I said, "You know what, let's get it all done now. I don't care."

The dentist looked at me in surprise. He said, "You're going to be in a lot of pain for the next couple of days." But I'd *been* in a lot of pain for weeks, and during the hour I'd been at this office, it had been steadily increasing.

The dentist left to create a financial estimate for the treatment. It felt like he took forever to come back. When he finally returned, he showed me an impossibly high number. It would be around $8,000 for the extraction, root canals, three crowns, anesthesia, and a list of medications and follow-ups that went on for pages. There was an option to pay the bill in monthly installments. I could see at a glance that I wouldn't be able to afford the down payment and interest rates, but all I could think was: "Let's do it. This pain is unbelievable." I was willing to take on the years of debt if it meant relief. But before I could sign off on the equivalent of a second car payment, I had to fill out one more form.

I remember exactly where it asked me for my Social Security number. I entered my tax ID number and, sure enough, the application was rejected. The receptionist couldn't tell me why, but I already knew the reason. I was a fraud in the eyes of the US healthcare system. The office gave me a second application with many of the same questions replicated and I raced through it, bouncing my knee in pain as I again entered the information that I hoped a computer would decide made me legitimate. But that application, too, was rejected.

By the time they gave me the third application—again asking the same questions about insurance and Social Security numbers in a slightly altered order—I'd texted my friend Vanessa. She'd once said that if I ever needed a cosigner for an expense, I could go to her. She has a great job and a stellar credit score. The third application didn't have a cosigner option, so the office looked for a fourth. The dentist found one with a cosigner option, but it still required that I provide my own Social Security number in order to proceed.

I started questioning why I was wasting the time of the people at this office, patiently trying to work with me. Through my blistering pain, I heard my undocumented identity asking: "Why are you doing this? You know why you are getting rejected. Vanessa's credit is obviously good. But you know that you don't have a number that proves that you are a human. You don't have a number that says you deserve treatment." I don't often cry, but in that moment I just melted down.

The dentist came back to see me bawling. I didn't even care. *Screw this shit. You want me to act like everything is fine when I am in intolerable pain and all your rules and policies and numbers are okay with that?* The dentist awkwardly told me he found a fifth application: "And this one *has* to be a good one," though I'm not sure who he was trying to reassure at that point. I filled it out and convinced myself that the fifth time would be the charm. But twenty minutes later, I was rejected again. When the dentist came back, his demeanor had changed. He told me, "I think you need to stop trying because I have another client and I'm wasting time. I wish I could help you." He gave me a prescription for antibiotics and painkillers. I went to the pharmacy and waited an additional two hours to get them filled.

By this time, it was dark out, and my mouth was starting to swell. I called every dentist in the area. Most were closed. I called clinics connected to local medical and dental schools, but they only offered routine care and had lengthy waiting lists. I asked friends if they might know anyone who might know anyone who could help me. I called friends in the medical field, friends who were migrant farmworkers, searching desperately for a lifeline.

Finally, a friend got back to me with a tentative lead. They'd heard about a place some distance away that might be willing to treat me. They said a friend of theirs had gone there, and did not actually recommend it. There would be no way for me to know if the people running this business were actually dentists. "But," my friend said, "if you think you are tough enough to go to this room and see somebody whose qualifications you don't know, then go for it."

There were no other choices. Of course I was going.

My friend gave me an address and a phone number.

I called this maybe dentist and described my situation. He spoke Spanish. He said he was too busy to see me the next day. In a shaky voice, I asked him when was the earliest I could come in. He must have heard the pain in my voice, because then he said that if I came early the next day, he could try to fit me in before his other appointments. He described his business as *very* under-the-table. I felt like I was buying drugs. But I graciously accepted the appointment. I felt oddly comforted by the fact that he spoke Spanish. If I was going to do something this shady, at least it would be with a Latino!

I remember thinking, unrhetorically, "What's the worst that could happen to me?" If this place had a dentist room in the back of a store, what else could they be selling there? I couldn't let my mind focus on anything other than a plan of action.

The maybe dentist warned me not to give out his address or phone number to anyone else. So when I walked into the hair salon, I reminded myself that the receptionist who greeted me was not really a receptionist. She was a nice lady who just happened to be sitting in the salon. She, too, reminded me to keep their secret: "Acuérdate que nada de lo que viste aquí lo puedes compartir con nadie. Al menos que sea alguien como tú que necesite ayuda." *You were not here, you didn't see anything. Remember to not share this place with anyone unless it's a person like you, who needs dental care.* Then I was ushered through the closet. When I went into the room, I giggled nervously at the sight of the huge TV blaring telenovelas.

A man came in wearing a surgical coat, face mask, hair net, and gloves. I barely could make out his dark brown eyes, and I knew that I wouldn't be able to identify him in public. He had a deep, serious voice, and as we conversed in Spanish, I noticed that his accent didn't sound Mexican.

I was terrified, shaking and giggling as I was subjected to another set of dental X-rays. He confirmed what the dentist from the previous day had said—I would need an extraction and multiple crowns and root canals. He said, "I can do the extraction today, and you can come back. I'll do a root canal tomorrow, and in two more weeks, I'll do the other one."

That wasn't going to happen. I was here now, and I didn't want to come back again. I said, "No, we need to get it all done today."

We had a "you don't understand" battle.

"You don't understand how much pain this process will take on your body."

"No, you don't understand the set of responsibilities I have ahead of me," I responded. "Let's get this over with."

He tried to tell me that "for girls, this pain is too much." I just gave him *the stare*. There have been too many times in my life when I hadn't felt brave in the moment but had been forced to move forward anyway. There was the time the man in a red truck had followed me home from school, or the time I'd landed in Georgia with AC, pretending our time in the US was temporary. There was the time I'd slept with scissors in my pocket in the house of the man who'd bullied my brother. There was the other time I'd slept with scissors in my pocket next to the man who'd attacked me. And there was the time I had said goodbye to my dad. Besides, it was a Friday, and I couldn't face a whole weekend of excruciating pain. My goal was to be back on my feet by Sunday morning.

He relented, and I was rewarded with the extractions and root canals I desired. Aside from the surreal location and *Mi amor!*'s blaring from the TV, it felt as routine as it could. It took two and a half hours.

After the surgery, the dentist apologized for being unable to prescribe any pain medication. Through my numbed mouth and thick tongue, I mumbled that the dentist I'd seen yesterday had taken pity on me and loaded me up with drug prescriptions.

I saw the kind squint of the dentist's eyes as he smiled, like this was a blessing. "I'm so glad that that happened." He talked to me for a few more minutes to make sure the anesthesia was wearing off and that I was good to drive home. I felt relieved and grateful. My body was coming down from an adrenaline high that I hadn't realized had been pumping through me.

"Hey," I said, "I really appreciate you taking me in today. I know that you had a very busy schedule and that you squeezed me in. I really appreciate that you are here for people like me."

When I said "people like me," he gave me a questioning look. Sometimes I share too much. I said, "I came here because this was an emergency, and I really appreciated finding somebody like you." In that moment, it didn't matter to me if this person was a real dentist or not. He had given me the care I had been begging for.

He said, "'People like you?' Todo lo que tenemos es a nosotros mismos." *All we have is each other.* "Sometimes we have to do these things to help our own people. At the end of the day, all we have is each other." I keep thinking about that "we." The US has certainly made it clear that I am not a part of its collective "we." I am a survivor, and we survivors find each other in the places where the world doesn't see us. This dentist was a total stranger to me, and he still spent hours pulling and digging at the horrors of my mouth. The world sees him as a criminal, as a fraud or a con man. That's how I first saw him. But we had both been making poor assumptions about each other. When I first came in, he'd thought I couldn't handle two root canals and an extraction. When I'd said "people like me," I could see that he'd assumed that I wasn't a person in need. Maybe he'd thought I'd just been hunting for a bargain when it came to dental surgery.

I paid him in cash: $700 for each root canal and $280 for the extraction. I would go on to get three crowns from him in the coming months, which would total $1,300 each.

Today, I still think about how this man had had to squeeze me in to his schedule, his time fully booked with similar appointments from people like me who have no other choice. All tough cookies. We are sick undocumented kids, undocumented people in ERs, hooked up to compassionate dialysis. We are undocumented people who have cancer.

It blows my mind how much a set of nine numbers (or lack thereof) can transform one's experience of the world. Nobody should have to go through this.

HISTORICALLY UNWELL

This country frames certain immigrants as nonhuman and "illegal." Policies and media depict immigrant communities as a threat to American health. These ideas make it acceptable to neglect our bodies. They convince people that we do not deserve human treatment. It's a tradition that goes to the core of America's settler-colonial foundation.

In *Fit to be Citizens? Public Health and Race in Los Angeles, 1879–1939*, Natalia Molina systematically breaks down how, more than a century ago, the Chinese, Japanese, and Mexican communities of Los Angeles were portrayed as health threats to the white gentry. Health officials created designated regions for the city's Mexican neighborhoods, Chinatown, and Little Tokyo. Racist assumptions of immigrants as "dirty" and "disheveled" meant they endured "inadequate medical care, exposure to raw sewage, and malnutrition." In other words, they faced pollutants, food deserts, and barricaded healthcare—all of which continue to threaten undocumented communities today.

Health perspectives of the nineteenth and twentieth centuries regularly portrayed Mexican women, in particular, as fertile beings who relied "on free birthing and medical services" and were "reliant on charity to support their newly expanded families."[7] As goes the nineteenth century, so goes the current day, when arguments against immigration are driven by fears of their growing families.

In 2020, the world was horrified by images of refugee children separated from their families and caged at the southern border. At the same time, the COVID-19 pandemic was revealing the true costs of immigrant health. We were placed most at risk while dutifully taking on the labor necessary to keep this country operating. While more affluent citizens sheltered in place, essential workers—many of them undocumented immigrants—continued to procure your food, care for your children, deliver your toilet paper, and keep this country afloat. We did this with little additional compensation for the risks we faced. While stimulus and rental-support checks were mailed across the country, undocumented individuals were barred from support.

In September 2020, wildfire smoke rolling in from Northern California turned my sky a dystopian orange.[8] The outside air was unhealthy to breathe. I saw eerie pictures of farmworkers, just an hour south of where I lived, continuing to work in the fields as they breathed in that shit. What are the long-term effects of breathing in air that an app on my phone says is "very unhealthy"?

I was reminded of the way immigrant health is exploited by the foundations of US supply chains. In the years since the pandemic began, epidemiologists have tried to determine the impact of COVID-19 on excess mortality.[9] That is, how many more people died "from all causes during a crisis above and beyond what we would have expected to see under 'normal' conditions." Excess mortality is hard to quantify. Some research suggests that the federal government's efforts to return the US to a "new normal" amount to attempts to "accustom the population to mass death in perpetuity."[10]

My life is on the cusp of excess mortality. Undocumented immigrants walk a tightrope of health scares while still working in the most unsafe conditions. Though some states have offered vaccination support and COVID guidance to immigrant communities, others, like Texas, have leveraged the pandemic to actively harm the undocumented. This was first done through dismantling in-state mask and vaccine requirements. In 2021, Texas governor Greg Abbott proclaimed, "The path forward relies on personal responsibility rather than government mandates."[11] Simultaneously, Abbott pandered to unfounded claims that undocumented immigrants were responsible for the pandemic surge. As Adam Serwer reported in *The Atlantic*, Abbott directed state troopers to surveil and stop "vehicles suspected of transporting undocumented immigrants." Serwer wrote: "The primary step Abbott has taken to reduce the spread of the coronavirus . . . is to encourage armed agents of the state to engage in racial profiling. You know, in the name of freedom."[12]

PRAYING FOR GASTRITIS

Recently, my body has started giving up on me again. More than a decade of physical and mental toil has caught up with me. Daily, I am taken over by extreme stomach pain. It's gone on long enough that I can no longer simply wish it away or try to adjust my diet. Throughout this book,

I've described the times I've failed to "listen to my gut." From messages from God to the warnings about abusive relationships, my gut has been a beacon trying to guide me. And now, it's blaring all of its Klaxons for me to heed its physical warnings. For the first time since coming to this country, I've missed multiple days of work, even as I hate disappointing the families depending on me.

Initial tests and antibiotics have not helped. Some days, I can't get out of bed, or I end up going home from work a few hours after showing up. I'm a shadow of the woman people have relied on. Instead, I'm merely a belly full of cramps and pain. As I write this, a doctor has told me that I urgently need to get an endoscopy, a colonoscopy, and a biopsy. I am bleeding internally from an unknown source. Even if I were to hand over all my savings, I would barely be able to afford one of these procedures.

The costs of health have been financially, spiritually, and physically draining. What's more, these costs aren't going away. They are increasing dramatically from day to day, an inflation that compounds on my life. I'm praying for a miracle—perhaps that all these symptoms turn out to be nothing more than gastritis. It feels funny to be crossing my fingers for a severe case of gastritis, but that's where I'm at. A more serious diagnosis could be unsurmountable.

CHAPTER 10

THE COST OF DREAMING

In the previous nine chapters, I've unfurled tens of thousands of words to tally the costs that this country has imposed on me. And yet, even if the framing of this book suggests I am only an object of the exploitation and abuse that rains down on those at the bottom of our social ladder, it is also true that I—and all of the other undocumented individuals I've met—have not been passive or idle.

In the same way I set aside and send money to my mother each month after my rent and other basic needs have been covered, I have been squirreling away time and relationships to support my dreams. For instance, there is the work that I do as a filmmaker and a storyteller. These aspects of my identity allow me to fully demonstrate my ability to change the world around me. And, although this is my first book, I regularly write op-eds about immigrant rights for newspapers like the *San Francisco Chronicle* and film and television scripts that speak to immigrant experiences.

The stories I tell—with my camera, with my keyboard, and with my voice—are my purpose. But my dreams are not convenient for the United States. Although I've been offered parts for shows and commercials, I have had to turn down these opportunities because of my status. Instead, on nights and weekends I collaborate on independent projects with other artists, many of whom are also immigrants hustling to the brink of exhaustion. For years, I have worked ten- and twelve-hour days as a nanny and then begun a second workday that went deep into the night, leading acting classes, mentoring other filmmakers, holding meetings to keep film productions on schedule, and planning shoots. My weekends were a tight choreography of early hours and all-day shoots, making movies with my friends and then finding a couple hours to rest before the week completed her revolution and started anew.

During the height of the pandemic, I spent many weekends traveling from the bay down to Los Angeles, where I was coproducing the short film *NorJack*. The film was a dramatic reimagining of the story of fabled plane hijacker D. B. Cooper. In 1971, he parachuted from a commuter jet with hundreds of thousands of dollars in ransom money and, to this day, has never been found. The composite police sketch of Cooper shows a generic-looking white man. As I sat inside the shell of the airplane cabin that we'd rented for our shoot, I thought of how Cooper's criminal actions transformed airport security. Pre-9/11 use of X-ray machines and metal detectors were a result of Cooper and subsequent copycat hijacking attempts. And though no longer needed on most modern planes, the Cooper vane device, named in his honor, was developed to prevent exits mid-flight. Cooper, the Patriot Act, and the ongoing villainization of people like me all add to the reasons it feels too risky for me to board airplanes in this country today.

In 2023, *NorJack* premiered at the TCL Chinese Theatre in Hollywood and has gone on to screen at many film festivals around the world. It was even short-listed for an Oscar. It is one of many films I've spent my time working on. I am proud of this work. One of the major projects I've been writing for several years now is a television series based on my life, reframing mainstream narratives about family, immigration, and cartel-fueled wars. I can't wait for you to watch it one day.

Weekend and late-night dreaming is incredibly taxing, and at this point, I am done with the guilt that accompanies hustle culture. I am done with the shame that has been instilled in me if I am not working with a pen or a broom or a baby's bottle in my hand. The "good immigrant" archetype means I'm only seen as valuable if I am constantly working.[1] Like Tricia Hersey and her viral movement, the Nap Ministry, which seeks to destigmatize rest and advocates for self-care as a form of political resistance, I understand that it is revolutionary for someone like me to rest and to dream.[2]

Today, I am in one of the most promising moments of my career (even as I am no closer to being "documented" in this country). I am an invited speaker at universities. I speak virtually to researchers and students across the country, and within California, I recently presented at Stanford University and UC Irvine. As a contracted consultant, I host writing workshops for teachers, community members, and other immigrants like me. And I coedit *La Cuenta,* where I help uplift undocumented voices, research, and resources. There is so much more to come. In fact, when I look at the kinds of things that I get to do with my life right now, I don't see a life that elicits pity. Instead, I am wealthy with purpose.

WEALTH AND DREAMING

Chicana and Chicano studies professor Tara Yosso has for many years challenged deficit views of historically marginalized communities, recognizing the harm that negative assumptions about young students' academic, linguistic, and social outcomes based on race and culture have caused for generations.[3] Her work rejects the assumptions that the only valuable perspectives are middle-class and white. Her 2005 article "Whose Culture Has Capital? A Critical Race Theory Discussion of Community Cultural Wealth" has served as a touchstone for how I articulate my resilience and dreaming. In this article, Yosso pushes against the conventional framing of "cultural capital" that sees people of color as deficient in the skills and competencies required to thrive in America.[4] She then introduces the idea of "community cultural wealth," an array of knowledge, skills, abilities, and contacts that communities of color use to survive macro- and micro-forms of oppression.[5] Yosso identifies six forms of capital that proliferate in Black, brown, and Indigenous communities, including linguistic capital ("the intellectual and social skills attained through communication experiences in more than one language and/or style") and familial capital ("those cultural knowledges nurtured among *familia* . . . that carry a sense of community history, memory and cultural intuition").

When I first read Yosso's article, I saw so many aspects of my life in it. It is the mirror image of the costs that are extracted from me throughout this book. Community cultural wealth describes the abundance I carry within me. One of these forms of wealth is particularly relevant to my identity as a speculative dreamer: aspirational capital. As Yosso explains:

> *Aspirational capital* refers to the ability to maintain hopes and dreams for the future, even in the face of real and perceived barriers. This resiliency is evidenced in those who allow themselves and their children to dream of possibilities beyond their present circumstances, often without the objective means to attain those goals.[6]

My undocumented community and I shoulder dreams in this country because it is how we will further change the world around us. I dream of a world where I am able to tell stories like the ones I've shared in this book without fear of any negative attention or hateful comments they might bring.

Tracey Flores, an associate professor at the University of Texas at Austin, mixes these forms of capital in her work. Her ongoing community-engaged research includes the intergenerational writing program Somos Escritoras/We Are Writers, which works "to support Latina girls to develop their writing while learning new tools to speak their truths, define themselves, and amplify their voices within a supportive community of Latina girls and women."[7] Flores brings together Latina girls and their parents so that they can dream and write together.

As Flores described the program to me, her voice quivered with emotion: "[The parents are] sometimes sharing stories for the first time with their daughters. And, because it's reciprocal, the parents are also learning new things about their daughters: what they care about, what matters to them, the things that they're struggling with day-to-day, fitting in, understanding that 'The world sees me in this way, but I don't see myself in this way.'" As these girls are able to fully share their lives, they get to see, she explained, that their parents "weren't always Mom and Dad. They were young. Their bodies were changing. They were activists. They did these things for *me.*"

Flores wept with pride as she described these families of writers. I told her about my own family of writers—from my daddy, who showed me how to hold a pencil to my brother for whom I did the same. Flores and I talked about the power of writing *into* a different future. "This is our lives," she reflected. "This is not just some fufu workshop I do. It's transformative." Opportunities like Somos Escritoras are transformative in that they break down assumptions about who we are and how we are seen. For instance, many Americans might take it for granted that my undocumented status makes me an outsider. But, in fact, my status is not something you can see, and it is not something that exists in any tangible way beyond the words and policies that created it in the not-too-distant past. Immigration policies may feel intractably embedded in the foundations of this society, but new worlds are dreamed up constantly. I can tell you about a world that would not chain me to a country that wants to watch me rot.[8] This is more than *aspirational*—this is my wealth as a dreamer.

I can dream, for example, of a world with open borders where I can make valued, visible, and acknowledged contributions to those around me. In this world, where my country of origin and a socially constructed immigration status do not define my personhood, I have a savings account that I am able to add to each month.

I live in a house that is comfortable but not lavish. I am able to afford the costs of modest living and keep my kitchen stocked with fresh, healthy food, bought from nearby stores and sourced from local agriculture. My car does not have multiple high-interest loans on which I make payments. It is a nondescript, pre-owned vehicle that reliably gets me where I need to go. When I drive, I do so cautiously but not fearfully.

In this world, I wake up knowing I have accrued sick time that allows me to attend to my and my family's health concerns as they arise. I have access to medical care that I can afford. I know that I can routinely visit a dentist and doctors. I know that if a medical catastrophe were to hit, I would be able to easily navigate a system that accommodates me. When I am stressed or feel the familiar weight of depression that has cloaked my mind in the past, I have a therapist and other holistic resources at my disposal.

In this not-impossible-world, I am a lawyer, fighting for human rights and social justice. I continue to work regularly and consistently, as a writer, storyteller, and filmmaker. I receive compensation for crafting narratives that affirm the lives of people who look and talk like me. I can complete my work within a regular business day, take breaks as I need them, and am trusted to make decisions for myself and my needs. My work fuels me creatively, and I am also able to set it aside when I go home and socialize with friends.

In this world, I can meet and date people without fear of disclosing my status. In all my relationships—romantic and otherwise—I can be the fullest version of myself if I choose to.

And, in this world, this world that is real in my heart and could be real for all of us if we choose to make it so, I am able to visit my family. I see my brother on a regular basis, and I travel to Mexico knowing I will not be hassled when I come back to the United States. My movements, both within the US, such as on freeways, and internationally, are unimpeded and do not come with undue stress. Perhaps I am worried my suitcase won't fit in the overhead compartment. I know that, in this world, if I leave my books and family photos behind, I will be able to go back and collect them.

The discussions around immigration policy in the United States feel impossibly shackled by ignorance and a lack of imagination. This is why speculative storytelling is an act of social transformation. From Afrofuturist and speculative storytellers like Octavia Butler and Nnendi Okorafor to the historical scholarship of researchers like Robin D. G. Kelley, Arturo Escobar, and Ruha Benjamin, speculation is a cornerstone to how I believe we will change this world for immigrant communities.[9] This kind of work is rooted in critical movements tied to race and gender.

In a 2014 lecture, scholar and activist Angela Davis said, "You have to act as if it were possible to radically transform the world. And you have to do it all the time."[10] It's a quote that has since circulated as a stand-alone meme, but the speech from which it was pulled is worth considering as well. Davis's statement came in the middle of a lengthy lecture on Reconstruction. The full power of possibility comes only from taking from a clear-eyed look at our past.

In "The Cost of Time," the first chapter of this book, I wrote about how there is no time period—past, present, or future—that offers any kind of reassurance or hope for me. My past contains the origins of my losses and a home I can no longer return to. The present is a hamster wheel of survival, trying to stay out of the sight of the state while making barely enough money to get by. And my future feels bleak: in the months that I've been writing this book in 2023 and 2024, the prospects of a pathway toward legally living in the US have gone from bad to worse. The modern anti-immigrant sentiment that has been alive and well since I first arrived in the US during the Obama administration has only escalated under presidents Trump and Biden. And so it is only my dreams that keep me moving forward. I dream along with the millions of other undocumented folks across the country. Our dreams contain possibilities that the United States may never fully know and that would only benefit this nation.

As you know, although I dream, I am not a Dreamer. That is, I am not a beneficiary of the Development, Relief, and Education for Alien Minors (DREAM) Act. Democrats have been introducing different versions of the Dream Act since 2001. Though limited components of the Dream Act, particularly Deferred Action for Childhood Arrivals (DACA), have been passed, the Dream Act as a whole has been consistently blocked by Republican legislators every time Congress has voted on it.

DACA recipients, as suggested in their name, are able to "defer" negative immigration actions. They may someday be at risk of deportation, especially as the program continues to face legal challenges. However, as I currently write this, individuals with DACA are authorized to work, access financial aid for higher education, and receive a Social Security number. These are vital elements to participating in public life in this country, and I am thrilled for the many friends I have who have received DACA. Among other requirements, to be eligible for DACA, individuals must have entered this country before they were sixteen years old. Because

I was not a childhood arrival, I am not eligible for DACA. And while DACA is an important component to how immigration is discussed in this country, it serves only a minority of the undocumented community—and even this sliver of opportunity is imperiled. The legal challenges to DACA have been incessant, working their way through various judicial circuits across multiple presidential terms. Because of these attacks, DACA has been rescinded and reinstated in varying ways. For DACA recipients, this has led to a constant state of uncertainty. Given the precarious nature of DACA, protecting this community remains imperative in immigrant rights movements. As I mentioned in earlier chapters, I campaigned for the Dream Act years before I became undocumented myself. It did not matter that I did not qualify for DACA or any of the legislative promises held in versions of the Dream Act. It was about bettering lives in my community.

DOCUMENTING DREAMS

Dreaming while undocumented means knowing the odds are always stacked against you. No matter how hard you might try to squirm out from under the heel of day-to-day survival, the social system and its various acronyms will try to kill every single piece of you, to keep you where people can take advantage of your intelligence, to keep you pinned to where they pillage your hard, cheap labor.

However, every obstacle this country has thrown at me has failed to defeat me. Every tragedy or abusive predator that I've encountered has simply led me here, where I am writing this to you now. I have been only fueled each time people took advantage of my good heart.

That's what society overlooks about all of us who are undocumented and dare to dream. At some point there was nothing left to take away from us, and that's how I've built myself up, piece by piece. Because when this country took away everything, it also took away my fear. So now, I am a survivor, a warrior, a walking miracle.

When I was young, I thought I was going to be a lawyer, fighting for human rights, and advocating for people who needed help. I thought I would use my law degree to help immigrants and to transform the world around me. But this country shot that possibility down. School was inaccessible, too expensive, and too time-consuming. But that didn't stop my *purpose*. My dreams remain unhampered. They grow untethered from any imaginary label that tries to lasso my strength.

I know that I will never get my daddy back. The version of the family that I once had no longer exists in the waking world. But I build new dreams now. I build a new future where nobody tells me what to do with my life or my ambitions. And I've finally gotten to feel how real love heals and gives life new meaning.

In January 2022, during the hardships described in these pages, I met Alexander, a handsome and gentle man. I knew right away he was everything I dreamed of finding. We dated for two years and even planned a summer wedding. Ultimately, though, despite how supportive and caring Alexander was, I realized that our love languages were fundamentally different. For the first time, I prioritized myself over a romantic relationship. I walked away from the man that I loved and the dream life he was offering me, not to mention the possibilities of "fixing" my legal status. I have never let my immigration status guide my heart. This country tries to make it otherwise, but undocumented people still marry for love.

This world tries to keep me and the undocumented community confined to children's nurseries or restaurant kitchens or processing plants or farmland. This world tries to saddle us with debt and the weight of the tools they give us to conduct backbreaking labor. But these are also the tools that we use to build a new world from the ground up. I learned not to allow the world and its stereotypes to define me. Societal judgment cannot corrupt my heart. I know the world would love for me to be bitter about the cruelty that I have experienced. However, not allowing these circumstances to transform me into a monster is my ultimate act of resistance. I have endured many battles that I never should have had to fight. I won every single one of them. I want you to know that you can fight and dream with me. I have no faith in the poisonous promises of politicians. The only way that we are going to transform the world is through uniting and making good on the realization of how fully we depend on one another. In the end, all we have is each other.

My biggest hope for this book is that it will open people's minds to the fact that, in a matter of seconds or with the smallest of mistakes, your life can change forever. That's what happened to me. Never in a million years did I think I would lose it all and be forced to be undocumented. But I promise you: my life won't be in vain. Our unity, love, and care for each other will get us through hardships. Fight for your neighbor, share the few or many things you've got. All of us were put on this earth with a purpose. The world needs what only you can offer. Our stories, especially now, are so necessary.

At some point, I will be able to reunite with my brother, AC. That's one of the tangible dreams I hold on to. I am going to give him the physical hug that FaceTime can never approximate. The day I reunite with AC will be the most beautiful day of my life. That kid is the reason I wake up every morning to dream anew. It's why I give myself permission to have dreams so large they can never be caged. I give myself permission to know you will see my work on movie and television screens soon and you will read more of my books in the future. I dream with certainty of fair wages for farmworkers. I dream with certainty that we will no longer live with the lie of being "illegal."

It doesn't matter how much this world hates us. My dreams of hope outshine them. Yours do too. If my words make you feel seen and loved, it will have made everything I've gone through worth it. I love you, and I thought of you as I wrote every word in this book. You, too, will survive.

I see so much brilliance and happiness in my future, not because it was given to me, but because I built it, because I didn't fold into the darkness. I crawled out of darkness, and I now know who I am. Yes, I lost it all in the process. I lost every single thing I owned. I lost every ounce of willingness to continue, at times. But in the process of losing it all, I found me.

RECKONING WITH
INHUMANE MATH

I am sitting in the emergency room, suffering and fearful. I feel a sadness deeper than any of the ongoing pain I have experienced over the last year of my life.[1] A strange noise gurgles from the IV attached to my body, and a lady in the next bed yells at the nurse for not being gentle enough with her. I understand her complaint: when the nurse inserted my IV, it was like the needle was an old USB cable and I was a laptop. But, despite the pain, I'm too drowsy from the drugs in my veins to raise my voice.

During the year that I finished the first draft of this book, 2023, the bottom fell out of my life. The stomach pain I'd been enduring for months became unbearable, and I was unable to see an abdominal specialist. After several all-day waits at a clinic, I was given a referral that promised the possibility of an appointment in six to eight weeks. But in that time, I've ended up in the emergency room on three different occasions, my heart palpitating from the pain.

So, here I am in the ER for the third time, drifting in and out of sleep. I see children and elderly patients come and go. I am filled with worry for all of my neighbors in this hospital, even as I ask God why I myself have ended up here. Of course, I know that people suffer every day, that nothing makes me an exception. However, I also know that if I had "good" insurance or reliable access to basic medical care, I wouldn't be sitting here now, dizzy with pain. My health wouldn't have gotten this bad. It is the label this country has placed on me that has led to the ongoing agony I feel in my body. I've seen (and paid) eight different doctors over the past year, with no answers to show for it.

I have continued to need emergency care and in the last year, I have visited the ER more times than I have gone to the mall. My bank account is empty from the mounting costs of medical tests, ER bills, and appointments with specialists. My debt is larger than the rash that has spread all over my body as a reaction to the antibiotic I was prescribed a week ago. Only two days ago, I was rushed to this same hospital, my pulse spiking, and my heart palpitating due to the allergic reaction. And now I am back here again.

A few hours ago, I became infuriated with my own body. How can it give up on me like this? I am still young. But then it hit me: My body is tired of this battle. I've spent the past decade trying to survive, and it is exhausting. My body is desperate to find peace and rest. But the only way I can take a break from my arduous work schedule is by being too sick to clock in. And so, my body became sick in order to force me to rest. Tears are falling from my face as I write this. I am so worn-out.

For months, I hid the fact that I was possibly facing a terrifying diagnosis. Several of the doctors I saw said that my symptoms strongly suggested that I had colon cancer. As mentioned at the end of chapter 9, I needed biopsies, a colonoscopy, and an endoscopy. The basic health insurance that undocumented immigrants in California became eligible to receive in 2023 did not cover these costs. It took me seven months to save up enough money to get these procedures done. I ate my fear for these months, not telling anyone how terrified I was. By the time I got the answer—I *didn't* have cancer, but my organs were severely inflamed—I had researched life insurance plans for undocumented individuals, trying to find a way to pay for my funeral and have money to go to my mother. I couldn't deal with the idea of my death being a burden for the people I love. Ultimately, it cost me more than $4,000 to find out I didn't have cancer, and I still didn't have clear answers about what was wrong.

When MDs were unable to give me conclusive answers, I started reaching out to holistic specialists, asking anyone and everyone for referrals to people who might help me. On top of the doctor-required tests, I paid for additional blood testing, CT scans, dieticians, and respiratory specialists. The team of doctors I worked with, after nearly a year of ongoing pain, finally determined that toxic black mold in my work environment—the family home in which I was nannying—had led to chronic inflammatory response syndrome (CIRS). When the doctor was able to finally confirm this diagnosis, she said, "You have one of the most American diseases. Most houses in this country have mold." The house I worked in every day had made me sick, and yet I had no access to workers' comp. The family offered me supportive words, but I have no benefits or legal recourse to draw from. There's nothing more American than slowly dying from the air of under-the-table labor. Tourists visiting Mexico are warned not to drink the water. I'd warn y'all not to breathe the air in the United States.

By the time I finally got my moldy answer (and an expensive treatment plan), I was broke and had staked my life on several high-interest loans. Because I'm unable to get loans from banks or other regulated programs, I'm forced to turn to predatory lenders with exorbitant interest rates waiting to prey on the needs of people like me. Right now, I am paying my life away in interest and fees in order to stay alive.

In order to pay for tests and have the time for all of my medical appointments, I have temporarily paused going to therapy. The money I would have spent on therapy for my mental wellness was diverted to keep my body from shutting down, and without any answers other than that I felt like garbage every day, I shut myself off from most of my friends. The cost of my health was thousands of dollars, my personal relationships, my mental health, and a year of shaken confidence. All of the costs in this book compound on top of one another, particularly in moments, or in this case, a year, of crisis. Even though parts of my professional career have been taking flight, undocumented survival means continually finding yourself flat-footed.

This is not an easy book to conclude. The resolution you might be looking for (and that I've been dreaming of) is nowhere in sight. As I look over the grand sum of costs and lived experiences that I've shared with you, I know that they don't add up to a neat portrait of my life. When a person is measured by what has been extracted from them, the picture is far from complete. It's based on the assumption that a person's value is only the extractable utility they offer. This book has shown you my bruises and tears from being a cog in the American Dream.

MISSING COSTS AND ABUNDANT LIFE

These chapters have accounted for ten costs that I chose in order to narratively illustrate my points. But in reality the costs don't end with the last chapter—they go on and on. There is also the cost of education; I dropped out of college to come here, and I spent a decade navigating the public education system as AC's guardian.

How do I tally the costs of rebuilding a relationship with my one remaining parent? For the first five years after I moved to California, I refused to have any contact with my mom, even as she regularly checked in on Cindy and AC. I couldn't shake the feelings of abandonment I had from her having left us stranded in this country for years. It's true that she herself was grieving, trying to pay off our debt, and save whatever remained of our property in Mexico. But I had been forced into her role as AC's mother. However, I eventually realized that I didn't want to carry the costs of resentment toward someone who also knew what it was like to lose it all. And so for the past eight years, I have been reinvesting in my relationship with my mother, healing our family.

Likewise, how do I account for the cost of being scared of people? Or the fact that this fear has only increased over time? My trust has been betrayed again and again by people who let me live with them, by romantic partners, colleagues, and church leaders. All this has only intensified my sense of suspicion and anxiety. In this current period in my life when I have needed help and a shoulder to lean on more than ever before, the world feels even more dangerous. This is the manifestation of what W. E. B. Du Bois called "double consciousness,"[2] a term he used nearly 120 years ago to describe the challenges facing the Black community in the United States. Du Bois's words are hauntingly relevant for marginalized communities in the US today: "It is a peculiar sensation, this double-consciousness, this sense of always looking at one's self through the eyes of others, of measuring one's soul by the tape of a world that looks on in amused contempt and pity."

I resonate with the "contempt and pity" Du Bois describes while also carrying pride in my Mexican strength and the promises I am furthering in my work as a storyteller. I am constantly terrified of how I am seen "through the eyes of others," a paranoia justified by my own histories of harm. It is this feeling that makes me look over my shoulder every time I am walking from my car.

Given the extreme precautions I've taken to keep myself and AC safe and out of the public eye, friends and family have asked why I would put so much of myself on these pages, offering a naked accounting of the details of my life. Why would I put these words out into a world I distrust? The answer is not a complicated one. I want you, reader, to know me. To know that there are so many people like me. A part of society and apart from society. Until you see and understand me, we cannot begin to build a freer world for all of us.

These pages are filled with grief, but I've learned that grief and hope can coexist. My life is full of beautiful moments, and I want you, reader, to know that too. Alongside the massive costs tallied in this book is a feeling of insurmountable love—the friendships and bonds that hold me up and continue to transform me.

I was a young woman trying to reach my dreams in Mexico, when life came along with other plans. In knowing me, you know that I've been pummeled into exhaustion. I didn't ask for the responsibilities placed upon me here in the United States, and I never planned to seek invisible refuge in this country. I invested *everything* into the happiness of my brother, our safety, and the dreams I still have. I know my dad would be so proud of me.

THE COST OF YOUR CONVENIENCE

In the pages that follow, I'm going to put a dollar amount to the costs detailed in this book. Like the incomplete picture of my life held within these pages, this figure can never fully encompass what I've lost. How do you put a price on embered dreams and betrayals that cut beneath the skin?

This total is not an amount that I am saying I am owed, or even an amount I have spent. Rather, this number is a combination of the bills and legal fees and unpaid wages and exploited labor that have accumulated over the twelve years described in this book. I'm putting a number on *my* life because too many of us are forced to bear these costs in order to make the United States operate affordably for everyone else. Every year, hundreds of individuals—far more than what is reported by the US Border Patrol—die simply trying to cross the US border.[3] How much were their lives worth to their families? This grotesque accounting also brings to mind the costs of the largest American law enforcement agency, the Department of Homeland Security, and the US Customs and Border Protection, one of the largest groups of police officers. In recent years, between $15 and $25 billion has been spent annually at the federal level on immigration-related enforcement.[4]

Far too many of us have, for far too long, endured harm, exploitation, illness, and death in order to keep this country afloat. All of us are so much more than the singular costs that have been pizza-sliced and served in this book. Our lives are uncontainable, and when we bring ourselves together, we are an incredible force to be reckoned with. Our wealth is beautifully abundant. This is why, with my coauthor Antero, I founded *La Cuenta*. Our online publication sustains a "we" that includes all of my immigrant community, giving us a space in which to relate, to be seen, and to help share the tallied costs of a life lived invisibly. I hope, if any of my life resonated with you, you'll join the *La Cuenta* community.

While my life—like all life—is priceless, professionals like adjusters, actuaries, forecasters, and analysts are trained to calculate how much a life, an injury, or an impairment are worth. These are centuries-old traditions, and in tallying this bill, I worked closely with a claims adjuster who specializes in workers' compensation. I consulted the American Medical Association's *Guides to the Evaluation of Permanent Impairment* and related materials from the World Health Organization.[5] The opening sentence of the *AMA Guides* tellingly describes the lens through which these practices operate: "Tolerance of and care for the sick and the disabled may be elemental components of our social fabric rooted in the very origins of human society."[6] This given premise of tolerance and care is then disseminated through a byzantine process of math, statistics, and reporting.

Many readers may have suspicions about the insurance companies who pay out these claims. My own sense, from the research I've done, is that this complex bureaucracy is meant to establish a baseline of objectivity and fairness for everyone. "The system of compensation does not see anyone's status—if they are undocumented or if they come from one racial background or not," the claims adjuster explained.

By distilling an individual's unique injury or impairment into a categorized class of severity (their "whole person impairment rating" in the parlance of the *AMA Guides*), the circumstances of harm become a single number. These "cultural differences" are still profound, of course. The opening chapters of the *AMA Guides* talk about how "Hispanics . . . generally prefer a social situation and are more comfortable if the [medical] encounter includes some conversation about family and some physical contact such as a handshake."[7] Similarly, these guides do not reflect the kinds of lived realities that many members of the undocumented community face. The Pain Disability Questionnaire, for example, asks individuals to give a zero to ten score for how their pain affects their lives.[8] It asks if the pain interferes "with your normal work inside and outside the home," "interferes with your traveling," or "interferes with your ability to see the people who are important to you as much as you would like." But how can I rate the pain of never seeing my loved ones again? Of being afraid to drive on freeways? How can I say that the pain in my lungs came from the "normal work" of caring for wealthy families' children?

Like Raj Chetty's research that estimates the real value of expert kindergarten teachers,[9] it is complex and speculative work. I took the tools of insurance companies that won't actually cover me and employers who won't actually hire me and adapted them to tally percentages of impairment and disability. I then added the costs of legal fees, of under-the-table medical care, and of out-of-pocket expenses incurred as a result of my undocumented status. A large cost I am including here is the cost of what I *haven't* been able to achieve. Each year I spent not finishing college (despite the tens of thousands of dollars of educational debt, reflected in the table) and being a nanny instead was another year of distance from the kind of job I wanted to have. If I had finished the final years of my bachelor's degree and then gone on to law school for three more years—my plan before my father died—I would likely have made more than twice my actual salary. This difference in earnings would have added to the US economy and positively benefited our shared society; we all share the burden of these costs. Additionally, as mentioned in chapter 1 of this book, undocumented individuals like me pay taxes each year, even if we don't benefit from them. Considering that some of these taxes fund healthcare I cannot access and immigration enforcement programs that seek to do me harm, I have included those tax payments in the tally.

"Being undocumented" made it impossible to provide the background checks that rental applications often required in Georgia and California. AC, Cindy, and I were relegated to the few rentals that would let our status skate by. We lived far below the US poverty line while in Georgia. Of course, we were not able to utilize government housing assistance, a cost reflected in the tally. Likewise, because churches and nonprofits could not hire me for the work I did for projects like Blue Ribbon, I donated thousands of dollars' worth of my own labor to run them. Likewise, I endured the ongoing sexual harassment of the manager at the Mexican restaurant in Georgia only because I knew how difficult it would be to get any other job. And because I, on a tourist visa, did not feel safe reporting him to the authorities, I endured a plight unique to undocumented individuals marginalized in our workforce.

In my discussions with Professor Bill Ong Hing, author of *Humanizing Immigration: How to Transform Our Racist and Unjust System*, he was not only unfazed by the final sum but wondered if, in fact, this number should be higher. As founding director of the University of San Francisco's Immigration and Deportation Defense Clinic and a professor of law and migration studies, Hing relies on contemporary research on the lasting impacts of adverse childhood experiences (ACEs) to stave off court decisions around deportation and separation for families. Referring to the lifelong impacts of immigrant precarity and the threat of deportation, Hing said the ongoing consequence of immigrant survival is "much more than just psychological trauma. It's neurological. It affects everything for the rest of your life."

Trauma carried by individuals like me impacts our entire family network, and does so across generations. I don't tally the costs of these traumas for AC or any of my other family members. However, invisible in charts and actuary tables and tallies like the one here are the incalculable costs of how efforts to resist family separation across different borders take an embodied toll on all of us.

I can't say if you'll see the derived figure here as a laughably high number, a paltry sum, or the expected cost of American progress. Know, however, that this one number is not far off from the similar costs incurred by the millions of other undocumented folks in our communities. All of us are worth far more than a single number.

THE COST OF MY SURVIVAL (2011–23)

ITEM & DESCRIPTION	COST
Wage theft (uncompensated hours working late for an abusive restaurant manager)	$600
Deliberate underpay (full-time work as a radio and television producer and host)	$51,000
Underpayment as a nanny (additional uncompensated hours, no overtime, last-minute cut hours)	$70,000
Late fees and penalties (accrued fees after families paid my salary up to two weeks late)	$500
Taxes (approximately 15 percent of my annual salary in taxes, nearly 75 percent of which funded programs I cannot access and anti-immigration law enforcement that seeks to do me harm)	$105,000
Salary differential of not being a lawyer (inclusive of three years of law school)[10]	$937,700
Legal fees (consultations about my immigration status and pathways toward a legal work permit at $280/hour)	$11,200
Time missed from work in order to meet with lawyers about my immigration status	$1,400
Time missed from work looking for new nannying jobs (approximately two weeks/year)	$25,200

(continues)

ITEM & DESCRIPTION	COST
Housing insecurity[11]	$21,600
Community college international student tuition and fees	$36,852
Driving while undocumented	Anxiety, missed social invites
Dental fees (cost for licensed practitioners and under-the-table providers)	$6,880 + permanent hearing loss
Time lost getting medical and dental care	$2,800
Uncompensated time (unpaid staff running church programs 10–15 hours/week for seven years)	$140,000
Sexual harassment[12]	$15,000 + insecurity, fear
Clothes, laptop, personal notebooks, and books left in Mexico	$5,000
Transportation costs (taxis, buses, and Ubers to get to work and take AC to soccer and other social activities without access to a state driver's license in Georgia)	$25,920
Bus fare (transportation to Los Angeles for film production to avoid Border Patrol checkpoints, $75 one way/monthly)	$9,000
Skipping meals to provide enough food for AC	Hunger, malnutrition
Lost wages (salary from film and acting jobs not able to accept without a Social Security number)	$30,000
Lost tips as a restaurant server from racist customers	$1,000
Blue Ribbon out-of-pocket expenses (food for recruitment events and food, clothes, etc., for patrons)	$5,000
Therapy ($150/hour and $50/hour, depending on financial means)	$27,500

ITEM & DESCRIPTION	COST
Complex post-traumatic stress disorder[13] (based on *AMA Guides* and including estimates for medical coverage, therapy, and ongoing treatment)	$75,000 + trauma, memory loss, panic attacks, feelings of hopelessness, dizziness, an eating disorder
Domestic violence[14] and not trusting going to legal authorities (includes coverage for psychological claims and treatment)	$12,000 + fear at home
Reference checks and housing application fees (additional requirements to be approved to rent an apartment)	$780
Hospital visits (specialists, emergency rooms, blood tests, prescriptions)	$48,000
Medical procedures (CT scans, endoscopies, colonoscopies)	$13,400
Chronic Inflammatory Response Syndrome (CIRS) caused by toxic mold in the house where I worked as a nanny[15] (based on *AMA Guides* for permanent impairment and treatment)	$225,000 + severe abdominal pain, loss of work
Interest paid on predatory, high-interest loans taken out to cover medical bills	$8,845
NONMONETARY TOTAL:	Anxiety, missed social invites, permanent hearing loss, insecurity, fear, hunger, malnutrition, trauma, memory loss, panic attacks, feelings of hopelessness, dizziness, an eating disorder, fear at home, severe abdominal pain, loss of work
MONETARY TOTAL:	$1,912,177

ACKNOWLEDGMENTS

F or this book, we spent years excavating the costs of undocumented survival. Still, our tally can never account for the cost of the hugs, goodbyes, and memories lost by immigrants who have been separated from their loved ones. For every person whose life has been burdened by borders, this book is for you.

The process of envisioning and writing this book was continually a challenge. At every step, our amazing agent, Jessica Papin, has been there with us. Thank you for believing in this work and guiding us through this process.

Catherine Tung has been an amazing editor. Her patience has sharpened our thinking and improved this text at every turn. We are grateful for the entire team alongside Catherine at Beacon Press.

The impetus for this book emerged from a Stanford Public Humanities workshop hosted by Mark Grief and Blakey Vermuele, and for that, as well as for the ongoing support from Natalie Jabbar, we are grateful. Additional institutional support for this work was provided by the Stanford Accelerator for Learning, and we are also grateful to Stanford Impact Labs for the opportunity to share preliminary aspects of this narrative with a public audience.

Hope Amico and her long-running Keep Writing project allowed us to explore the theme of this book in postcard form. Thank you.

While we worked with myriad individuals for this project, we are particularly appreciative of scholarly expertise from Ramón Martínez, Jonathan Rosa, Leigh Patel, Cati de los Ríos, Tracey Flores, Rocío Rosales, José Luis Cano Jr., Christopher Moriates, and Bill Ong Hing.

We also drew on guidance and support from Eve Ewing, Rafael Agustin, Nicole Mirra, Anni Quintero, Stephanie Robillard, Karli Stander, Emily Farrell, and Aure Shrock. Thank you all for your belief in this work.

To United We Dream, the Young Center, UndocuProfessionals, Define American, and all other organizations that are supporting the needs and centering the humanity of the undocumented community, thank you.

Research support was provided by Laura Villalobos and Christían Peña. Thank you both for your steadfast guidance for this book and for sharing your own perspectives to enrich the narrative. And, of course, thank you for helping *La Cuenta* flourish.

I would like to acknowledge Stella and Joey—*Stelwah* and *JoJo* when this book first began! It is the pursuit of making this world a better one for you that keeps me writing each day.

This has been one of the most challenging and vulnerable projects I've worked on. Thank you, Alix, for trusting me with your experiences and for teaching me all along this journey.

There are innumerable costs related to completing this book and you, Ally, have shouldered more of them than you ever imagined. You have been an unwavering steward of this work, even when that stress was particularly heavy. Thank you for supporting me and believing in us.

—ANTERO

I would like to thank all of the people who have loved and carried me over the years. I could fill many more pages expressing my gratitude. Your generosity and support have saved my life.

Very few people have impacted me as much as Antero has. Working together all these years has been an honor. I have been writing since I was a kid, but he is the reason this book is possible. Antero, there are not enough words to thank you for building this with me.

Thank you to the people who sacrificed so much to help me: Tía Vianney, Tía Martha Ortiz, Patty Delgado and Luis Delgado Tamez, Pastor Jacob Pereida, Elvia Ramos, and Kathya Rios.

To my wonderful friends who have pushed me harder to pursue my calling in life and love me unconditionally: Angelica Bingham, Leah Galarza, Gabriella Fox, Alyssa Pasquel, Elizabeth Hernandez, Jen Popp, Megan Elizabeth Cantu, Andrea Sandoval, Hector Sandoval, Yadira Diaz, Walter Perez, Manuel Reyes, Sandra Giraldo, Ian Pineda, Vee Chhun, Juliana Ireland, Alyssa Shaheen, Negin Nourani, Thom McCallum, Hugo Soto-Martínez, Alexis Delgado, and Omar Barragán.

Thank you, Alicia McCallum, for encouraging me to pursue filmmaking. You are the reason I make films. I am grateful for your endless love and support.

Jorge Xolalpa, thank you for being my tamal and allowing me to make films with you.

Jazbleidy Cadavid, thank you for dreaming with me and being the cheerleader I needed.

Daliana Cadavid, you constantly reminded me that our dreams are possible.

Thank you, Susanna Rogers, for the endless support in all I do. You sprinkle happiness on everything you encounter.

Thank you to my wonderful therapist, Martin MC; to the best holistic care provider, Dr. Lacey; and to my incredible physical therapist, Ada Batun, for helping me get healthy again.

Thank you, Alicia Peque and Tío Javi, for helping us through the years.

To the family that changed my life forever—La Familia Valdez—Jesse, Janice, Christina Lisa, Vanessa, Tía Cynthia, and Priscilla: it doesn't matter what kind of distance separates us, you will always be my family.

Thank you, Lia Hernandez. When I felt like the whole world had left me, you were always there. Your love got me through the hardest days.

Brenda Graciano, my guardian angel, thank you for carrying me when I couldn't.

Debbii Dawson, you saw all of this long before I could see it myself. You are my family and the other half of my heart. And to your parents, David S. Dawson and Sharon Dawson, thank you for being my safe place and letting me be your daughter.

Thank you to my mom, for not letting the cruelty of the world corrupt your heart.

Thank you, Cindy. Your love, patience, and bravery are the reason we are still a family. Thank you for never giving up on AC and me. And thank you, Eduardo Santana, for being the best brother-in-law. You are a gift to our family.

Nana and Tata, for taking care of me, even from a distance, thank you.

Thank you to my daddy. You will never be a distant memory. The love you gave me still gets me through life.

Thank you to the reason for my existence, God. Whenever I wanted to give up, you showed up just in time.

And to AC, to whom I dedicate this book. If I had to choose a lifetime, I would still pick this one, just to be your sister. You are my pride and joy.

—ALIX

NOTES

A NOTE ON OUR RESEARCH PROCESS

1. See Garcia, *Good Reception*; Garcia, *All Through the Town*; and Mirra, Garcia, and Morrell, *Doing Youth Participatory Action Research*.

2. Relationality and positionality are complex, overlapping, and never quite accounted for in the methods sections of much scholarly work. In this work, we considered de los Ríos and Patel's repositioning of how our identities shape our work; de los Ríos and Patel, "Positions, Positionality, and Relationality in Educational Research," 1–12. See also Espino, "Positionality as Prologue," 1–16, and Garcia, "When Seeing Is Not Enough."

3. Our approach and adaptation of this work is informed by Fierros and Bernal, "Vamos a platicar," 98–121; Guajardo and Guajardo, "The Power of Plática," 159; Hannegan-Martinez, "Pláticas as a Methodological Praxis of Love," 1702–13; and Ochoa, "Learning and Being in Community," 246–58.

4. This intentionally references Gutiérrez et al., "Replacing Representation with Imagination," 30–60, and Garcia et al., "Glimmers of Care," 337–54.

5. Fierros and Bernal, "Vamos a platicar," 102.

6. Hannegan-Martinez, "Pláticas as a Methodological Praxis of Love."

7. Patel expands on this in written work such as "Pedagogies of Resistance and Survivance," 397–401, and *No Study Without Struggle*.

8. Kinloch and San Pedro, "The Space Between Listening and Storying," 42.

9. Cruz, "Toward an Epistemology of a Brown Body," 657–69.

10. Such work gets to a broader civic foundation of how we might interact as a team and as a collective society. This work reflects a large focus of Antero's research; we also considered the intentional scholarship on civic learning of youth and adults labeled undocumented including Escudero, *Organizing While Undocumented*; Parkhouse, "Lessons on Citizenship and Democratic Power Literacy from Undocumented Youth"; and Rogers et al., "Civic Lessons," 201.

11. See Febos, *Body Work*, and Humphreys, *The Qualified Self*.

12. Chee, *How to Write an Autobiographical Novel*; Febos, *Body Work*; Huerta, *Magical Habits*; and Rhee, *Decolonial Feminist Research*.

13. See Brown and Dreby, *Family and Work in Everyday Ethnography*, and Hernández, *Frameworks and Ethics for Research with Immigrants*.
14. There are myriad other examples of harmful research practices. These are the examples most widely known by the general public. For readers interested in details about Stanford's history in this work, see Harris, *Palo Alto*.
15. Matthew Desmond resisted the first person in *Evicted*: "But first-person narration is not the only technique available to us. In fact, it may be the least well-suited vehicle for capturing the essence of a social world because the 'I' filters all."
16. Kimmerer, *Braiding Sweetgrass*.
17. We are reminded of Arundhati Roy's prophetic, if overlooked, description of the pandemic as a portal in "The Pandemic Is a Portal."

INTRODUCTION: THE BALANCE
1. Only a small number of states in the US allow undocumented individuals to apply for driver's licenses. Like many other policies covered throughout this book, they change from one year to another, one state to the next.
2. Chetty et al., "$320,000 Kindergarten Teachers," 22–25; Chetty et al., "How Does Your Kindergarten Classroom Affect Your Earnings?" 1593–1660.
3. Snyder et al., *Digest of Education Statistics 2017*.
4. Rosales, *Fruteros*.
5. Patel, *No Study Without Struggle*, 98.
6. I draw on Black feminist scholarship about intersectionality here, particularly Crenshaw, "Demarginalizing the Intersection of Race and Sex," 23–51. Additionally, see Combahee River Collective, *The Combahee River Collective Statement*; Collins, *Intersectionality as Critical Social Theory*; and Lorde, *Sister Outsider*.
7. This book is inspired by the words and writing of Jose Antonio Vargas as well as other memoirs and broader reflections on immigrant life; see Vargas, *Dear America*. Work particularly from other undocumented or formerly undocumented writers includes Agustin, *Illegally Yours*; Arce, *My (Underground) American Dream*; Arce, *You Sound Like a White Girl*; Cornejo Villavicencio, *The Undocumented Americans*; Grande and Guiñansaca, *Somewhere We Are Human*; and Zamora, *Solito*.
8. This complicated nature of how empathy can be at odds with movements for justice is informed by Davis, *The Other Side of Empathy*.
9. There is a plethora of studies related to undocumented schooling and education, including powerful work from current and formerly undocumented scholars. Some of the titles I consulted in this book include Abrego and Negrón-Gonzales, *We Are Not Dreamers*; Dyrness, *Mothers United*; Rodriguez and McCorkle, "On the Educational Rights of Undocumented Students," 1–34; and Rodriguez Vega, *Drawing Deportation*.

10. Maria Franquiz, in her 2023 presidential address at the National Council of Teachers of English convention, referred to the idea of words as a *consejo* to offer to readers. This framing draws on the words of children's author René Colato Laînez; see Colato Laînez, "The Gift of Telling Our Stories," 363–65.

CHAPTER 1: THE COST OF TIME

1. For additional perspectives on the role of Mexican drug cartels in the global economy, in culture, and in the shaping of contemporary Mexican life, I consulted Bonello, *Narcas*; Grillo, *El Narco*; and Hernández, *Narcoland*.

2. De los Ríos's work related to corridos includes "'Los Músicos': Mexican Corridos, the Aural Border, and the Evocative Musical Renderings of Transnational Youth," 177–200, and "Toward a *Corridista* Consciousness," 455–71.

3. Merrell, *The Impact of Unauthorized Immigrants on the Budgets of State and Local Governments*.

4. Blau and Mackie, *The Economic and Fiscal Consequences of Immigration*; Caplan and Weinersmith, *Open Borders*.

5. Le Guin, "National Book Foundation Medal: Ursula's Acceptance Speech."

6. Research on the community of individuals who are labeled undocumented and aging primarily comes from Center for Social Innovation, *The Health Needs of Undocumented Older Adults*; Enriquez et al., "Mental Health and COVID-19 Pandemic Stressors Among Latina/o/x College Students with Varying Self and Parental Immigration Status," 282–95; Flores Morales, "Aging and Undocumented," e12859; Migration Policy Institute, *Profile of the Unauthorized Population*; and Nuila, "Home: Palliation for Dying Undocumented Immigrants," 2047–48.

7. Center for Social Innovation, *The Health Needs of Undocumented Older Adults*.

8. Nuila, "Home: Palliation for Dying Undocumented Immigrants."

9. Migration Policy Institute, *Profile of the Unauthorized Population: United States*.

10. The field of psychology is still determining the meaning, causes, and definitions of pre-TSD and its relationship to global conflict and climate collapse. Research in this area includes Berntsen and Rubin, "Pretraumatic Stress Reactions in Soldiers Deployed to Afghanistan," 663–74, and Kaplan, "Is Climate-Related Pre-Traumatic Stress Syndrome a Real Condition?" 81–104.

CHAPTER 2: THE COST OF BEING MEXICANA

1. So far, I have avoided the complicated nature of how I identify (Latina/o/x/e) or the varied political interpretations of these labels. I am, as made clear in this chapter, a proud Mexicana. However, society labels me depending on its whims. The history of the use of "Latinos" is messy and often

racist. For this chapter, I move forward as a Mexicana but acknowledge the historical and scholarly work that allows me to do so, including Chavez, *The Latino Threat*; Gómez, *Inventing Latinos*; and Ramos, *Finding Latinx*.

2. Throughout this chapter, my exploration of research related to female identity, body image, and Mexican families included Abrego, *Sacrificing Families*; Andrews, *Undocumented Politics*; Galarte, *Trans Figurations*; González-López, *Erotic Journeys*; Longoria, *Living Beyond Borders*; Mojica Rodríguez, *For Brown Girls with Sharp Edges and Tender Hearts*; Oliveira, *Motherhood Across Borders*; Pitts, Ortega, and Medina, *Theories of the Flesh*; and Soto, *Girlhood in the Borderlands*.

3. See also Mojica Rodríguez, *For Brown Girls with Sharp Edges and Tender Hearts*.

4. For additional consideration around the role of skin color and colorism, see Cox, *Shapeshifters*; Crenshaw, "Demarginalizing the Intersection of Race and Sex"; Mojica Rodríguez, *For Brown Girls with Sharp Edges and Tender Hearts*; and Rios, *Punished*.

5. Work in this section on the exoticization of Black and brown bodies includes Bonello, *Narcas*; Davis, *The Other Side of Empathy*; Díaz, *Manufacturing Celebrity*; and Molina-Guzmán, *Dangerous Curves*.

6. See Bonello, *Narcas*.

7. Smith et al., *The National Intimate Partner and Sexual Violence Survey*.

8. Right to Be, *Cornell International Survey on Street Harassment*.

CHAPTER 3: THE COST OF LIVING IN A CARTEL WAR

1. Like the previous chapter, some of the resources consulted for the perspectives in this section include Bonello, *Narcas*; Grillo, *El Narco*; and Hernández, *Narcoland*. In addition, US contexts related to the impacts of global empire, strife, and commerce include Cole and Durham, *Figuring the Future*; Galeano, *Open Veins of Latin America*; Martinez, *The Injustice Never Leaves You*; Povinelli, *Between Gaia and Ground*; Povinelli, *Economies of Abandonment*; and Stuelke, *The Ruse of Repair*.

2. The complexities of narco politics meant it was convenient for someone like Amado Carrillo Fuentes to be assumed dead. His death was often spoken of with skepticism, the quotation marks around "dead" silent but understood.

3. This section of the chapter is informed by research on raising children in a socially toxic environment; see Garbarino, "Raising Children in a Socially Toxic Environment." It also includes work related to critical hope; see Duncan-Andrade, "Note to Educators," 181–94. Other work on trauma and intergenerational stress includes Haines, *The Politics of Trauma*; Menakem, *My Grandmother's Hands*; and Van der Kolk, *The Body Keeps the Score*.

4. For an overview of this data, see American Psychological Association, Task Force on the Sexualization of Girls, *Report of the APA Task Force on the Sexualization of Girls*.

5. For an overview of the tensions of the drug trade on both sides of the border, see Andreas, *Border Games*; Dilanian, "Drug War Allies U.S. and Mexico Aren't Getting Along"; and Office of Public Affairs, *Cooperation Between United States and Mexican Law Enforcement Leads to Significant Actions Against Transnational Drug Trafficking Organization*. Additionally, I read regionally for the relationship between the Mexican drug trade and where I lived in East Palo Alto, starting with descriptions and resources in Harris, *Palo Alto*, including *Palo Alto Online*, "Agents Target Heroin-Trafficking Ring, Arrest 12"; State of California Department of Justice, *Brown Announces Seizure of $7 Million Worth of Heroin in East Palo Alto*; and US Department of Justice National Drug Intelligence Center, *Northern California High Intensity Drug Trafficking Area Drug Market Analysis, 2011*.

6. US Department of Justice Drug Enforcement Administration, *National Drug Threat Assessment 2024*; News Nation, "Mexican Cartels Wiped Out Competition in US Fentanyl Market."

7. Again, these findings are shaped by Harris, *Palo Alto*; *Palo Alto Online*, "Agents Target Heroin-Trafficking Ring, Arrest 12"; and State of California Department of Justice, *Brown Announces Seizure of $7 Million Worth of Heroin in East Palo Alto*.

8. Lia's story doesn't end in tragedy. It isn't mine to tell, but I can tell you that she did leave Sinaloa and its "boring bitches" and boulevard massacres. She enrolled in school elsewhere, and eventually found full-time work in the US. As I write this, we both live in Los Angeles, and we try to see each other as often as life allows.

CHAPTER 4: THE COST OF BORDER CROSSING

1. Contemporary research theorizing the meaning of borders and transnationalism shaped much of this portion of this chapter. Work in this area includes Amaya, *Citizenship Excess*; Andreas, *Border Games*; Anzaldúa, *Borderlands*; Chouliaraki and Georgiou, *The Digital Border*; Degollado, Nuñez, and Armijo Romero, "Border Literacies," 456–64; Dick, *Words of Passage*; Dreby, *Divided by Borders*; Dyrness and Sepúlveda, *Border Thinking*; Hernandez, *Migra!*; Lowe, *The Intimacies of Four Continents*; Mignolo, *Local Histories/Global Designs*; Minian, *Undocumented Lives*; Ngai, *Impossible Subjects*; Rodríguez, *A Kiss Across the Ocean*; Schmidt Camacho, *Migrant Imaginaries*; Walia, *Border and Rule*; and Wynter, "Unsettling the Coloniality of Being/Power/Truth/Freedom," 257–337. In addition, research on the everyday life of undocumented communities was informed by Asad, *Engage and Evade*; Chavez, *Shadowed Lives*; García, *Legal Passing*; Gomberg-Muñoz, *Becoming Legal*; Gonzales, "Learning to Be Illegal," 602–19; and Sandoval-Strausz, *Barrio America*.

2. Graeber, "The Possibility of Political Pleasure."

3. Dunbar-Ortiz, *Not "A Nation of Immigrants."* Related work on empire and settler colonialism informing this chapter includes Hernández, *Bad Mexicans*; Mignolo and Walsh, *On Decoloniality*; paperson, *A Third University Is Possible*; Patel, "Pedagogies of Resistance and Survivance"; Rothstein, *The Color of Law*; and Tuck and Yang, "Decolonization Is Not a Metaphor," 1–40. In addition, we are reminded of the intentional relationship between Indigenous communities and the land they lived upon as described in Anderson, *Tending the Wild*.

4. Andreas, *Border Games*.

5. US Customs and Border Protection, *About CBP*.

6. García, *Legal Passing*.

7. Kotlowitz, "Our Town."

8. Rosa's work on raciolinguistics includes *Looking Like a Language, Sounding Like a Race*; see also Rosa and Flores, "Unsettling Race and Language," 621–47.

9. For critical perspectives related to English, bilingualism, and multilingualism, see García et al., "Rejecting Abyssal Thinking in the Language and Education of Racialized Bilinguals," 203–28; Lozano, *An American Language*; Pennycook, "English in the World/The World in English"; Rosa, *Looking Like a Language, Sounding Like a Race*; and Rosa and Flores, "Unsettling Race and Language."

10. For additional work from Martínez, see "Spanglish as Literacy Tool," 124–49, and "Reading the World in Spanglish," 276–88, and Palmer et al., "Reframing the Debate on Language Separation," 757–72.

11. Grosjean, *Life as a Bilingual*.

12. Research on the limitations of schooling opportunities for students labeled as English learners includes Altavilla et al., "Disentangling Educational Structural Inequality," 6, and Biernacki et al., "Long-Term English Learners' Mathematics Course Trajectories," 122–38.

13. Rojas, "Immigrants a Largely Hidden Segment of L.A.'s Homeless Population."

14. Cano, "El Retén Fronterizo."

15. American Civil Liberties Union, "Know Your Rights: 100 Mile Border Zone."

16. García, *Legal Passing*.

CHAPTER 5: THE COST OF EMPLOYMENT

1. The majority of this chapter details the three different kinds of jobs I've had while living in the United States. With much of this chapter focusing on my personal experiences, I want to be clear, here, that undocumented and immigrant labor in this country is tantamount to the operation of this country. Interrelated scholarship about undocumented labor for this chapter includes García, *Legal Passing*; Loza, *Defiant Braceros*; Lubrano, *Limbo*; and Rosales, *Fruteros*. Additional data about the general impact of undocu-

mented labor on the US economy includes Bonn and Schiff, *Immigrants and the Labor Market*; Gelatt, *Unblocking the U.S. Immigration System*; and US Bureau of Labor Statistics, *Job Openings and Labor Turnover Summary*.

2. For the months I worked at the radio station, I took home $300 each week.

3. This is a fundamental point *across* US history. See, for example, Abrego, *Sacrificing Families*; Loza, *Defiant Braceros*; Rosales, *Fruteros*; Sennett and Cobb, *The Hidden Injuries of Class*; Villa-Nicholas, *Data Borders*; and Villa-Nicholas, *Latinas on the Line*.

4. See Land, *Maid: Hard Work, Low Pay, and a Mother's Will to Survive*.

5. Hackman, "Arrests, Deportations of Immigrants Illegally in U.S. Increased in 2022"; Sacchetti, "Deportations of Migrants Rise to More Than 142,000 Under Biden."

6. See Carcamo, "He's Diabetic."

7. Gu et al., "The Role of Conspiracy Theories in the Spread of COVID-19 Across the United States," 3843; Mochkofsky, "The Latinx Community and Covid-Disinformation Campaigns."

8. Office of Governor Gavin Newsom, "Governor Gavin Newsom Issues Stay at Home Order."

CHAPTER 6: THE COST OF LOVE

1. There are several key studies on the role of relationships and immigration. The work that informed how I considered the context of my relationships as part of a broader backdrop of undocumented vulnerability included Abrego, *Sacrificing Families*; Dreby, *Everyday Illegal*; Enriquez, *Of Love and Papers*; García, *Legal Passing*; Lekas Miller, *Love Across Borders*; and Soto, *Girlhood in the Borderlands*. Additionally, my conceptions of love in this chapter are informed by Chapman, *The 5 Love Languages*; hooks, *All About Love*; and Nhất Hạnh, *How to Love*.

2. See Enriquez, "Gendering Illegality," 1153–71; Enriquez, "Multigenerational Punishment," 939–53; and Enriquez, *Of Love and Papers*.

3. Catalano, *Intimate Partner Violence, 1993–2010*; Leemis et al., *The National Intimate Partner and Sexual Violence Survey*.

4. Adams and Campbell, "Being Undocumented & Intimate Partner Violence (IPV)," 15–34; National Network to End Domestic Violence, *Immigration Policy*.

5. Enriquez, *Of Love and Papers*.

CHAPTER 7: THE COST OF FAITH

1. The research on Christianity and religion throughout this chapter is shaped by work critical of contemporary forms of US Christianity. Aside from Hoover, most of this research focuses on broad forms of marginalization, on the subjugation of Black people, and on the role of settler colonialism in shaping current Christianity; see Hoover, *Immigration and*

Faith. This scholarship includes Butler, *White Evangelical Racism*; Cone, *God of the Oppressed*; Du Mez, *Jesus and John Wayne*; House, "The Long History of How Jesus Came to Resemble a White European"; LaDuke, *Recovering the Sacred*; Mason, *Woke Church*; Morrison, *Be the Bridge*; Stewart, *Shoutin' in the Fire*; and Tisby, *The Color of Compromise*.

2. Genesis 12:1.

3. Butler, *White Evangelical Racism*.

4. Du Mez, *Jesus and John Wayne*.

5. Roberts et al., "God as a White Man," 1290–1315. For further writing about the identity and race of Jesus, see also BBC News, "What Did Jesus Really Look Like?"; Blum and Harvey, *The Color of Christ*; and House, "The Long History of How Jesus Came to Resemble a White European."

6. Tripodi, "Searching for Alternative Facts."

7. Tripodi, "Searching for Alternative Facts."

8. Stewart's articulation of Jesus committed to collective liberation is particularly relevant to this section of the chapter. See Stewart, *Shoutin' in the Fire.*

9. Because of the nature of my work with Elizabeth, I am using Blue Ribbon as a pseudonym for the organization I created.

CHAPTER 8: THE COST OF MENTAL HEALTH

1. This chapter focuses on specific forms of mental health struggles I've faced. They are broadly similar to some of the references shared in chapter 2 and additional work, including Clare, *Brilliant Imperfection*; Haines, *The Politics of Trauma*; Medford, *My Body and Other Crumbling Empires*; Menakem, *My Grandmother's Hands*; and Van der Kolk, *The Body Keeps the Score.*

2. *Romeo and Juliet* would be a fulfilling story of wholesome romance, if Shakespeare had only cut the final act or so.

3. See Artiga and Ubri, "Living in an Immigrant Family in America," and Garcini et al., "Undocumented Immigrants and Mental Health."

4. Fair, "FTC Says Online Counseling Service BetterHelp Pushed People into Handing Over Health Information."

5. "Complex post-traumatic stress disorder (Complex PTSD) is a disorder that may develop following exposure to an event or series of events of an extremely threatening or horrific nature, most commonly prolonged or repetitive events from which escape is difficult or impossible (e.g., torture, slavery, genocide campaigns, prolonged domestic violence, repeated childhood sexual or physical abuse)," according to *International Classification of Diseases for Mortality and Morbidity Statistics, 6B41 Complex Post Traumatic Stress Disorder,* World Health Organization, 2022. Importantly, as noted by Brewin ("Complex Post-Traumatic Stress Disorder," 145–52), C-PTSD was not formally adopted by the International Classification of Diseases and World Health Organization until 2022. In investigating histories of C-PTSD and codependency, I am struck by how forms of trauma

experienced by non-male populations have only in recent years started to receive formal scrutiny.

6. "'But when we sit together, close,' said Bernard, 'we melt into each other with phrases. We are edged with mist.'" Woolf, *The Waves*.

7. Leung, *Imagine Us, the Swarm*, 52.

CHAPTER 9: THE COST OF HEALTHCARE

1. Trump, *Presidential Proclamation on the Suspension of Entry of Immigrants Who Will Financially Burden the United States Healthcare System*.

2. Artiga and Ubri, "Living in an Immigrant Family in America." Updated and corroborating results include Pillai et al., *Health and Health Care Experiences of Immigrants*.

3. Stillman, "The Migrant Workers Who Follow Climate Disasters." Related, descriptive work on the impacts of the environment and labor on immigrant communities includes Cornejo Villavicencio, *The Undocumented Americans*, and Dunbar-Hester, *Oil Beach*.

4. Reporting on COVID and the immigrant community includes Angawi, "Immigrants, Health, and the Impact of COVID-19," 176; Đoàn et al., "Immigrant Communities and COVID-19," S224–31; and Immigration History Research Center, *Immigrants in Covid America*.

5. Related work on compassionate dialysis includes Gray, "Cruel Carousel," E778–779; Gupta and Fenves, "Dialysis in the Undocumented," 417–19; and Nguyen et al., "Association of Scheduled vs. Emergency-Only Dialysis with Health Outcomes and Costs in Undocumented Immigrants with End-Stage Renal Disease," 175.

6. Moriates, Arora, and Shah, *Understanding Value-Based Healthcare*.

7. Molina, *Fit to Be Citizens?*

8. Fuller, "Wildfires Blot Out Sun in the Bay Area."

9. Mathieu et al., "Coronavirus Pandemic (COVID-19)."

10. Giattino et al., "Excess Mortality During the Coronavirus Pandemic."

11. Serwer, "Greg Abbott Surrenders to the Coronavirus."

12. Serwer, "Greg Abbott Surrenders to the Coronavirus."

CHAPTER 10: THE COST OF DREAMING

1. Shukla and Suleyman, *The Good Immigrant*.

2. Hersey, *Rest Is Resistance*.

3. Yosso, "Whose Culture Has Capital?" 69–91. Additionally, related work around critical race theory for this section includes Aguilar, "Undocumented Critical Theory," 152–60, and Yosso, *Critical Race Counterstories Along the Chicana/Chicano Educational Pipeline*.

4. Here Yosso takes Pierre Bourdieu's framing of cultural and social capital as a starting place for her analysis. See Bourdieu, Passeron, and Bourdieu, *Reproduction in Education, Society and Culture*.

5. Yosso, "Whose Culture Has Capital?" 77.
6. Yosso, "Whose Culture Has Capital?" 77–78.
7. Flores, "Writing the Threads of Our Lives," 209–23; Flores, "Somos Escritoras/We Are Writers," 1730–56.
8. While this chapter centers on my purpose as a storyteller, this section frames *all* human beings as natural storytellers. Robin Kimmerer reminds us that this is a unique contribution we humans make to the broader more-than-human ecosystem we live within; see Kimmerer, *Braiding Sweetgrass.*
9. Benjamin, *Viral Justice*; Butler, *Parable of the Sower*; Escobar, *Designs for the Pluriverse*; Kelley, *Freedom Dreams.* Additionally, this section is shaped by the work of coauthor Antero Garcia's scholarship around speculative education and related research in the field of education. See Garcia and Mirra, "Other Suns," 1–20; Garcia and Mirra, *Speculative Pedagogies*; and Mirra and Garcia, "Guns, Schools, and Democracy," 345–80.
10. Davis, "Lecture at Southern Illinois University Carbondale."

CONCLUSION
1. This opening reflection was adapted from an essay I first published on *La Cuenta.* Dick, "Reflections from the Emergency Room."
2. Du Bois, *Souls of Black Folk.*
3. US Government Accountability Office, *Southwest Border.*
4. USA Facts, *Government Immigration and Border Security Spending*; US Customs and Border Protection, *About CBP.*
5. Rondinelli et al., *AMA Guides to the Evaluation of Permanent Impairment, 2023*; World Health Organization, *International Classification of Functioning, Disability and Health.*
6. Rondinelli et al., *AMA Guides to the Evaluation of Permanent Impairment, 2023*," 1.
7. Rondinelli et al., *AMA Guides to the Evaluation of Permanent Impairment, 2023*," 27.
8. Anagnostis et al., "The Pain Disability Questionnaire," 2290–2302.
9. Chetty et al., "$320,000 Kindergarten Teachers," 22–25; Chetty et al., "How Does Your Kindergarten Classroom Affect Your Earnings?" 1593–1660.
10. According to the US Bureau of Labor, the mean salary for attorneys in the US in 2023 was $163,770.
11. Although this figure doesn't include the stressors related to experiencing homelessness, it is based on the cost of twelve months of average apartment rentals in Fulton County, GA.
12. This sum for workplace sexual harassment was based on persistence, severity, and processes for treating a psychological claim through workers' comp. It does not include harassment at home or in nonwork settings.

13. This figure does not include apportionment of prior conditions, understanding that multiple sources lead to C-PTSD.
14. This is based solely on estimates for psychological insurance claims and temporary treatment.
15. This figure includes permanent impairment and consideration of future medical care, including medication and treatment.

REFERENCES

Abrego, Leisy J. *Sacrificing Families: Navigating Laws, Labor, and Love Across Borders*. Stanford, CA: Stanford University Press, 2014.

Abrego, Leisy J., and Genevieve Negrón-Gonzales, eds. *We Are Not Dreamers: Undocumented Scholars Theorize Undocumented Life in the United States*. Durham, NC: Duke University Press, 2020.

Adams, Margaret E., and Jacquelyn Campbell. "Being Undocumented & Intimate Partner Violence (IPV): Multiple Vulnerabilities Through the Lens of Feminist Intersectionality." *Women's Health and Urban Life* 11, no. 1 (2012): 15–34. https://tspace.library.utoronto.ca/handle/1807/32411.

Aguilar, Carlos. "Undocumented Critical Theory." *Cultural Studies↔Critical Methodologies* 19, no. 3 (June 2019): 152–60. https://doi.org/10.1177/1532708618817911.

Agustin, Rafael. *Illegally Yours: A Memoir*. 1st ed. New York: Grand Central Publishing, 2022.

Altavilla, J. M., P. J. Biernacki, G. Solano-Flores, G. Valdés, and R. M. Garcia-Fontana. "Disentangling Educational Structural Inequality: Spanning Tree of Mathematics Course-Taking Trajectories in a High School." *Educational Measurement: Issues and Practice* 39, no. 1 (2020): 6.

Amaya, Hector. *Citizenship Excess: Latinas/Os, Media, and the Nation*. Critical Cultural Communication. New York: New York University Press, 2013.

American Civil Liberties Union. "Know Your Rights: 100 Mile Border Zone," 2024. https://www.aclu.org/know-your-rights/border-zone.

American Psychological Association, Task Force on the Sexualization of Girls. *Report of the APA Task Force on the Sexualization of Girls*, 2007.

Anagnostis, Christopher, Robert J. Gatchel, and Tom G. Mayer. "The Pain Disability Questionnaire: A New Psychometrically Sound Measure for Chronic Musculoskeletal Disorders." *Spine* 29, no. 20 (2004): 2290–2302. https://doi.org/10.1097/01.brs.0000142221.88111.0f.

Anderson, Kat. *Tending the Wild: Native American Knowledge and the Management of California's Natural Resources*. Berkeley: University of California Press, 2005.

Andreas, Peter. *Border Games: The Politics of Policing the U.S.-Mexico Divide.* 3rd ed. Ithaca, NY: Cornell University Press, 2022.

Andrews, Abigail. *Undocumented Politics: Place, Gender, and the Pathways of Mexican Migrants.* Oakland: University of California Press, 2018.

Angawi, Khadijah. "Immigrants, Health, and the Impact of COVID-19: A Narrative Review." *F1000Research* 12 (November 20, 2023): 176. https://doi .org/10.12688/f1000research.130085.2.

Anzaldúa, Gloria. *Borderlands: La Frontera: The New Mestiza.* 4th ed. San Francisco: Aunt Lute Books, 2012.

Arce, Julissa. *My (Underground) American Dream: My True Story as an Undocumented Immigrant Who Became a Wall Street Executive.* 1st ed. New York: Center Street, 2016.

————. *You Sound Like a White Girl: The Case for Rejecting Assimilation.* 1st Flatiron Books paperback edition. New York: Flatiron Books, 2023.

Artiga, Samantha, and Petry Ubri. "Living in an Immigrant Family in America: How Fear and Toxic Stress Are Affecting Daily Life, Well-Being & Health." Menlo Park, CA: Kaiser Family Foundation (2017).

Asad, Asad L. *Engage and Evade: How Latino Immigrant Families Manage Surveillance in Everyday Life.* Princeton, NJ: Princeton University Press, 2023.

BBC News. "What Did Jesus Really Look Like?" December 24, 2015, sec. Magazine. https://www.bbc.com/news/magazine-35120965.

Benjamin, Ruha. *Viral Justice: How We Grow the World We Want.* Princeton, NJ: Princeton University Press, 2022.

Berntsen, Dorthe, and David C. Rubin. "Pretraumatic Stress Reactions in Soldiers Deployed to Afghanistan." *Clinical Psychological Science* 3, no. 5 (2015): 663–74. https://doi.org/10.1177/2167702614551766.

Biernacki, Paulina J., Jennifer Altavilla, Klint Kanopka, Hsiaolin Hsieh, and Guillermo Solano-Flores. "Long-Term English Learners' Mathematics Course Trajectories: Downstream Consequences of Early Remediation on College Preparation." *International Multilingual Research Journal* 17, no. 2 (April 3, 2023): 122–38. https://doi.org/10.1080/19313152.2022.2137910.

Blau, Francine D., and Christopher D. Mackie, eds. *The Economic and Fiscal Consequences of Immigration.* Washington, DC: National Academies Press, 2017.

Blum, Edward J., and Paul Harvey. *The Color of Christ: The Son of God & the Saga of Race in America.* Chapel Hill: University of North Carolina Press, 2012.

Bonello, Deborah. *Narcas: The Secret Rise of Women in Latin America's Cartels.* Boston: Beacon Press, 2023.

Bonn, Sarah and Eric Schiff. *Immigrants and the Labor Market.* Public Policy Institute of California, 2011, https://www.ppic.org/wp-content/uploads/ content/pubs/jtf/JTF_ImmigrantsLaborJTF.pdf.

Bourdieu, Pierre, and Jean-Claude Passeron. *Reproduction in Education, Society and Culture.* 2nd ed. Reprinted. Theory, Culture & Society. London: Sage, 2000.

Brewin, Chris R. "Complex Post-Traumatic Stress Disorder: A New Diagnosis in ICD-11." *BJPsych Advances* 26, no. 3 (May 2020): 145–52. https://doi .org/10.1192/bja.2019.48.

Brown, Tamara Mose, and Joanna Dreby, eds. *Family and Work in Everyday Ethnography*. Philadelphia: Temple University Press, 2013.

Butler, Anthea D. *White Evangelical Racism: The Politics of Morality in America*. Chapel Hill: University of North Carolina Press, 2021.

Butler, Octavia E. *Parable of the Sower*. New York: Grand Central Publishing, 2019.

Cano, José Luis, Jr. "El Retén Fronterizo: Un Foto Ensayo/The Border Checkpoint: A Photo Essay." *Latinx Talk*. https://latinxtalk.org/2023/03/13/el -reten-fronterizo-un-foto-ensayo-the-border-checkpoint-a-photo-essay/.

Caplan, Bryan Douglas, and Zach Weinersmith. *Open Borders: The Science and Ethics of Immigration*. New York: First Second, 2019.

Carcamo, Cindy. "He's Diabetic. He Works a High-Risk Job. But to Pay Rent, He Has No Choice." *Los Angeles Times,* May 22, 2020. https://www.latimes. com/california/story/2020-05-22/coronavirus-immigrants-worker-migrant -paycheck-health-choice.

Catalano, Shannan. *Intimate Partner Violence, 1993–2010*. Bureau of Justice Statistics, 2015. https://bjs.ojp.gov/content/pub/pdf/ipv9310.pdf.

Center for Social Innovation. *The Health Needs of Undocumented Older Adults: A View on Health Status, Access to Care, and Barriers*. UC Riverside, 2019. https://socialinnovation.ucr.edu/health-needs-undocumented-older-adults -view-health-status-access-care-and-barriers.

Chapman, Gary D. *The 5 Love Languages: The Secret to Love That Lasts*. Chicago: Northfield Publishing, 2015.

Chavez, Leo R. *Shadowed Lives: Undocumented Immigrants in American Society*. Case Studies in Cultural Anthropology. Fort Worth, TX: Harcourt Brace College Publishers, 1998.

———. *The Latino Threat: Constructing Immigrants, Citizens, and the Nation*. 2nd ed. Stanford, CA: Stanford University Press, 2013.

Chee, Alexander. *How to Write an Autobiographical Novel: Essays*. Boston: Houghton Mifflin Harcourt, 2018.

Chetty, Raj, et al. "$320,000 Kindergarten Teachers." *Phi Delta Kappan* 92, no. 3 (2010): 22–25. https://doi.org/10.1177/003172171009200306.

———. "How Does Your Kindergarten Classroom Affect Your Earnings? Evidence from Project Star." *Quarterly Journal of Economics* 126, no. 4 (2011): 1593–1660. https://doi.org/10.1093/qje/qjr041.

Chouliaraki, Lilie, and Myria Georgiou. *The Digital Border: Migration, Technology, Power*. Critical Cultural Communication. New York: New York University Press, 2022.

Clare, Eli. *Brilliant Imperfection: Grappling with Cure*. Durham, NC: Duke University Press, 2017.

Colato Laînez, René. "The Gift of Telling Our Stories." *Language Arts* 99, no. 5 (2022): 363–65. https://doi.org/10.58680/la202231797.

Cole, Jennifer, and Deborah Lynn Durham, eds. *Figuring the Future: Globalization and the Temporalities of Children and Youth.* 1st ed. School for Advanced Research Advanced Seminar Series. Santa Fe, NM: School for Advanced Research Press, 2008.

Collins, Patricia Hill. *Intersectionality as Critical Social Theory.* Durham, NC: Duke University Press, 2019.

Combahee River Collective. *The Combahee River Collective Statement*, 1978.

Cone, James H. *God of the Oppressed.* Rev. ed. Maryknoll, NY: Orbis Books, 1997.

Cornejo Villavicencio, Karla. *The Undocumented Americans.* One World Trade paperback ed. New York: One World, 2021.

Cox, Aimee Meredith. *Shapeshifters: Black Girls and the Choreography of Citizenship.* Durham, NC: Duke University Press, 2015.

Crenshaw, Kimberlé. "Demarginalizing the Intersection of Race and Sex: A Black Feminist Critique of Antidiscrimination Doctrine, Feminist Theory and Antiracist Politics." In *Feminist Legal Theories*, ed. Karen Maschke. New York: Routledge, 2013, pp. 23–51.

Cruz, Cindy. "Toward an Epistemology of a Brown Body." *International Journal of Qualitative Studies in Education* 14, no. 5 (September 2001): 657–69. https://doi.org/10.1080/09518390110059874.

Davis, Angela. "Lecture at Southern Illinois University Carbondale." 2014, https://www.youtube.com/watch?v=6s8QCucFADc.

Davis, Jade E. *The Other Side of Empathy.* Durham, NC: Duke University Press, 2023.

Degollado, Enrique David, Idalia Nuñez, and Minea Armijo Romero. "Border Literacies: A Critical Literacy Framework from Nepantla." In *The Handbook of Critical Literacies*, ed. Jessica Zacher Pandya et al. New York: Routledge, 2021, pp. 456–64.

de los Ríos, Cati V. "'Los Músicos': Mexican Corridos, the Aural Border, and the Evocative Musical Renderings of Transnational Youth." *Harvard Educational Review* 89, no. 2 (June 1, 2019): 177–200. https://doi.org/10.17763/1943-5045-89.2.177.

———. "Toward a *Corridista* Consciousness: Learning from One Transnational Youth's Critical Reading, Writing, and Performance of Mexican Corridos." *Reading Research Quarterly* 53, no. 4 (October 2018): 455–71. https://doi.org/10.1002/rrq.210.

de los Ríos, Cati, and Leigh Patel. "Positions, Positionality, and Relationality in Educational Research." *International Journal of Qualitative Studies in Education* (October 14, 2023): 1–12. https://doi.org/10.1080/09518398.2023.2268036.

Desmond, Matthew. *Evicted: Poverty and Profit in the American City.* 1st paperback ed. New York: B\D\W\Y Broadway Books, 2017.

Díaz, Vanessa. *Manufacturing Celebrity: Latino Paparazzi and Women Report-ers in Hollywood*. Durham, NC: Duke University Press, 2020.

Dick, Alix. "Reflections from the Emergency Room." *La Cuenta*, 2023. https://lacuenta.substack.com/p/reflections-from-the-emergency-room.

Dick, Hilary Parsons. *Words of Passage: National Longing and the Imagined Lives of Mexican Migrants*. 1st ed. Austin: University of Texas Press, 2018.

Dilanian, Ken. "Drug War Allies U.S. and Mexico Aren't Getting Along. What Happened?" NBC News, March 17, 2023. https://www.nbcnews.com/politics/national-security/no-cooperation-us-mexico-drug-war-rcna75093.

Đoàn, Lan N., Stella K. Chong, Supriya Misra, Simona C. Kwon, and Stella S. Yi. "Immigrant Communities and COVID-19: Strengthening the Public Health Response." *American Journal of Public Health* 111, no. S3 (October 2021): S224–31. https://doi.org/10.2105/AJPH.2021.306433.

Dreby, Joanna. *Divided by Borders: Mexican Migrants and Their Children*. Berkeley: University of California Press, 2010.

———. *Everyday Illegal: When Policies Undermine Immigrant Families*. Oakland: University of California Press, 2015.

Du Bois, W. E. B. *Souls of Black Folk*. New York: Modern World Library, 1903.

Du Mez, Kristin Kobes. *Jesus and John Wayne: How White Evangelicals Corrupted a Faith and Fractured a Nation*. New York: Liveright Publishing, 2021.

Dunbar-Hester, Christina. *Oil Beach: How Toxic Infrastructure Threatens Life in the Ports of Los Angeles and Beyond*. Chicago: University of Chicago Press, 2023.

Dunbar-Ortiz, Roxanne. *Not "A Nation of Immigrants": Settler Colonialism, White Supremacy, and a History of Erasure and Exclusion*. Boston: Beacon Press, 2021.

Duncan-Andrade, Jeffrey. "Note to Educators: Hope Required When Growing Roses in Concrete." *Harvard Educational Review* 79, no. 2 (2009): 181–94. https://doi.org/10.17763/haer.79.2.nu3436017730384w.

Dyrness, Andrea. *Mothers United: An Immigrant Struggle for Socially Just Education*. Minneapolis: University of Minnesota Press, 2011.

Dyrness, Andrea, and Enrique Sepúlveda. *Border Thinking: Latinx Youth Decolonizing Citizenship*. Minneapolis: University of Minnesota Press, 2020.

Emerson, Robert M., Rachel I. Fretz, and Linda L. Shaw. *Writing Ethnographic Fieldnotes*. 2nd ed. Chicago Guides to Writing, Editing, and Publishing. Chicago: University of Chicago Press, 2011.

Enriquez, Laura E. "Gendering Illegality: Undocumented Young Adults' Negotiation of the Family Formation Process." *American Behavioral Scientist* 61, no. 10 (September 2017): 1153–71. https://doi.org/10.1177/0002764217732103.

———. "Multigenerational Punishment: Shared Experiences of Undocumented Immigration Status Within Mixed-Status Families." *Journal of Marriage and Family* 77, no. 4 (August 2015): 939–53. https://doi.org/10.1111/jomf.12196.

————. *Of Love and Papers: How Immigration Policy Affects Romance and Family*. Oakland: University of California Press, 2020.

Enriquez, Laura E., Alberto Eduardo Morales, Victoria E. Rodriguez, Karina Chavarria, and Annie Ro. "Mental Health and COVID-19 Pandemic Stressors Among Latina/o/x College Students with Varying Self and Parental Immigration Status." *Journal of Racial and Ethnic Health Disparities* 10, no. 1 (February 2023): 282–95. https://doi.org/10.1007/s40615-021-01218-x.

Escobar, Arturo. *Designs for the Pluriverse: Radical Interdependence, Autonomy, and the Making of Worlds*. New Ecologies for the Twenty-First Century. Durham, NC: Duke University Press, 2018.

Escudero, Kevin. *Organizing While Undocumented: Immigrant Youth's Political Activism under the Law*. Latina-o Sociology Series. New York: New York University Press, 2020.

Espino, Michelle M. "Positionality as Prologue: Encountering the Self on the Journey to Transforming Latina/o/x Educational Inequities." *Teachers College Record: The Voice of Scholarship in Education* 120, no. 14 (December 2018): 1–16. https://doi.org/10.1177/016146811812001413.

Fabian, Johannes. *Time and the Other: How Anthropology Makes Its Object*. New York: Columbia University Press, 2002.

Fair, Lesley. "FTC Says Online Counseling Service BetterHelp Pushed People into Handing Over Health Information—and Broke Its Privacy Promises." Federal Trade Commission, 2023. https://www.ftc.gov/business-guidance/blog/2023/03/ftc-says-online-counseling-service-betterhelp-pushed-people-handing-over-health-information-broke.

Febos, Melissa. *Body Work: The Radical Power of Personal Narrative*. New York: Catapult, 2022.

Fierros, Cindy O., and Dolores Delgado Bernal. "Vamos a platicar: The Contours of Pláticas as Chicana/Latina Feminist Methodology." *Chicana/Latina Studies* (2016): 98–121.

Flores, Tracey T. "Somos Escritoras/We Are Writers: Latina Mothers and Daughters Writing and Sharing 'En Convivencia.'" *Urban Education* 57, no. 10 (December 2022): 1730–56. https://doi.org/10.1177/00420859211003920.

————. "Writing the Threads of Our Lives: Stories from a Bilingual Family Writing Project." In *Culturally Sustaining and Revitalizing Pedagogies: Language, Culture, and Power*, ed. Cathy Coulter and Margarita Jimenez-Silva. Leeds, UK: Emerald Publishing, 2017, pp. 209–23.

Flores Morales, Josefina. "Aging and Undocumented: The Sociology of Aging Meets Immigration Status." *Sociology Compass* 15, no. 4 (2021): e12859. https://doi.org/10.1111/soc4.12859.

Fuller, Thomas. "Wildfires Blot Out Sun in the Bay Area." *New York Times*, September 9, 2020. https://www.nytimes.com/2020/09/09/us/pictures-photos-california-fires.html.

Galarte, Francisco J. *Brown Trans Figurations: Rethinking Race, Gender, and Sexuality in Chicanx-Latinx Studies.* 1st ed. Latinx. Austin: University of Texas Press, 2021.

Galeano, Eduardo. *Open Veins of Latin America: Five Centuries of the Pillage of a Continent.* 25th anniversary ed. New York: Monthly Review Press, 1997.

Garbarino, James. "Raising Children in a Socially Toxic Environment." *Family Matters* 50 (1998).

García, Angela S. *Legal Passing: Navigating Undocumented Life and Local Immigration Law.* Oakland: University of California Press, 2019.

Garcia, Antero. *All Through the Town: The School Bus as Educational Technology.* Minneapolis: University of Minnesota Press, 2023.

———. *Good Reception: Teens, Teachers, and Mobile Media in a Los Angeles High School.* John D. and Catherine T. MacArthur Foundation Series on Digital Media and Learning. Cambridge, MA: MIT Press, 2017.

———. "When Seeing Is Not Enough: Hearing for Truth in an Era of Disinformation and Pandemic." *Teachers College Record*, 2021. https://www .tcrecord.org/Content.asp?ContentId=23884.

Garcia, Antero, and Nicole Mirra. "Other Suns: Designing for Racial Equity Through Speculative Education." *Journal of the Learning Sciences* 32, no. 1 (2023): 1–20.

Garcia, Antero, and Nicole Mirra, eds. *Speculative Pedagogies: Designing Equitable Educational Futures.* New York: Teachers College Press, 2023.

Garcia, Antero, Aaron Guggenheim, Kristina Stamatis, and Bridget Dalton. "Glimmers of Care: Attending to the Affective Everyday in Ninth-Grade Literacy Classrooms." *Reading Research Quarterly* 56, no. 2 (2021): 337–54.

García, Ofelia, et al. "Rejecting Abyssal Thinking in the Language and Education of Racialized Bilinguals: A Manifesto." *Critical Inquiry in Language Studies* 18, no. 3 (2021): 203–28.

Garcini, Luz M., et al. "Undocumented Immigrants and Mental Health: A Systematic Review of Recent Methodology and Findings in the United States." *Journal of Migration and Health* 4 (2021): 100058. https://doi.org/10.1016 /j.jmh.2021.100058.

Gelatt, Julia. *Unblocking the U.S. Immigration System: Executive Actions to Facilitate the Migration of Needed Workers.* Migration Policy Institute, 2023. https://www.migrationpolicy.org/sites/default/files/publications/mpi -global-skills-us-executive-actions-2023_final.pdf.

Giattino, Charlie, et al. "Excess Mortality During the Coronavirus Pandemic (COVID-19)." *Our World Date* (2021).

Glaser, Barney G., and Anselm L. Strauss. *Awareness of Dying.* New Brunswick, NJ: Aldine Transaction, 2005.

Gomberg-Muñoz, Ruth. *Becoming Legal: Immigration Law and Mixed-Status Families.* New York: Oxford University Press, 2017.

Gómez, Laura E. *Inventing Latinos: A New Story of American Racism*. Paperback ed. New York: New Press, 2022.

Gonzales, Roberto G. "Learning to Be Illegal: Undocumented Youth and Shifting Legal Contexts in the Transition to Adulthood." *American Sociological Review* 76, no. 4 (August 2011): 602–19. https://doi.org/10.1177/0003122411411901.

González-López, Gloria. *Erotic Journeys: Mexican Immigrants and Their Sex Lives*. Nachdr. Berkeley: University of California Press, 2010.

Graeber, David. "The Possibility of Political Pleasure: David Graeber at TEDxWhitechapel." 2013. https://www.youtube.com/watch?v=5eR_95slEFw.

Grande, Reyna, and Sonia Guiñansaca, eds. *Somewhere We Are Human: Authentic Voices on Migration, Survival, and New Beginnings*. 1st HarperVia ed. New York: HarperVia, 2022.

Gray, Nathan A. "Cruel Carousel: The Grim Grind of 'Compassionate' Dialysis." *AMA Journal of Ethics* 20, no. 8 (2018): E778–79. https://doi.org/10.1001/amajethics.2018.778.

Greenhouse, Carol J. *A Moment's Notice: Time Politics Across Cultures*. Ithaca, NY: Cornell University Press, 1996.

Grillo, Ioan. *El Narco: Inside Mexico's Criminal Insurgency*. Paperback ed. New York: Bloomsbury Press, 2012.

Grosjean, François. *Life as a Bilingual: Knowing and Using Two or More Languages*. Cambridge: Cambridge University Press, 2021.

Gu, Fu, et al. "The Role of Conspiracy Theories in the Spread of COVID-19 Across the United States." *International Journal of Environmental Research and Public Health* 18, no. 7 (2021): 3843. https://doi.org/10.3390/ijerph18073843.

Guajardo, Francisco, and Miguel Guajardo. "The Power of Plática." *Reflections: A Journal of Public Rhetoric, Civic Writing, and Service Learning* 13 (2013): 159.

Gupta, S., and A. Z. Fenves. "Dialysis in the Undocumented: The Past, the Present, and What Lies Ahead." *Seminars in Dialysis* 30, no. 5 (2017): 417–19. https://doi.org/10.1111/sdi.12622.

Gutiérrez, Kris D., et al. "Replacing Representation with Imagination: Finding Ingenuity in Everyday Practices." *Review of Research in Education* 41, no. 1 (2017): 30–60. https://doi.org/10.3102/0091732X16687523.

Hackman, Michelle. "Arrests, Deportations of Immigrants Illegally in U.S. Increased in 2022." *Wall Street Journal*, December 30, 2022. https://www.wsj.com/us-news/arrests-deportations-of-immigrants-in-u-s-illegally-increased-in-2022-11672419628.

Haines, Staci K. *The Politics of Trauma: Somatics, Healing, and Social Justice*. Berkeley, CA: North Atlantic Books, 2019.

Hammersley, Martyn, and Paul Atkinson. *Ethnography: Principles in Practice*. 3rd ed. London: Routledge, 2007.

Hannegan-Martinez, Sharim. "Pláticas as a Methodological Praxis of Love." *International Journal of Qualitative Studies in Education* 36, no. 9 (2023): 1702–13. https://doi.org/10.1080/09518398.2023.2181437.

Harris, Malcolm. *Palo Alto: A History of California, Capitalism, and the World.* 1st ed. New York: Little, Brown, 2023.

Hernández, Anabel. *Narcoland: The Mexican Drug Lords and Their Godfathers.* Updated paperback ed. London: Verso, 2013.

Hernández, Kelly Lytle. *Bad Mexicans: Race, Empire, and Revolution in the Borderlands.* 1st ed. New York: W. W. Norton & Company, 2022.

———. *Migra! A History of the U.S. Border Patrol.* American Crossroads 29. Berkeley: University of California Press, 2010.

Hernández, María G., ed. *Frameworks and Ethics for Research with Immigrants.* New Directions for Child and Adolescent Development 141. San Francisco, CA: Jossey-Bass, 2013.

Hersey, Tricia. *Rest Is Resistance: A Manifesto.* 1st ed. New York: Little, Brown Spark, 2022.

hooks, bell. *All About Love: New Visions.* 1st William Morrow paperback ed. New York: William Morrow, 2018.

Hoover, Brett C. *Immigration and Faith: Cultural, Biblical, and Theological Narratives.* Mahwah, NJ: Paulist Press, 2021.

House, Anna Swartwood. "The Long History of How Jesus Came to Resemble a White European." *The Conversation,* July 17, 2020. http://theconversation.com/the-long-history-of-how-jesus-came-to-resemble-a-white-european-142130.

Huerta, Monica. *Magical Habits.* Durham, NC: Duke University Press, 2021.

Humphreys, Lee. *The Qualified Self: Social Media and the Accounting of Everyday Life.* Cambridge, MA: MIT Press, 2018.

Immigration History Research Center. *Immigrants in Covid America.* Regents of the University of Minnesota, 2023. https://immigrantcovid.umn.edu/home.

International Classification of Diseases for Mortality and Morbidity Statistics. *6B41 Complex Post Traumatic Stress Disorder.* World Health Organization, 2022. https://icd.who.int/browse11/l-m/en#/http://id.who.int/icd/entity/585833559.

Kaplan, E. Ann. "Is Climate-Related Pre-Traumatic Stress Syndrome a Real Condition?" *American Imago* 77, no. 1 (2020): 81–104. https://doi.org/10.1353/aim.2020.0004.

Kelley, Robin D. G. *Freedom Dreams: The Black Radical Imagination.* Twentieth anniversary. Revised and expanded ed. Boston: Beacon Press, 2022.

Kimmerer, Robin Wall. *Braiding Sweetgrass: Indigenous Wisdom, Scientific Knowledge and the Teachings of Plants.* 1st paperback ed. Minneapolis: Milkweed Editions, 2013.

Kinloch, Valerie, and Timothy San Pedro. "The Space Between Listening and Storying: Foundations for Projects in Humanization." *Humanizing*

Research: Decolonizing Qualitative Inquiry with Youth and Communities 21 (2014): 42.

Kotlowitz, Alex. "Our Town." *New York Times*, August 5, 2007. https://www.nytimes.com/2007/08/05/magazine/05Immigration-t.html.

LaDuke, Winona. *Recovering the Sacred: The Power of Naming and Claiming*. Chicago: Haymarket Books, 2016.

Land, Stephanie. *Maid: Hard Work, Low Pay, and a Mother's Will to Survive*. New York: Hachette, 2019.

Leemis, Ruth W., et al. *The National Intimate Partner and Sexual Violence Survey: 2016/2017 Report on Intimate Partner Violence*, 2022.

Le Guin, Ursula K. "National Book Foundation Medal: Ursula's Acceptance Speech," 2014. https://www.ursulakleguin.com/nbf-medal.

Lekas Miller, Anna. *Love Across Borders: Passports, Papers, and Romance in a Divided World*. Chapel Hill, NC: Algonquin Books of Chapel Hill, 2023.

León Portilla, Miguel, ed. *The Broken Spears: The Aztec Account of the Conquest of Mexico*. Expanded and updated ed. Boston: Beacon Press, 2007.

Leung, Muriel. *Imagine Us, the Swarm*. New York: Nightboat Books, 2021.

Longoria, Margarita, ed. *Living Beyond Borders: Growing Up Mexican in America*. New York: Philomel Books, 2021.

Lorde, Audre. *Sister Outsider: Essays and Speeches*. Berkeley, CA: Crossing Press, c2007.

Lowe, Lisa. *The Intimacies of Four Continents*. Durham, NC: Duke University Press, 2015.

Loza, Mireya. *Defiant Braceros: How Migrant Workers Fought for Racial, Sexual, and Political Freedom*. Chapel Hill: University of North Carolina Press, 2016.

Lozano, Rosina. *An American Language: The History of Spanish in the United States*. American Crossroads 49. Oakland: University of California Press, 2018.

Lubrano, Alfred. *Limbo: Blue-Collar Roots, White-Collar Dreams*. Hoboken, NJ: Wiley, 2004.

Martinez, Monica Muñoz. *The Injustice Never Leaves You: Anti-Mexican Violence in Texas*. Cambridge, MA: Harvard University Press, 2018.

Martínez, Ramón Antonio. "Reading the World in Spanglish: Hybrid Language Practices and Ideological Contestation in a Sixth-Grade English Language Arts Classroom." *Linguistics and Education* 24, no. 3 (2013): 276–88.

———. "Spanglish as Literacy Tool: Toward an Understanding of the Potential Role of Spanish-English Code-Switching in the Development of Academic Literacy." *Research in the Teaching of English* 45, no. 2 (2010): 124–49.

Mason, Eric. *Woke Church: An Urgent Call for Christians in America to Confront Racism and Injustice*. Chicago: Moody Publishers, 2018.

Mathieu, Edouard, et al. "Coronavirus Pandemic (COVID-19)." *Our World in Data*, 2020.

Medford, Lyndsey. *My Body and Other Crumbling Empires: Lessons for Healing in a World That Is Sick*. Minneapolis: Broadleaf Books, 2023.

Menakem, Resmaa. *My Grandmother's Hands: Racialized Trauma and the Pathway to Mending Our Hearts and Bodies*. Las Vegas: Central Recovery Press, 2017.

Merrell, Melissa. *The Impact of Unauthorized Immigrants on the Budgets of State and Local Governments*. US Congress, Congressional Budget Office, 2007.

Mignolo, Walter. *Local Histories/Global Designs: Coloniality, Subaltern Knowledges, and Border Thinking*. Princeton Studies in Culture/Power/History. Princeton, NJ: Princeton University Press, 2012.

Mignolo, Walter, and Catherine E. Walsh. *On Decoloniality: Concepts, Analytics, Praxis*. On Decoloniality. Durham, NC: Duke University Press, 2018.

Migration Policy Institute. *Profile of the Unauthorized Population: United States*, 2019. https://www.migrationpolicy.org/data/unauthorized-immigrant-population/state/US.

Minian, Ana Raquel. *Undocumented Lives: The Untold Story of Mexican Migration*. Cambridge, MA: Harvard University Press, 2020.

Mirra, Nicole, and Antero Garcia. "Guns, Schools, and Democracy: Adolescents Imagining Social Futures Through Speculative Civic Literacies." *American Educational Research Journal* 59, no. 2 (2022): 345–80.

Mirra, Nicole, Antero Garcia, and Ernest Morrell. *Doing Youth Participatory Action Research: Transforming Inquiry with Researchers, Educators, and Students*. Language, Culture, and Teaching. New York: Routledge, 2016.

Mochkofsky, Graciela. "The Latinx Community and Covid-Disinformation Campaigns." *New Yorker*, January 14, 2022. https://www.newyorker.com/news/daily-comment/the-latinx-community-and-covid-disinformation-campaigns.

Mojica Rodríguez, Prisca Dorcas. *For Brown Girls with Sharp Edges and Tender Hearts: A Love Letter to Women of Color*. 1st trade paperback ed. New York: Seal Press, 2022.

Molina, Natalia. *Fit to Be Citizens? Public Health and Race in Los Angeles, 1879–1939*. American Crossroads 20. Berkeley: University of California Press, 2006.

Molina-Guzmán, Isabel. *Dangerous Curves: Latina Bodies in the Media.* Critical Cultural Communication. New York: New York University Press, 2010.

Moriates, Christopher, Vineet Arora, and Neel Shah, eds. *Understanding Value-Based Healthcare*. New York: McGraw-Hill Education, 2015.

Morrison, LaTasha. *Be the Bridge: Pursuing God's Heart for Racial Reconciliation*. 1st ed. Colorado Springs, CO: WaterBrook, 2019.

National Network to End Domestic Violence, *Immigration Policy*, 2017. https://nnedv.org/content/immigration-policy/.

New International Version. (2011). BibleGateway. www.biblegateway.com/passage/?search=Luke%2010%3A25–37&version=NIV.

News Nation. "Mexican Cartels Wiped out Competition in US Fentanyl Market: DEA." May 20, 2024. https://www.newsnationnow.com/us-news /immigration/mexican-cartels-fentanyl-competition/.

Ngai, Mae M. *Impossible Subjects: Illegal Aliens and the Making of Modern America.* Princeton, NJ: Princeton University Press, 2014.

Nguyen, Oanh Kieu, et al. "Association of Scheduled vs. Emergency-Only Dialysis with Health Outcomes and Costs in Undocumented Immigrants with End-Stage Renal Disease." *JAMA Internal Medicine* 179, no. 2 (February 1, 2019): 175. https://doi.org/10.1001/jamainternmed.2018.5866.

Nhất Hạnh, Thich. *How to Love.* Berkeley, CA: Parallax Press, 2015.

Nuila, Ricardo. "Home: Palliation for Dying Undocumented Immigrants." *New England Journal of Medicine* 366, no. 22 (2012): 2047–48. https://doi.org /10.1056/NEJMp1201768.

Ochoa, Gilda. "Learning and Being in Community: A Latina Feminist Holistic Approach to Researching Where We Live." *International Journal of Research & Method in Education* 45, no. 3 (May 27, 2022): 246–58. https:// doi.org/10.1080/1743727X.2022.2043842.

Odell, Jenny. *Saving Time: Discovering a Life Beyond the Clock.* 1st ed. New York: Random House, 2023.

Office of Governor Gavin Newsom. "Governor Gavin Newsom Issues Stay at Home Order," Executive Office, State of California, 2020. https://www.gov .ca.gov/wp-content/uploads/2020/03/3.19.20-attested-EO-N-33-20-COVID -19-HEALTH-ORDER.pdf.

Office of Public Affairs. *Cooperation Between United States and Mexican Law Enforcement Leads To Significant Actions Against Transnational Drug Trafficking Organization.* US Department of Justice, 2023. https://www .justice.gov/opa/pr/cooperation-between-united-states-and-mexican-law -enforcement-leads-significant-actions.

Oliveira, Gabrielle. *Motherhood Across Borders: Immigrants and Their Children in Mexico and New York.* New York: New York University, 2018.

Palmer, Deborah K., et al. "Reframing the Debate on Language Separation: Toward a Vision for Translanguaging Pedagogies in the Dual Language Classroom." *Modern Language Journal* 98, no. 3 (September 2014): 757–72. https://doi.org/10.1111/modl.12121.

Palo Alto Online, "Agents Target Heroin-Trafficking Ring, Arrest 12." May 16, 2012. https://www.paloaltoonline.com/news/2012/05/16/agents-target -heroin-trafficking-ring-arrest-12.

paperson, la. *A Third University Is Possible.* Minneapolis: University of Minnesota Press, 2017.

Parkhouse, Hillary. "Lessons on Citizenship and Democratic Power Literacy from Undocumented Youth." *Critical Education* 8, no. 5 (March 15, 2017). https://doi.org/10.14288/CE.V8I5.186125.

Patel, Leigh. "Pedagogies of Resistance and Survivance: Learning as Marronage." *Equity & Excellence in Education* 49, no. 4 (2016): 397–401.

——. *No Study Without Struggle: Confronting Settler Colonialism in Higher Education.* Boston: Beacon Press, 2021.

Pennycook, Alastair. "English in the World/The World in English." In *Power and Inequality in Language Education*, ed., James W. Tollefson. Cambridge: Cambridge University Press, 1995.

Pillai, D., et al. *Health and Health Care Experiences of Immigrants: The 2023 KFF/LA Times Survey of Immigrants*, 2023.

Pitts, Andrea J., Mariana Ortega, and José M. Medina, eds. *Theories of the Flesh: Latinx and Latin American Feminisms, Transformation, and Resistance.* New York: Oxford University Press, 2019.

Povinelli, Elizabeth A. *Between Gaia and Ground: Four Axioms of Existence and the Ancestral Catastrophe of Late Liberalism.* Durham, NC: Duke University Press, 2021.

——. *Economies of Abandonment: Social Belonging and Endurance in Late Liberalism.* Durham, NC: Duke University Press, 2011.

Pratt, Mary Louise. *Imperial Eyes: Travel Writing and Transculturation.* 2nd ed. London: Routledge, 2008.

Ramos, Paola. *Finding Latinx: In Search of the Voices Redefining Latino Identity.* New York: Vintage Books, 2020.

Rhee, Jeong-eun. *Decolonial Feminist Research: Haunting, Rememory and Mothers.* London: Routledge, 2021.

Right to Be. *Cornell International Survey on Street Harassment*, 2015. https://righttobe.org/research/cornell-international-survey-on-street-harassment/.

Rios, Victor M. *Punished: Policing the Lives of Black and Latino Boys.* New Perspectives in Crime, Deviance, and Law Series. New York: New York University Press, 2011.

Roberts, Steven O., et al. "God as a White Man: A Psychological Barrier to Conceptualizing Black People and Women as Leadership Worthy." *Journal of Personality and Social Psychology* 119, no. 6 (December 2020): 1290–1315. https://doi.org/10.1037/pspi0000233.

Rodríguez, Richard T. *A Kiss Across the Ocean: Transatlantic Intimacies of British Post-Punk & US Latinidad.* Durham, NC: Duke University Press, 2022.

Rodriguez, Sophia, and William McCorkle. "On the Educational Rights of Undocumented Students: A Call to Expand Teachers' Awareness of Policies Impacting Undocumented Students and Strategic Empathy." *Teachers College Record* 122, no. 12 (2020): 1–34.

Rodriguez Vega, Silvia. *Drawing Deportation: Art and Resistance Among Immigrant Children.* New York: New York University, 2023.

Rogers, John, Marisa Saunders, Veronica Terriquez, and Veronica Velez. "Civic Lessons: Public Schools and the Civic Development of Undocumented

Students and Parents." *Northwestern Journal of Law and Social Policy* 3 (2008): 201.

Rojas, Leslie Beresten. "Immigrants a Largely Hidden Segment of L.A.'s Homeless Population." KQED, September 23, 2016. https://www.kqed.org/news /11100554/immigrants-a-largely-hidden-segment-of-l-a-s-homeless -population.

Rondinelli, Robert D., et al. *AMA Guides to the Evaluation of Permanent Impairment, 2023*. In *AMA Guides to the Evaluation of Permanent Impairment*. 6th ed. American Medical Association, 2023.

Rosa, Jonathan. *Looking Like a Language, Sounding Like a Race: Raciolinguistic Ideologies and the Learning of Latinidad*. Oxford Studies in the Anthropology of Language. New York: Oxford University Press, 2019.

Rosa, Jonathan, and Nelson Flores. "Unsettling Race and Language: Toward a Raciolinguistic Perspective." *Language in Society* 46, no. 5 (2017): 621–47.

Rosales, Rocío. *Fruteros: Street Vending, Illegality, and Ethnic Community in Los Angeles*. Oakland: University of California Press, 2020.

Rothstein, Richard. *The Color of Law: A Forgotten History of How Our Government Segregated America*. New York: Liveright Publishing, 2018.

Roy, Arundhati. "The Pandemic Is a Portal." *Financial Times*, April 3, 2020. https://www.ft.com/content/10d8f5e8-74eb-11ea-95fe-fcd274e920ca.

Sacchetti, Maria. "Deportations of Migrants Rise to More Than 142,000 Under Biden." *Washington Post*, December 29, 2023. https://www.washington post.com/immigration/2023/12/29/immigrants-ice-border-deportations -2023/.

Sandoval-Strausz, A. K. *Barrio America: How Latino Immigrants Saved the American City*. 1st ed. New York: Basic Books, 2019.

Schmidt Camacho, Alicia R. *Migrant Imaginaries: Latino Cultural Politics in the U.S.-Mexico Borderlands*. Nation of Newcomers. New York: New York University Press, 2008.

Sennett, Richard, and Jonathan Cobb. *The Hidden Injuries of Class*. New York London: W. W. Norton, 1972.

Serwer, Adam. "Greg Abbott Surrenders to the Coronavirus." *The Atlantic*, August 12, 2021. https://www.theatlantic.com/ideas/archive/2021/08/texas -politics-are-dangerously-broken/619725/.

Shukla, Nikesh, and Chimène Suleyman, eds. *The Good Immigrant: 26 Writers Reflect on America*. 1st ed. New York: Little, Brown, 2019.

Smith, Sharon G., et al. *The National Intimate Partner and Sexual Violence Survey: 2015 Data Brief—Updated Release*, 2018.

Snyder, Thomas D., Cristobal De Brey, and Sally A. Dillow. *Digest of Education Statistics 2017, NCES 2018–070*. National Center for Education Statistics, 2019.

Soto, Lilia. *Girlhood in the Borderlands: Mexican Teens Caught in the Crossroads of Migration*. New York: New York University Press, 2018.

State of California Department of Justice. *Brown Announces Seizure of $7 Million Worth of Heroin in East Palo Alto*, 2009. https://oag.ca.gov/news /press-releases/brown-announces-seizure-7-million-worth-heroin-east -palo-alto.

Stewart, Danté. *Shoutin' in the Fire: An American Epistle*. New York: Convergent, 2021.

Stillman, Sarah. "The Migrant Workers Who Follow Climate Disasters." *New Yorker*, November 1, 2021. https://www.newyorker.com/magazine/2021 /11/08/the-migrant-workers-who-follow-climate-disasters.

Stuelke, Patricia. *The Ruse of Repair: US Neoliberal Empire and the Turn from Critique*. Durham, NC: Duke University Press, 2021.

Tisby, Jemar. *The Color of Compromise: The Truth About the American Church's Complicity in Racism*. Grand Rapids, MI: Zondervan Reflective, 2019.

Townsend, Camilla. *Fifth Sun: A New History of the Aztecs*. New York: Oxford University Press, 2019.

Traweek, Sharon. *Beamtimes and Lifetimes: The World of High Energy Physicists*. Cambridge, MA: Harvard University Press, 1988.

Tripodi, Francesca. "Searching for Alternative Facts." *Data & Society* (2018).

Trump, Donald J. *Presidential Proclamation on the Suspension of Entry of Immigrants Who Will Financially Burden the United States Healthcare System*. White House, 2019. https://trumpwhitehouse.archives.gov/presidential -actions/presidential-proclamation-suspension-entry-immigrants-will- financially-burden-united-states-healthcare-system.

Tuan, Yi-Fu. *Space and Place: The Perspective of Experience*. Minneapolis: University of Minnesota Press, 2002.

Tuck, Eve, and Wayne K. Yang. "Decolonization Is Not a Metaphor." *Decolonization: Indigeneity, Education & Society* 1, no. 1 (2012): 1–40.

USA Facts. *Government Immigration and Border Security Spending*, 2023. https://usafacts.org/state-of-the-union/immigration/.

US Bureau of Labor Statistics. *Job Openings and Labor Turnover Summary*, 2023. https://www.bls.gov/news.release/jolts.nr0.htm.

US Customs and Border Protection. *About CBP*, 2023. https://www.cbp.gov /about.

US Department of Justice Drug Enforcement Administration. *National Drug Threat Assessment 2024*. US Department of Justice, 2024. https://www.dea .gov/sites/default/files/2024-05/NDTA_2024.pdf.

US Department of Justice National Drug Intelligence Center. *Northern California High Intensity Drug Trafficking Area Drug Market Analysis 2011*. US Department of Justice, 2011. https://www.justice.gov/archive/ndic/dmas /Northern_CA_DMA-2011(U).pdf.

US Government Accountability Office. *Southwest Border: CBP Should Improve Data Collection, Reporting, and Evaluation for the Missing Migrant Program*, 2022. https://www.gao.gov/products/gao-22-105053.

Van der Kolk, Bessel A. *The Body Keeps the Score: Brain, Mind and Body in the Healing of Trauma*. New York: Penguin Books, 2015.

Vargas, Jose Antonio. *Dear America: Notes of an Undocumented Citizen*. 1st Dey Street paperback ed. New York: Dey St., 2019.

Villa-Nicholas, Melissa. *Data Borders: How Silicon Valley Is Building an Industry Around Immigrants*. Oakland: University of California Press, 2023.

———. *Latinas on the Line: Invisible Information Workers in Telecommunications*. Latinidad: Transnational Cultures in the United States. New Brunswick, NJ: Rutgers University Press, 2022.

Walia, Harsha. *Border and Rule: Global Migration, Capitalism, and the Rise of Racist Nationalism*. Chicago: Haymarket Books, 2021.

Wilkerson, Isabel. *Caste: The Origins of Our Discontents*. 1st ed. New York: Random House, 2020.

Woolf, Virginia. *The Waves*. London: Hogarth, 1931.

World Health Organization. *International Classification of Functioning, Disability and Health: ICF*. World Health Organization, 2001.

Wynter, Sylvia. "Unsettling the Coloniality of Being/Power/Truth/Freedom: Towards the Human, After Man, Its Overrepresentation—An Argument." *CR: The New Centennial Review* 3, no. 3 (2003): 257–337.

Yosso, Tara J. "Whose Culture Has Capital? A Critical Race Theory Discussion of Community Cultural Wealth." *Race Ethnicity and Education* 8, no. 1 (March 2005): 69–91. https://doi.org/10.1080/1361332052000341006.

———. *Critical Race Counterstories Along the Chicana/Chicano Educational Pipeline*. The Teaching/Learning Social Justice Series. New York: Routledge, 2006.

Zamora, Javier. *Solito: A Memoir*. London: Hogarth, 2023.

INDEX

AB 60, California, 102
Abbott, Greg, 157
accents, language, 29
activism and outreach, 119–26, 166
address, proof of, 1, 78
American Medical Association, *Guides to the Evaluation of Permanent Impairment*, 174–75
Arce, Julissa, 5
Arizona Senate Bill 1070, 56
aspirational capital, 162
Aztec Empire, 17

Benjamin, Ruha, 164
Bernal, Dolores Delgado, viii
Biden, Joe, 165
birth certificates, 78
Blue Ribbon (pseudonym; nonprofit organization), 121–26, 178
body image and beauty standards, 23–27, 28–29
Border Patrol, 2, 57–58, 68, 174. *See also* ICE (US Immigration and Customs Enforcement)
borders, linguistic, 19, 58. *See also* US-Mexico border
Bourdieu, Pierre, 193n4
buchona look, 28–29
Butler, Anthea, 118
Butler, Octavia, 164

Cano, José Luis, Jr., 69
cartels. *See* Mexican drug cartels
catcalling, 30, 46
Chetty, Raj, 2, 175
Chicana feminist scholarship, viii
Christian faith: activism and outreach, 119–26; conservative values, 10, 43, 93, 97, 133; evangelicalism as anti-immigrant, 116–20; prayer, 115–16, 120, 124, 138; strength and perseverance, 113–14, 126–27, 138, 143
chronic inflammatory response syndrome (CIRS), 171, 179
claims adjudication, insurance, 174–75
Colato Laínez, René, 187n10
"colored people time" trope, 18
colorism and skin color, 26–27
community cultural wealth, 161–62
"compassionate" healthcare, 149
complex-PTSD (C-PTSD), 140, 179, 192n5
Cooper, D. B., 160
Cornejo Villavicencio, Karla, 5, 148
corridos (narrative ballad genre), 11
Costs of Care (nonprofit organization), 150
costs of undocumented labor, overview, 2–4, 173–79

COVID-19 pandemic, 88–89, 141, 148–49, 156, 157
Cruz, Cindy, ix

DACA (Deferred Action for Childhood Arrivals), 6, 165–66
Davis, Angela, 164–65
Declaration of Independence, 57
de los Ríos, Cati, 11–12
dental care, 145–46, 150–55, 178
deportation, 19, 66, 67–68, 88, 99–100, 165, 176
depression, 52–53, 59, 94, 129–30, 138–40
Desmond, Matthew, 186n15
diet culture, 24–25
domestic abuse and violence, 60–62, 105–12, 134–35, 179
domestic labor. *See* nannying
double-consciousness, 172–73
DREAM Act (Development, Relief, and Education for Alien Minors), 119, 165
driver's licenses, 1, 102, 186n1
drug cartels. *See* Mexican drug cartels
Du Bois, W. E. B., 172–73
Du Mez, Kristin Kobes, 118
Dunbar-Ortiz, Roxanne, 57

eating disorders, 24–25
economic crisis (2008), 10–11
education: access to, for undocumented immigrants, 31, 165–66, 167; cost of, 178; language, 63–64
elderly undocumented immigrants, 18–20
employment: and DACA, 165; dangerous and unhealthy workplaces, 148–49, 156–57; documentation for, 74, 77–78; essential workers, 88–89, 156–57; labor abuse, 76–77, 79, 82–83, 177; and language, 77, 78–79; nannying routine, 85–88; sexual harassment, 79–80, 176,

178; "strong work ethic" trope, 73–74, 160–61; under-the-table, 74–76, 77, 81; workers' compensation, 174–75
English, learning, 59, 63–64, 75
Enriquez, Laura E., 101, 108
Escobar, Arturo, 164
Escobar, Pablo, 37
essential workers, 88–89
ethnographic research methodology, viii–xii
evangelicalism, 116–20
E-Verify, 74
excess mortality, 157
exoticization, 28–30

faith. *See* Christian faith
family: and cost of memory, 2–3; domestic abuse and violence, 60–62, 105–12, 179; and familial capital, 161; fertile Mexican woman trope, 156; goodbyes, 14, 50, 52–53, 139; raising and supporting, 59, 61–62, 63, 64–66, 75, 93, 95, 136–37, 172; transnational dynamics, 30–31. *See also* romantic relationships
fat shaming, 23–25
fentanyl, 49–50
Fierros, Cindy O., viii
financial crisis (2008), 10–11
Flores, Tracey, 162–63
Franquiz, Maria, 187n10
Fuentes, Amado Carrillo, 37–38, 41, 188n2
Fuentes, Vicente, 38
future, uncertainty of, 20–22

García, Angela, 58, 69
Garcia, Antero, 194n9
gendered labor, 86. *See also* women
Graeber, David, 56
green cards, and marriage, 99–101, 134, 167
Greenhouse, Carol, 17

healthcare: barriers to, for undocumented immigrants, 146–48, 149–52, 169–71; and claims adjudication, 174–75; cost of, 145, 146, 151, 155, 178, 179; illicit medical treatment, 145–46, 152–55; and vulnerable groups, 19–20, 89, 141, 148–49, 156–57. *See also* mental health
hearing loss, 147
Hersey, Tricia, 160–61
Hing, Bill Ong, 176
homelessness, 64–67, 121, 178
hustle culture, 73–74, 160–61

ICE (US Immigration and Customs Enforcement), 69, 100, 111
identity. *See* Mexicana identity
Individual Taxpayer Identification Number (ITIN), 16, 77–78
institutional review boards (IRBs), xi–xii
insurance company claims adjudication, 174–75

Jesus, and migration, 117–18, 120
Jewish scripture, 117
jobs. *See* employment

Kelley, Robin D. G., 164
Kimmerer, Robin, xiv, 194n8
Kotlowitz, Alex, 58

labor abuse, 76–77, 82–83
La Cuenta (online publication), xiv, 6–7, 161, 174
language: and accents, 29; and employment, 77, 78–79; and healthcare access, 19; learning English, 59, 63–64, 75; linguistic borders, 19, 58; linguistic capital, 161; raciolinguistics, 58
Latinos, as label, 187–88n1
legal fees, 50, 177
Le Guin, Ursula, 17–18

loans, predatory, 171, 179
love. *See* family; romantic relationships

marriage, and green cards, 99–101, 134, 167
Martínez, Ramón, 64
medical care. *See* healthcare; mental health
member checking, xi
memory: cost of, 2–3; and trauma, 141
mental health: and body image/beauty standards, 23–27; coping mechanisms, 142–43; depression and suicide, 52–53, 59, 94, 129–30, 138–40; therapy, 140–41, 171, 178; trauma, 20, 131–33, 140, 141, 176–77, 179, 192n5
Mexicana identity: *vs.* American identity, 69–70; body image and beauty standards, 23–27, 28–29; and double-consciousness, 172–73; and labels, 187–88n1; people-pleasing expectations, 27–28, 30, 108, 135; and robbed girlhood, 30–32; survival and resiliency, 32–33, 161–62; and whiteness, 26–27, 69
Mexican border. *See* US-Mexico border
Mexican drug cartels: and buchona look, 28–29; Fuentes family, 37–38, 41; glorification of, 11–12, 38; money laundering, 12, 44; Sinaloa as center of, 10, 11, 35–37; threat of violence, 12–13, 15, 30, 35, 38–39, 49, 52; United States impacted by, 49–50
migration, in religious texts, 117–18
mirror method, ix, xi
Molina, Natalia, 156
Moriates, Christopher, 149–50
mortality, excess, 157

nannying: daily routine, 85–88; positive and negative experiences, 81–85
narcocorridos (cartel narrative ballads), 11

narcos. *See* Mexican drug cartels
Newsom, Gavin, 88
NorJack (short film), 160
Nulia, Ricardo, 19

Obama, Barack, 165
Okorafor, Nnendi, 164
outreach and activism, 119–26, 166

pandemic, COVID-19, 88–89, 141,
    148–49, 156, 157
passports, 55, 78, 96. *See also* tourist
    visas
Patel, Leigh, ix, xiii, 4
pláticas, viii–x
predatory loans, 171
pre-traumatic stress disorder
    (pre-TSD), 20, 187n10
proof of address, 1, 78
Proposition 187, California, 147

racial profiling, 69, 157
raciolinguistics, 58
racist stereotypes: in conceptions
    of time, 18; and cultural capital,
    161; "dirty" immigrant trope,
    156; Mexican women archetypes,
    29–30; and profiling, 69, 157;
    "strong work ethic" trope, 73–74,
    160–61. *See also* Mexicana identity;
    whiteness
radio programming employment,
    75–76, 191n2
refugee status, 2, 50, 156
relationships. *See* family; romantic
    relationships
religion. *See* Christian faith
restaurant employment, 77–80, 178
Roberts, Steven, 119
romantic relationships: codependent,
    133, 135, 140; domestic abuse
    and violence, 105–12, 134–35,
    179; ideal *vs.* reality, 91–93;
    long-distance, 93–99, 101–4; mar-
    riage, and green cards, 99–101,

134, 167; and trauma, 131–33;
    undocumented status dynamics,
    108, 111, 133–34
Rosa, Jonathan, 3, 58
Rosales, Rocío, 2–3

schools. *See* education
Serwer, Adam, 157
sexual harassment, 29–30, 46–49,
    79–80, 176, 178. *See also* domestic
    abuse and violence
Sinaloa, Mexico, 9–11, 12, 15, 23,
    35–38, 49
skin color and colorism, 26–27
Social Security numbers, 16, 59, 74,
    146, 148, 151–52, 165
social services, as unavailable to un-
    documented immigrants, 17, 66,
    147, 176
Somos Escritoras/We Are Writers
    (writing program), 162–63
Soto, Lilia, 30–31
speculative storytelling, 164
Stillman, Sarah, 148
suicide, 52, 130, 138–40. *See also*
    depression

taxes, 16–17, 176, 177
temporary checkpoints, 68–69
therapy, 140–41, 171, 178
time, conceptions of, 17–18
tourist visas, 55–56, 59, 60, 66, 67–68,
    101
transportation costs, 178
trauma, 20, 131–33, 140, 141, 176–77,
    192n5
Tripodi, Francesca, 119
Trump, Donald, 89, 99–100, 118, 147,
    165
2008 financial crisis, 10–11

undocumented immigrants, as label, 6
unhoused immigrants, 64–67, 121
US Immigration and Customs Enforce-
    ment (ICE), 69, 100, 111

US-Mexico border: checkpoints, 68–69; collective acceptance of, 56, 57; federal budget to police, 174; militarization of, 57–58

Vargas, Jose Antonio, 5, 186n7
violence: domestic abuse and, 60–62, 105–12, 134–35, 179; Mexican drug cartels, 12–13, 15, 30, 35, 38–39, 49, 52
visas, tourist, 55–56, 59, 60, 66, 67–68, 101

wage theft and underpayment, 76, 77, 79, 82, 177
Watson, Lilla, 7
welfare programs, as unavailable to undocumented immigrants, 17, 66, 147, 176

whiteness: and beauty standards, 24, 26–27; and employment, 77, 78; and evangelicalism, 118–19; immigration checkpoints, 69
wildfires, California, 156–57
Wilkerson, Isabel, 27
women: body image and beauty standards, 23–27, 28–29; domestic abuse and violence, 105–12, 134–35, 179; fertile Mexican trope, 156; and gendered labor, 86; robbed girlhood, 30–32; sexual harassment, 29–30, 46–49, 79–80, 176, 178
work. *See* employment
writing, power of, 162–63

Yosso, Tara, 161–62, 193n4